1857

A Great Rebellion

1857
A Great Rebellion

Dr. Raj Kumar

RAJ

RAJ PUBLICATIONS
New Delhi-110 002

1857 - A Great Rebellion

First Published in 2007

ISBN 81-86208-49-6

Published by : Poonam Goel
Raj Publications
108, 4855/24, Ansari Road
Darya Ganj, New Delhi-110002
Tel. : 011 - 30120939

Laser Typesetting by : Kumar Computers, Delhi

Printed at : Sachin Printers, Delhi-

Contents

Preface

History has yet to pronounce its final verdict on the rebellion of 1857. Wether it was the first war of independence against foreign occupation forces or, as the British themselves considered it, an unsuccessful mutiny among the armed forces. But Indian rightly commemorate those who fell in that attempt to overthrow British rule as martyrs.

Scholars working on the subject have attributed various causes of the rebellion. The Enfield cartridges were seen as a threat to caste and religion. Army based on caste system, seniority, brigading, terms of enlistments, centralization and staff system were accessed also as causes of the mutiny. Colonial writers feel that at one time there had been one British to every three Indian soldiers in India. In 1856, the ratio had fallen to one in more than six. This is seen as one of the causes of the mutiny. There was widespread belief that the British were attempting to convert the inhabitants to Christianity. This situation, writes, William Dalrymple, provided the backdrop to the revolt in which the ideological lead was taken by Islamic jihadis. Moreover colonialism had brought with it violence, exploitation plunder, imprishment, loss of identity and Lapes Doctrine. Lord Canning had said in 1855:

> "We must not forget that in the Sky of India, serene as it is, a small cloud may arise, at first no bigger than a man's hand, but which growing bigger and bigger, may at last threaten to overwhelm us with ruin."

The revolt, as forwarned above, soon assumed the proportions of a country wide uprising and the British hold on the country tottered everywhere for over an year. It was on June 17, 1858 that Rani Lakshmi Bai of Jhansi fell in the heroic defence of Gwalior, besieged by the British forces and Tantia Topi, commander of the revolutionary forces fled. That broke the back of the revolt.

The Lok Sabha in Delhi began its first session after the election with a two minutes silent tribute to the fallen martyrs of the 1857 revolution.

All over, people gathered, to commorate the 150th century in every town of importance, prabhat pheries, marched in procession to the singing of national songs and the National Flag was hoisted. In many places, the special flag of the 1857 revolutionaries - a green flag with a golden sun - was unfurled by the side of the Indian national tricolour. A colourful march was organised from Meerut to Delhi to awaken the spirit of those great patriots of India who died so that India could awake to freedom.

Aim of this book is to give a panormic view of this great event. It will be useful and handy for every patriotic Indian citizen and a mine of easy to grasp knowledge to any one who wants to have essence of this important episode. We have included some extremely important essays by renowned authorities on the subject to enhance its usefulness to the researchers as well.

We record our indebtrdness to the authorities on the subject. We cann't adequelty thank the Librarians and their staffmembers for kindness and help.

Last but not the least my publishers deserve appreciation for making this important material on this important past event in Indian history, for wider intellectual persuits.

----- Dr. Raj Kumar

1

1857 - A Historical Perspective

In May 1857 the clear sunshine of India was darkened by mutinous clouds which broke in lightning and anarchy, and a "continent" was wrapped in the arms of fire. There were only twenty thousand soldiers and citizens of the ruling race to quench the flames. To fan them were a hundred thousand of their own well-trained soldiers, and a population of some millions armed and in revolt. The great Moghul capital, a large number of the chief cities, some of the fortresses and principal arsenals, were in the hands of the insurgents.

All trace of British administration had vanished throughout the extent of great provinces. The mighty fabric of Empire was shaken to the foundations. But the men of the class who had erected it, schooled by a century of victory and government, determined it should stand reformed. Heroic deeds and great achievements began to pierce the gloom.

The story told here is how for more than twelve weeks a

small force of besiegers fought more than thirty well-contested combats against a disciplined host, and, were with disease, reduced in numbers, how they stormed in the face of day the strongly fortified Moghul capital; how half a British regiment, a few loyal sepoys, and a motley gathering of civilians defended against enormous odds, against increasing loss, against hope deferred, the fragile range of the Residency of Lucknow; how Havelock and his veterans, after four days' hard fighting, reached Cawnpore; how, though baffled at first, they broke the strength and spirit of a highly-disciplined army, and delivered from death a host of women and children. The vital struggle for supremacy closed with the storming and capture of Delhi (14th September 1857) and the relief of Lucknow by Havelock (25th September). The political and moral effects of Havelock's desperate venture were prodigious. A native leader of the Mutiny states: "Our first cause for regret was the early recapture of Cawnpore—that fact caused the Nepaulese to waver; a little later and our negotiations would have been completed. To the people of Oudh the first relief of Lucknow was the boldest act the English have ever undertaken, and from the date of the entry into the Bailey Guard all our hopes of overcoming the garrison except by starvation were given up."

The tale is also told how Colin Campbell, by a series of operations which will always be of compelling interest, relieved Outram and Havelock and removed the gallant garrison and the women and children from the Residency; how with a force of five thousand men he totally defeated at Gawnpore an army of twenty-five thousand men, numbering in its ranks the most perfectly equipped and organised force in India; how he besieged and captured Lucknow—an operation which will always be considered a striking illustration of the art of war.

But even after the capture of Lucknow (March 1858)

whole armies were still against us and entire kingdoms in insurrection. In the ancient province of Behar, occupying the north-western corner of Bengal, the Rajput chief, Koer Singh, still headed the revolt; in the Rohilcund, the vast tract bounded on the north by the Himalayas, on the south-west by the Ganges, and on the east by Oudh, Khan Bahadur, Khan of Bareilly, held sway; in Central India the authority, not only of the British Government but of the two leading Maratha chiefs, Scindia and Holkar, had almost vanished.

In the events on the Central Indian Campaign, one of the most glorious achievements recorded in the military annals of England, is told from the despatches of Sir Hugh Rose and the respective commanders and brigadiers. They have been collated with diaries and letters, and certain errors rectified and obscure points cleared.

In the Central Indian Campaign no army, but a small body of good fighting men, led by a chief always ready to face tremendous risks, marched in the hottest and most deadly season of the year from the confines of Western India to the waters of the Jumna, a distance of a thousand miles. They made their way across rugged plateaux where roads were mere tracks and towns few and far between;they toiled through dense jungles where the Bhil hunter roamed undisturbed;they crossed broad rivers, swollen with the rain which fell on the mountains; they forced formidable passes;they fought and won pitched battles, and they stormed the strongest forts.

The capture of Jhansi must rank with, the great actions recorded in British annals. A force consisting of an incomplete division had laid siege to a strong fortress and a walled city, defended by a desperate and disciplined garrison more than double its number, and supplied with all the munitions of war. The Bombay Sepoy and the Madras Sapper vied with the British soldier in patience, endurance of privation, and fatigue. Then, in light of day, this handful of men stormed the lofty walls, and, after four days' strenuous fighting, the city was captured.

The taking of Calpee, a natural fortress on a high bald rock rising from the Jumna, completed the plan which the Government of India had drawn up for the Central India Field Force. But the occupation of Gwalior by Tantia Tope and the Rani of Jhansi compelled Sir Hugh Rose, leaving a small garrison at Calpee, to make a very rapid march in summer heat to Gwalior with the remainder of his troops, and to fight and gain two actions on the road, one at Morar Cantonments, the other at Kotah-ka-Serai.

They arrived, from great distances and by bad roads, at their posts before Gwalior on the day appointed, the 19th of June; and on that same day carried by assault all the enemy's positions on strong heights and in most difficult ground; taking one battery after another, twenty-seven pieces of artillery in the action, twenty-five in the pursuit, besides the guns in the fort, the old city, the new city, and finally the rock of Gwalior,held to be one of the most important and strongest fortresses in India. On the 28th of June Sir Eobert Napier marched from Gwalior in pursuit of the enemy, and by a daring feat of arms closed the Central Indian Campaign.

On the 2nd of April 1858 Sir Hugh Rose captured Jhansi; on the 28th of April Sir Colin Campbell entered Rohilcund. The account of the Rohilcund Campaign is mainly constructed from the despatches of Sir Colin Campbell and of the respective commanders of the columns. Sir Colin Campbell showed at the capture of Bareilly the same great power of planning a combination which he desplayed in the siege and capture of Lucknow.

The concentration of the work was executed with marvellous precision. Slowly but surely they were brought to bear on a great city which, though without walls, was filled by thousands of fanatics who only desired to die in a hand-to-hand struggle with the infidel. And the combination resulted in its occupation with much economy of life.

After the account of the Rohilcund Campaign the scene is shifted to Bengal, and the operations rendered necessary for the suppression of the revolt in Behar. The curtain rises on the outbreak in the city of Patna, followed by the mutiny of the Sepoys at Dinapore (25th July 1857), and the march to Arrah. The tale is told again of the defence of the little house at Arrah—a noble exploit shining on a by-path of the history of the Indian Mutiny. The rescue of the few defenders by Major Vincent Eyre, his defeat of Koer Singh's army, and the capture of the Rajput Chiefs citadel, were the main incidents of a "glorious little campaign," to use the words of Outram. The occupation of Azimghur by Koer Singh, Lord Mark Kerr's rapid march from Benares with a small force, and the stubborn fight by which he made his way into the beleaguered cantonment, are recorded in these pages.

A detailed account, based on the official records, is also given of the subsequent operations under Sir Edward Lugard and the pursuit of the rebels by Brigadier Douglas, and their surprise and final defeat in the Kaimur hills. In Western Behar the operations did not result in any great victory, but they illustrated the true greatness of the British soldier's character.

From Bengal the narrative turns to Oudh, and the campaign which brought to an end the long and stern contest for supremacy in that kingdom. During the brief winter campaign some hundreds, of forts were destroyed, about one hundred and fifty guns captured, and 150,000 armed men, of whom at least 35,000 were disciplined soldiers, were subdued. The success of the operations was due in great part to Lord Clyde's capacity for combination, and his accuracy and energy of execution. It was the old campaigner's last campaign. The stone that covers his grave in Westminster Abbey tells the passer - by that of his own deserts through fifty years of arduous service, from the earliest battles of the Peninsular War to the pacification of India in 1858, he rose to the highest rank in the British army.

In the end, the pursuit of Tantia Tope—a striking example of that form of military activity known as "guerilla war." Of all the leaders who acted an important part in the Mutiny he possessed the greatest talent for organisation, the greatest enterprise as regards initiation; but in execution he was wanting in promptitude and decision, and on the field of battle he lacked the courage belonging to the Maratha race.

At the battle of the Betwa he planned with considerable skill the most formidable attack with which Sir Hugh Rose had to contend, but he galloped off the field at the very beginning of the contest. After the decisive defeat of the rebels by Sir Robert Napier, Tantia commenced the marvellous series of operations which continued for ten months. The commanders opposed to him are the best evidence of his extraordinary skill.

He occupied positions of strategic importance, he seized cities, obtained fresh stores, collected new guns and fresh recruits. He kept his irregular force in constant motion, often marching sixty miles a-day in order to keep the British columns apart until the Nana could break through the cordon in Oudh and join him. Then with the adopted son of the last Peshwa, who was regarded as the legitimate head of the Maratha confederacy, he intended to enter the Baroda state governed by a Maratha dynasty, make a dash at such a rate as would defy pursuit into the Deccan,and raise the true Maratha provinces.

But the Nana could not break through Lord Clyde's net. Tantia found the pursuing columns were closing round him. He made a swift and sudden race through a wild country to the Nerbudda and crossed it. It was a skilful, daring manoeuvre. He placed a full turbid river between himself and his pursuers, and he changed the theatre of operations.

The best course then to have followed would have been the resolute pursuit of his great object. But he hesitated, and his return to Rajpootana from the Tapte was a fatal blunder.

The British troops were now accustomed to endure hardship and make long marches. Brigadier Somerset to overtake Tantia did 230 miles in nine days. Tantia, finding that he could not shake off his pursuers, and that his force decreased in numbers every day, threw himself into the jungle, was betrayed and captured.

He was tried by court-martial for having been in rebellion, and for having waged war against the British Government, was found guilty, sentenced justly under the law to death, and paid the full penalty. In the statement giving an account of his career which he dictated when he was a prisoner, he denied all complicity in the Cawnpore massacre. But they are the words of one that is desperate, which are as the wind. The evidence leaves not a shadow of doubt.

The dispersion of the last strong organised rebel force in Central India marks the close of the main operations for the suppression of the great revolt. It was not, however, till November 1859 that the last body of rebels in Northern Oudh surrendered to a British force, and for some time considerable bands of rebels, who had become bandits, had to be hunted out of the dense jungles and deep glens of Central India. The Bengal army was annihilated, and the authority of the British Government was fully established over the continent.

It has been the fashion to write as if the Indian army had thrown off its allegiance, but it was only an important fraction. The Madras army and the Bombay army, with a few exceptions, remained true to their colours. It has been my privilege to record in this volume the patient endurance of privation and fatigue, and the undaunted courage of the Madras Sapper and the Bombay Sepoy. The devotion and loyalty of some even of the Bengal Sepoys is a relief to the terrible features of a reign of terror. Let us also be liberal toward those who so grievously sinned. The bravery and devotion they had shown, and the faithful service the Bengal army had rendered for nearly a century, must not be interred.

Writers and administrators of the time have warmly disputed about the origin of the mutiny of the Bengal soldiers, followed by widespread revolt, and a struggle as furious and relentless as any recorded in history. Many solutions have been put forward.

It was the greased cartridge; it was the land-revenue system; it was the policy of annexation; it was the refusal to allow the right of adoption; it was the lack of discipline in the Bengal army, and the humiliating memories of the First Afghan War; it was the fanaticism of the Brahmin and the Moslem.

All these interpretations have heen examined by the light of official records and the enormous mass of evidence collected at the time, but to analyse the evidence in these pages, and to state fully the conclusions founded on them, would expand this volume to four.

The First Afghan War was a primary influence. In the

East a victory is soon forgotten, but the slightest disaster is exaggerated and remembered. The Cabul disaster was greatly exaggerated. No army perished in Afghanistan, as is so often stated, but a weak brigade was destroyed. Cabul was easily retaken and the guilty city received its due punishment. But Pollock and Nott returned to India, and to the Oriental any retrograde movement means defeat. Five hundred mutilated and crippled camp-followers and sepoys of the destroyed brigade accompanied the march of Pollock's victorious forces. On reaching India they were sent to their homes, and throughout the land they spread the news that English prestige had perished, thus sowing the first tares of the Indian Mutiny.

Soon after the victorious British force left Cabul the belief spread in Afghanistan itself that we had been driven out of the country, and in every bazaar in India it was accepted as a fact that our armies had been annihilated and our power destroyed.

Forty years had not passed since the British Government had become the sovereign paramount of India, and the Chiefs and Princes began to wonder if it were beyond dispute. Their tone became more lofty and arrogant. A generation had not passed since the Maratha had disputed our supremacy and the Maratha Court of Gwalior showed itself openly hostile to the interests of the British Government. It had an army of 30,000 men, mainly composed of Brahmin or Rajpoot corps, with a numerous artillery. The army of the Khalsa,or Sikh commonwealth, numbering 70,000 soldiers and 300 guns, loomed formidable on our north-western frontier.

During the Afghan War the Sikhs had attempted to corrupt our sepoys and detach them from the service. An invasion of the British Provinces had often been vauntingly talked of in the Punjab. The fame of the British arms had now been diminished. The Sikh State was partly a combination of Hindu sectaries; and an alliance between the Hindu army of Gwalior and the army of the Khalsa to establish Hindu supremacy in Hindustan was no remote possibility.

On December 29, 1843, at Maharajpore the English once more encountered the Marathas. They fought with all their ancient valour, but after a desperate resistance had to yield to British bayonets. The same day another British force encountered another portion of the Maratha army at Punniar, twelve miles from Gwalior. It was well for India that Lord Ellenborough, by his prompt action, destroyed the Gwalior army before the inevitable collision with the Sikhs came.

On the 6th of December 1846, eleven years before the Mutiny, the Punjab Sikh army crossed the Sutlej—an act of war—and the Sikhs fought fiercely on its banks. After a bloody and obstinate contest, in which we only held our own, and two hard-won successes, twenty thousand British troops occupied the capital of the Punjab. Ranjeet Singh's young son was put on the throne, and a Regency, with treaty stipulations intended to secure the administration of the Punjab under the general superintendence of British administrators, was established. The new arrangements were bound to be as ineffectual as the English occupation of Afghanistan. The Sikh army had been defeated, not crushed; the Khalsa had submitted, but had not been inspired with the fear or strength of our power. We declared our sojourn to be temporary. No Government of foreigners can afford to treat the title, morality, or durability of its rule as an open question. It leads to fallacies, dangerous illusions, and disappointment.

The Queen-Mother and the Chiefs of the Punjab were

soon deep in a plot, not only against the new arrangement, but for the complete destruction of British rule. The Rani opened secret communication with Cabul, Candhar, and Cashmere. She strove to unite the Princes of Rajpootana and the Maratha Chiefs in a Hindu conspiracy against the English. She roused the patriotic zeal of the Sikh troops in the Durbar army. She attempted to destroy the allegiance of our native troops, by troubling the dark spirit of fanaticism which dwelleth in the Oriental mind. She sent emissaries to every native regiment to inform them of the riots which had taken place at Lahore, owing to the killing of a cow by a European soldier. The poisoners of the Sepoy mind succeeded in sowing the seeds of a suspicion that our Government intended to destroy the Brahmin soldier's caste. After the outbreak at Multan in April 1848 the plot was discovered, the Rani was conveyed across the Sutlej and sent a state-prisoner to Banares. No worse spot could have been chosen than the sacred city, the centre of the hierarchy of Hindu religious fraternities. The Rani entered into communication with the Maratha Brahmins who resided there, and through them with the exiled Peshwa and his retinue at Cawnpore. The centre of the conspiracy for Hindu supremacy was transferred from the capital of the Punjab to Cawnpore, Benares, and Poona. The local outbreak at Multan, like the outbreak at Meerut, upset the plan of the leaders of the movement for a simultaneous revolution throughout India. The *emeute* at Multan led to a general rising of the military classes in the Punjab, and the old Sikh army reassembled to fight again for the independence of the Khalsa. The Sikhs hoped that the Bengal troops would join in a war against the Government that they had begun to believe was hostile to their religion. But the canker of disloyalty, which ultimately destroyed the Bengal army, had not then infected the whole body. At Chillianwalla (January 1849) some of the regiments fought with gallantry, but some by their treachery nearly produced terrible disaster. It was averted by the valour of the British soldier. The treachery of some of the Native Regiments was reported to the Military Board, but no action was taken. The fatal policy of weakness and hush was followed. The Sepoy was nattered, the British soldier ignored. The Asiatic mercenary came to the conclusion that he was the flaster of India. Soon after the annexation of the Punjab a sepoy in the Province asked an officer what he would do without them.

When after a protracted war-time there came a calm, the Bengal sepoy turned his attention to two subjects which are always of vital interest to the mercenary soldier—pay and privileges. He resented that the victories which his foreign rulers told him he mainly had helped to gain should result in a pecuniary loss to himself. The conversion of the Punjab into a British province entailed the loss of extra allowances, and the sepoys in the Punjab, and those who had been ordered there, quietly agreed to strike for higher pay. The official documents prove that at this time native regiments began to communicate with one another by emissaries on the subject of their real or supposed grievances, and had established by an understood general consent an armed unions.

The rigid enforcement of a financial resolution passed some years before, which resulted in a petty economy at the sepoy's cost, increased his annoyance and shook his belief in the good faith of the Government. Five regiments openly evinced a dangerous mutinous spirit; one attempted to seize a strong fortress, and when Sir Charles Napier, by a prompt and daring measure, contrived to extinguish the flame ere it had spread over the Empire, he was told it did not exist.

'I have confronted," wrote the Governor- General, "the assertions of the Commander-in-Chief on this head with undisputed facts and with the authority of recorded documents. Fortified by these facts and documents, and my convictions strengthened by the information which the Government commands, I desire to record my entire dissent from the statement that the army has been in mutiny and the Empire in danger."

A year after the foregoing was written, the Governor-General requested the 38th Regiment to proceed to Burma. They refused on account of caste prejudice. The Governor-General, and the Commander-in-Chief who succeeded Sir Charles Napier, succumbed. The 38th was not disbanded. In every cantonment it was known that the Governor - General had suffered a repulse.

Lord Dalhousie prepared the general enlistment - order, which his successor Lord Canning passed, that in future every recruit of the Bengal army should "at the time of his enlistment distinctly undertake to serve beyond sea, whether within the territories of the Company or beyond them."

The order was discussed in every regimental line by the Brahmin soldier, and it was regarded as a fresh illustration of the intention of Government to destroy their religion and caste.

A loyal Native officer, tracing the causes of the Mutiny, stated: "When the old sepoys heard of this order, they were much frightened and displeased. They said: 'Up to this day those men who went to Afghanistan have not been readmitted to caste; how are we to know where the English may not force us to go? They will order us next to London."

Ten years before the Mutiny a sepoy remarked to an officer in the Punjab, when he heard that Scinde was to be joined to Bengal:"Perhaps there will be an order to join London to Bengal."

Lord Canning wrote home that there was no symptom that the enlistment order was unpopular, or that the sepoys enlisted on the old terms regarded it as a first step towards breaking faith with themselves— an instructive instance of a ruler being told only what is pleasant.

The sepoy objected to annexation because each new province added to the Empire widened his sphere of service. But it also increased his power; as each new province was added the cry arose for "more troops." It is too often forgotten that it is possible to arm and discipline too many native troops, which may become a source of difficulty and danger—costly in themselves and doubly costly when they jmust be watched by European regiments.

The Bengal army was gradually increased, while the European force gradually decreased. At the close of Lord Dalhousie's rule the Native army was 233,000, while the European force numbered 45,322. Lord Dalhousie saw — what Lord Gough had so urgently pressed upon the Government some years before—that this relative proportion of British to native troops was dangerously small.

On the 28th of February, the last day he presided at the Council of India, he laid on its table nine minutes containing his views and proposals on military subjects. In these minutes he insisted on the European force as "the essential element of our strength,"and advocated "an increase in our Europeanand a substantial decrease in our native army.

The recommendations were neglected; the minutes never reached Parliament or the British public, with whom rests the ultimale control of Indian affairs. The result in this case was that owing to the paucity British troops the principal arsenals and military posts were garrisoned by the Bengal

Lawrence, the great soldier-statesman not only called attention to the numerical disproportion of the native to the European force, but also to the system by which they were locatecd.

In the Punjab were gathered the British bayonets, between Agra and Calcutta were two European regiments; the newly-annexed kingdom of Oudh was guarded by one weak European regiment. The high military commands of the favoured and for-midable Bengal troops were given to men whose only claim rested on seniority. The nerves of discipline were relaxed by the sepoys being encouraged to make frivolous complaints to Headquarters, and they became impatient of any subordination.

The murmurs regarding regimental grievances swelled to seditious clamour. The spirit of discontent and disaffection increased, and when the occasion came it broke into a general revolt. Some of the causes of the Bengal army mutiny are still at work and ought not to be allowed to remain.

Among the many causes to which the great conflagration is attributed, the resentment of the people at the deposition of their princes has been regarded as one of the most important. During the decade preceding the revolt of the Bengal army the Kingdom of Punjab and the Kingdom of Pegu were acquired by conquest. Oudh was annexed on the just ground of intolerable misgovernment. Various chiefships and separate tracts were brought under the sway of the British Government by the vigorous enforcement of the rule that, in cases where natural heirs failed, the sovereignty of subordinate states should not descend to an adopted son but lapse to the paramount authority.

Neither the doctrine of escheat nor the practice was new, but it was never so systematically enforced. This policy was regarded as a fresh illustration that the British Government intended to outrage the feelings, laws, and usages of the Hindu people, and that their earth-hunger was insatiable. The majority of the chiefs, though they regarded with suspicion and distrust the confiscation of kingdoms, did not join in the revolt.

The native officers made a blunder when they waited on the Moghul Emperor in the Imperial Hall of Special Audience and "promised to establish his rule throughout the whole country." The great Hindu chiefs had no incentive to restore the paramount power of the Moghul Caesars. The great principalities of Rajpootana, who for some centuries had maintained a gallant struggle against the Delhi sovereigns, had no desire to be again under the obligations of allegiance, tribute, and military service to the Moghul Emperor.

They also had not forgotten the extortions and indignities of the Maratha predatory rulers, and they had no wish to revive the power of the Maratha Confederacy. The powerful lieutenants of the Great Moghuls, like the Nizam, who had carved out independent kingdoms, had no inclination to be again in the grip of the Moghul central power. They, remembered the time when the Maratha the land, ransacked cities, and annexed fertile provinces. No ruler had any desire to taste bitterness of military tyranny.

The chiefs and princes had a difficult and delicate part to play. They had in their civic courts nobles who were anxious that they should join in the destruction of the British power. Certain of them had large bodies of troops, commanded and trained by British officers and recruited from the same class as the Bengal sepoy, who were on the verge if not in the heroes of rebellion. They had to deal with a priesthood fomenting hatred against the Nazarene. They confronted the dangers which beset them with firmness and dexterity, and they overcame them by a resolute bearing, the fidelity of their own troops and the feeling of reverence and loyalty which (Orientals have for a personal sovereign).

It is described how Maharaja Scindia, a born soldier, amidst many trials and temptations, was found faithful in the hour of need. The suspicion and distrust which the doctrine of escheat had created had been removed by the distinguished cordiality with which Lord Canning welcomed the young sovereign when he visited Calcutta, and the most emphatic assurance' that the Governor-General gave him that the British Government would ever rejoice in the prosperity of the Gwalior State under the rule of its hereditary chief.

In these pages are also recorded the important services rendered by the great chiefs of Rajpootana, representatives of ancient houses. The Mutiny revealed to us the advantage of native states as (to use the words of *Lord Canning) "breakwaters to the storm which would otherwise have swept over us in one great wave."*

At the close of the storm the native chiefs saw clearly that the British Government was the paramount power in India, and that the maintenance of their rights and interests was identical with British supremacy. By the valour of her soldiers, by the ministry of the brave military and civil officers of the East India Company, Queen Victoria became in fact Empress of India.

A new era was introduced in India by the Queen's Proclamation (1st November 1858), which announced that "We shall respect the rights, dignity, and honour of native princes as our own; and we desire that they, as well as our own subjects, should enjoy that prosperity and that social advancement which can only be secured by internal peace and good government.

The "adoption Sanad" which Lord Canning gave to the chiefs were in accordance with the Queen's utterances. The royal warrants stated that "Her Majesty being desirous that the governments of the several princes and chiefs of India, who now govern their own territories, should be perpetuated, and that the representation and dignity of their houses should be continued,"conveyed to them the assurance that, in the case of the Hindu states the succession of an adopted son would be confirmed, and in the case of Mahomedan states any succession legitimate according to the Mahomedan law.

"Be assured," were the closing words of the Sanad, "that nothing shall disturb the egagement just made to you so long as your house is loyal to the crown and faithful to the treaties, grants, and engagements which records its obligations to the British Government.

The influence of the Sanads extended far beyond those who received them. "There is a reality in the suzerainty of the sovereign of England," wrote Lord Canning, "which has never existed before, and which is not only felt but eagerly acknowledged by the chiefs. "The reality grew stronger as the long and beneficent reign advanced, and the chiefs became acquainted with the private and personal virtues of a queen whose wish was to see them strong and their subjects prosperous.

Twenty years after the Mutiny, on the historic plain of Delhi, the Viceroy, surrounded by the great chiefs and princes of the continent, formally proclaimed Her Majesty the Queen to be Empress of India, and thus permanently and publicly fixed Her Majesty's suzerain power in India.

Kirig Edward by his fine tact and wide sympathetic nature made the great chiefs feel proud of being royal feudatories of a sovereign whose dominion extends to every quarter of the globe. On the 12th of December 1911, at the imperial city, the King Emperor and Queen Empress were crowned in Durbar, and the chiefs and princes of India did homage to a crown older and more illustrious than any Moghul Caesar's.

Although the impartial historian must acknowledge the propriety of some of Lord Dalhousie's annexations, and record with gratitude the valuable assistance rendered us by the great chiefs in the suppression of the rebellion, he must also record the fact that the policy of annexation carried out under the doctrine of lapse supplied fresh vigour and new leaders to the conspirators who had been working for the restoration of the Peshwa and the destruction of the paramount power.

The King of Oudh, the Begum of Oudh, and the Rani of Jhansi joined it because they saw a chance of recovering lost dominions. It is impossible to trace exactly the form and working of the conspiracy, but there is sufficient evidence to show that the Nana and these leading conspirators communicated and corresponded. Azimoolah Khan, a clever Mahomedan adventurer, who, had been to London and the Crimea just after the repulse of the allies, was the chief channel of communication between the Mahomedan and Brahmin conspirators. Both the Mahomedan and the Hindu sepoy had to be won over for the success of the conspiracy.

John Lawrence, in his letter on the trial of the King of Delhi, states that "the mutiny was not attributable to any external conspiracy whatever"; a mass of Sepoy correspondence had been inspected, the records ofIhe Moghul palace had been ransacked, "and yet no trace of such a detailed plan" was found.

It is strange that Lord Lawrence with all his experience should not have known that the corres pondence of the conspiracy would not be the public post, but conveyed by private hands such as fakeers and other religious mendicants who were the agents of the disaffected.

It was these missionaries of sedition who, working the surface, passed up and down the country foretelling ruin, disaster, and the wrath of God, and announcing the near destruction of a power that was destroying their religion and their caste.

They revived the memory of the old prophecy that the iron age of British supremacy would last only a century after the rout of Plassey (1757).

Ominous symptoms of unrest and agitation now began to appear among the masses. It is a difficult task to decide to what extent the revolt can be connected with popular discountent. "In no case", says John Lawrence, "did popular tumult precede the military outbreak; but invariably where it occurred at all, it ensued upon a mutiny, like cause following effect." But in some cases after the mutiny of the troops at Meerut and the capture of Delhi, the populace rose before the sepoys.

The religious mendicant who caused people to believe that "the English are people who overthrew all religions," aroused the fanatical passions of the rural classes; but there were other forces at work, and other questions involving their rights and interests in the soil, which excited them.

After the annexation of Oudh the rights and position of the barons of the kingdom,s were ignored. With a few exceptions the Talookdars went against us, and what is most important to remember - the people followed them *en masse*. The settlement of Oudh had been founded on the lines of the settlement of the older and bordering North-Western Provinces.

When we gained these provinces we found numerous

village proprietary bodies whose title we maintained, and we also found proprietors of large estates built up of numerous villages, often of villages the original proprietary bodies of which had placed themselves under these proprietors for the sake of protection against the exactions con-current with misrule. The power and influence of these superior proprietors were a factor of immense importance, demanding careful handling in the settlement of a large province by a new power.

Sir Auckland Colvin, who had spent his official life in the province and governed it for five years, tells us—"Not a few who at the commencement of British rule had owned large estates now found themselves ousted. "Many of these ancient titles had been adjudged defective. The administrators of the Upper Provinces, driving at the welfare of the actual cultivator or the occupying owner, also made the mistake of ignoring the inferior proprietor, whose goodwill it was their interest to win.

The British Government introduced the power of public and private sale—a power which was formerly unknown—and the estates of families of rank fell into the hands of shopkeepers and money-lenders. A "Magistrate and Collector" in charge of a large district at the informs us—"These men, in a vast majority of instances, were also absentees, fearing or disliking to reside on their purchases, where they were looked upon as interlopers and unwelcome intruders.

The ancient proprietary of these alienated estates were again living as tenantry on the lands once theirs; by no means reconciled to their change of position, but maintaining their hereditary hold as strong as ever over the sympathies and affections of the agricultural body, who were ready and willing to join their feudal superiors in any attempt to recover their lost position and regain possesion of their estates. "When the province was in a blaze, the old proprietors strove to eject the moneyed classes who had supplanted them, and they were assisted by their former tenants.

It required a small spark to kindle a blaze in a society passing through a period of religious and economic unrest. The greased cartridge which the Mahomedan and Brahmin sepoy honestly believed to have been greased with the fat of swine or of the cow, was the spark which fell on combustible materials.

The Government refused to believe that they had to deal with a genuine feeling of discontent founded on a substantial grievance. At Meerut, the sepoys who would not receive their cartridges were treated as criminals, and with unnecessary degradation delivered up to the penalties of military law.

On Sunday, the fatal 10th of May, there was a military outbreak at that great and important cantonment. Then fanaticism, bigotry, reverence of caste, poverty, and discontent with land settlements blazed out, and flames of consuming fire swept over the land.

Fifty years have passed since the great revolt. The land is again passing through a state of transformation, economic, intellectual, and religious, the same dark and mysterious forces are stirring beneath the surface.

The story of the Mutiny conveys many lessons how the problems of the future should be solved and in what spirit they should be faced. Power and strength there must always be to discipline peace. The crowning of the King - Emperor and Queen - Empress at the imperial city is a noble and chivalrous endeavour to bind the myriads of India, not by the bonds of material improvement and administrative efficiency, but by the living roots of faith, hope, charity, and loyalty.

2

January - March 1857

JANUARY: At the beginning of this year the East India Company had a composite force of European and Indian troops to guard its interests in India. By a coincidence the European troops were abnormally below establishment, and amounted to some 4 regiments of Cavalry, 31 regiments of Infantry and 64 batteries or companies of Artillery, the latter were composed only partly of British troops. There were 6,170 officers and 39,352 men in these units. They were armed with the Enfield rifle, and the artillery had 6pdr and 9pdr field guns, 18pdr and 24pdr heavy field guns, and 24pdr siege guns with 8inch howitzers and mortars. The Indian troops, who were armed with the old 'Brown Bess' musket, were divided into three armies, based in Madras, Bombay and Bengal. The Bengal Army alone mutinied: it consisted of some 34 regiments of Cavalry (regular and irregular). 119 regiments of Infantry (regular and irregular), 32 companies of Artillery and 6 companies of Engineers, with a total strength of some 135,767 troops of all ranks. It is difficult to compute, with any accuracy, the exact number of these troops that actually mutinied, but the figure probably approaches 100,000 trained soldiers. The preponderance of Brahmins in the Bengal Army was very great, and a high proportion of these had been recruited from Oude[Awadh], chiefly the Byswira and Banoda Divisions of that province. Indian troops outnumbered Europeans by a factor of 25 to 1 in Bengal.

This month saw the beginning of the phenomenon known as the 'passing of the *chapaties.*' These small unleavened cakes circulated through certain districts of the North West Provinces, no attempt was made to hide the matter, indeed many were brought to British officers and an explanation sought as to their meaning. The latter is still not clear, but it may be that it was a signal sent *by* those intending revolt, the pattern was fairly similar- the *chowkidar* (village watchman) would receive two (or one) *chapaties* with instruction to make ten (or six) more and distribute them two by two or one by one to neighbouring villages. Rather like a chain letter the 'news' (though no one knew what it was) spread like wildfire. Some villagers in fact thought it was Government that was circulating the *chapaties!* An interesting account of the phenomenon is to be found in Khodang Godur. the diary of Mainudin Husain. set forth in Charles Metcalfe's. *Two Native Narratives of the Mutiny in Delhi.* London. 1898.

JANUARY 22 : A *lascar* attached to the magazine at Dum Dum near Calcutta, asked a sepoy of the garrison to give him a drink of water from his *lota:* the sepoy indignantly refused, saying that the vessel would be contaminated by the lips of a low-caste man; nettled by this reply the

The Cartridge

lascar retorted that the sepoy would soon be deprived of his caste altogether, for Government was busy manufacturing cartridges greased with the fat of cows and swine, and the sepoys would have to bite the forbidden substance before loading their weapons. This is possibly the or gin of the greased cartridge controversy: certainly the tale spread rapidly among the sepoys of the Bengal Army, and for many this is regarded as the true origin of the 'mutiny'. There was some foundation for what the *lascar* said. The manufacture of greased cartridges to be used with the new Enfield rifle which was to replace the 'Brown Bess' musket had long been going on. and the grease contained tallow of doubtful origin.

Had the cartridges been handled in the old way then there might not have been a problem, but the drill devised for the Enfield rifle entailed the sepoy *biting off the end of the cartridge with his teeth* before upending it and ramming it down into his weapon. It was this drill rathe;than the grease itself (for Indian artillerymen of high caste had long used such grease on their guns) which was thought to be damaging: the high caste Hindu would be contaminated by the fat of cows, the Muslim sepoy or trooper would be defiled by the touch of pig fat. For further investigation of this matter of greasing the cartridges see T. Rice Holmes.*A History of the Indian Mutiny*, London,1904. Appendix W, and P.J.O.Taylor. *A Companion to the 'Indian Mutiny' of 1857*, Delhi,1996, p 70. Within a week of this incident being reported

General Hearsey

the manufacture of these cartridges ceased at Dum Dum, and General Hearsey the Divisional Commander ordered that the sepoys be allowed to prepare their own grease, but it was too late. Trust had been destroyed, the belief that Government had entered a great conspiracy to deprive the sepoys of their caste and forcibly convert them to Christianity had taken hold upon the imagination of a large part of the Bengal army. In Dum Dum itself where there was a Musketry Depot for training in the use of the new Enfield rifle, the sepoys *apparently* accepted the reassurance of Government, at least until the month of May.

JANUARY 26: A Treaty was signed at Peshawar (literally the ceremony took place at the entrance to the Khyber Pass), with Dost Mohamed the Amir of Afghanistan, agreeing to assist him against Persia. The Shah had claims upon the territory of Herat and was busy intriguing with rebels there to oust the Afghans. The treaty owed much to the vision and character of the Commissioner of Peshawar. Herbert Edwardes: it was agreed that the British should furnish the Amir with 4,000 stand of arms, and a subsidy of a lakh of rupees a month, and that, in return, the Amir should maintain an army of 18,000 men to act against Persia, and allow a British mission to enter his country to watch over the expenditure of the subsidy. 'I have made an alliance, said Dost Mahomed, with the British Government, and, come what may, I will keep it till death. He remained true to this vow, and his friendship during the period of the 'Mutiny' was to be of crucial importance to the British cause.

JANUARY 27: A consequence of the alliance and friendship that had been established between the British Government in Calcutta and the Amir of Afghanistan. Dost Mohamad was that the East India Company became involved in that was to he its last war. This was a campaign against Persia.

Troops from India (Bombay) reached the Persian Gulf on 7 December 1856, under the command of Major General Stalker. The town of Bushire was taken without difficulty and two 'battles' fought and won by the British. Major-General Sir James Outram arrived on this day and took command, with Brigadier-General Henry Havelock as his chief subordinate commander. The campaign was swiftly over, the Shah making peace (in Paris) and withdrawing all his claims to Herat etc. The British force withdrew after a few months, Outram and Havelock arrived back in India in late May to hear that the 'Mutiny' had broken out. The 'Persian War', marked by so few battles, is notable for the suicide of two senior British officers, both of whom were apparently oppressed by the responsibility of high command: Major-General Stalker, and Commodore Ethersley (who had been placed in command of the Indian Navy in the Persian Gulf).

JANUARY 28: General Hearsey reported to-the Governor General that there was ill-feeling among his men. Incendiarism at Barrackpore and Raniganj included the burning of public buildings and officers' bungalows. Rumblings of discontent and insubordination had begun.

FEBRUARY 6: The cartridge grievance was inquired into at Barrackpore, close to Calcutta, where the 34th BNI were stationed. Despite assurances and analysis of the cartridge paper the sepoys refused to accept the official denial that grease had been applied to the cartridges during manufacture; the paper was shiny and the gloss looked suspiciously like grease.

FEBRUARY 9: Hearsey paraded the 34th BNI and tried to convince them they had nothing to fear. Despite his eloquence - and he was fluent in their language - they remained sceptical of government's good faith.

FEBRUARY 11: General Hearsey again warned Government about disaffection. It began to be rumoured in Calcutta that a mutiny of the sepoys could be expected, ***and had already been arranged,*** and that the cartridges were just an excuse.

FEBRUARY 26: The 19th Bengal N.I. were stationed at Berhampore, under their Commanding Officer Colonel Mitchell. Some detachments of the 34th BNI from Barrackpore arrived on transfer and they very soon spread their fears about the cartridges to the 19th, and there was a riot. Mitchell attempted to overawe them with cavalry and artillery, but he had no British troops and was in an impossible position. His angry speeches to the regiment merely confirmed in their eyes that the British did have something to hide in the matter of the cartridges, but for the time being they resumed their duties apparently with obedience and punctuality. It was clear however that their riot would be punished.

MARCH 2: Canning, the Governor General, sympathised with the doubts of the sepoys and announced a 'concession' to the effect that they would henceforth be allowed to pinch off the end of the cartridge instead of biting it, but it was to no avail: the sepoys objected that habit would make them use their teeth in stead of their fingers.

Lord Canning

MARCH 17: Hearsey tried again to address his men, in particular the 34th at Barraakpore. He assured them there was no design against their caste or their religion and as they had not been convicted of any crime they would not be punished: this however tended to make them even more fearful, as they contemplated the fate of the mutinous 19th.

MARCH 19: General Anson, the Commander-in-Chief, arrived at Ambala on his tour of inspection, accompanied by the 36th BNI. Two NCOs of the regiment who had been at the musketry depot there ran out to meet their comrades, but instead of a cheery welcome were railed at as perverts and Christians because they had handled the accursed cartridges.

MARCH 20: Lieutenant Martineau who was the musketry instructor at the Ambala Depot, and who thus saw small parties of sepoys from many different regiments, reported that 'the entire Bengal army is labouring under the dread of forcible conversion' ie to Christianity. Anson was undecided as to what to do. he was loth to be severe: the decision was placed in Canning's hands.

MARCH 29: In some opinions this day sees the true outbreak of the mutiny proper; ie the Mangal Pande incident. The 34th BNI had a British Sergeant-Major. Hewson by name, attached to it, and he was told that a sepoy *by* the name of Mangal Pande had come out of the lines with his musket loaded, which was against standing orders. In turn he informed the adjutant Lieutenant Baugh. Hewson and Baugh found Mangal Pande outside the quarter-guard calling on his comrades to help him strike a blow for their religion: he fired at Baugh and brought down his horse, and then took on both Hewson and Baugh with his *tulwar* and was a match for them both. The sepoy was clearly under the influence of some drug, although he was of previously good character. The guard of twenty sepoys looked on unconcerned, only one. Sheik Paltu came to the aid of the Europeans and held Mangal Pande while they escaped. Colonel Wheeler of the 34th came up and ordered the guard to arrest the mutineer but no one obeyed him. Similarly Brigadier Grant came up and was ignored. Mangal Pande was continuing to taunt his comrades. Hearsey and his two sons then rode up and Hearsey with some courage threatened the guard with his revolver and forced them to move against the mutineer, but the latter turned his musket against himself: he fell wounded and was arrested and taken off to the hospital.

MARCH 30: The 19th BNI inarched down from Berhampore to Barrackpore and were met by some of the 34th who urged them to join in with the slaughter of the European officers, but they refused.

MARCH 31: The 19th BNI were paraded at Barrackpore in the presence of all the troops the could be mustered, and informed that the regiment was to be disbanded. In obedience to orders they piled their arms: they were then given their last pay and dismissed. Hearsey gave them a sad but kind farewell address, and, somewhat surprisingly, they cheered him heartly as they left the parade-groud.

3

April - May 1857

APRIL : During this month before the outbreak of the rebellion, many rumours were spread. It was whispered that the British were attempting to defile both Hindu and Muslim (and thus make conversion to Christianity easier) by mixing the ground bones of cattle and pigs with *alia* on sale in the bazar. The story appears to have originated in Meerut near to which, at mills in Bhola, the *atta* was ground before being sent down to Kanpur for sale. Although government had, from first to last, nothing to do with this flour which was in the hands of contractors and merchants, the rumours - and resultant panic - soon spread rapidly and were difficult to contain. See W.H.Carey *The Mahomedan Rebellion,* 1857, and *Mutiny Narratives,* esp. F. Williams. *Narrative of Events attending the Outbreak of Disturbances and the Restoration of Authority in the District of Meerut in 1857-58.* See also FSUP Vol I, p 395 *et seq.*

APRIL 4: Canning now decided that government had made

enough concessions, concluding, probably rightly, that they were being regarded as a sign of weakness. Native officers at Ambala were telling Anson that although their own fears might have been removed the general fears of the army remained, and that if any troops used the cartridges they would be cast out of the society of their comrades and even of their own families. But the decision was now taken not to withdraw the cartridges.

APRIL 6: Mangal Pande, who had survived his self-inflicted wound, was tried and sentenced to be hanged at Barrackpore. At his court martial he declared that he had been taking *bhang* and opium of late and had not been aware at the time of what he was doing. He refused to give the names of those who had incited him to mutiny, but declared he had done it of his own free will. This refusal has been interpreted as implying that there *were* others involved, and for his refusal to betray them he has been made into a hero. Hearsey believed him to have acted alone, but to have been motivated by religion as much as by drugs. For details see Sir George Forrest. *Selections from the Letters, Dispatches and other State Papers of the Military Department of the Government of India 1857-58,* Calcutta, 1893-1912, Vol I.

APRIL 8: Mangal Pande was hanged.

APRIL 10: The troops at Lucknow were also becoming restless as the rumours continued to spread. Dr Wells was the surgeon of the 48th BNI (commanded by Lt. Colonel Palmer). His claim to notoriety is that he was insensitive enough to offend the caste prejudices of the sepoys of his regiment. 'Having occasion to visit the medicine store of the hospital, and feeling at the same time indisposed, he incautiously applied to his mouth a bottle taken from the hospital medicines containing a carminative.' No high-caste Hindu could afterwards have partaken of the contents of the bottle: the doctor's incautious 'swig' caused an outcry, a refusal by the sepoys to take any medicine, and an addition to the legend that the English were intending to convert all the sepoys to Christianity.

APRIL 11: The Jemadar of the guard at Barrackpore who had refused the order to arrest Mangal Pande was put on trial by court martial, and sentenced to be hanged.

APRIL 16: Dr Wells's bungalow in Lucknow was burnt down, and although it was known to have been done by sepoys of the 48th BNI nothing could be proved and no action was taken. See Martin Gubbins. *The Mutinies in Oudh,* London, 1858, chapter 1.

APRIL 17: An immediate result of Canning's decision on the cartridges, when it became known to the men, was that fires broke out in the cantonment of Ambala, especially in government buildings and officers' bungalows. It was later established that this type of incendiarism regularly accompanied the beginnings of mutiny, but at Ambala this was not then understood, and Courts of Enquiry were convened but were unable to establish causes as no one would come forward to give evidence. zIn the next few days there were a number of tit for tat burnings, of the huts of sepoys attached to the musketry depot, and of huts belonging to the 60th BNI. Later a Sikh was to give evidence that the men had sworn to burn down every bungalow in the station, in revenge for the order to use the cartridges. See J. Cave-Browne, *The Punjab and Delhi in 1857.* Edinburgh 1861, Vol I p 42-50, and Kaye, *History of the Sepoy War.* Vol. I. p 412.

APRIL 22: Isri Pande the Jemadar of the 34th BNI who had been in charge of the quarter-guard when Mangal Pande mutinied was today hanged, without further incident, before the troops at Barrackpore, although on the scaffold he called for them to come to his aid. He confessed to the existence of a conspiracy. Kaye. *History of the Sepoy War,* Vol. I. p 429.

APRIL 24: At Meerut were stationed the 11th and 20th Regiments B.N.I. and the 3rd Native Cavalry; also in cantonment were H.M.'s 60th Rifle Regiment, a Regiment of Dragoons, and large bodies of horse and foot artillery, the strongest European force at any station in the North-Western Provinces. Colonel Carmichael Smyth, a hard and unpopular officer, commanded the 3rd Cavalry, and he determined to test his troops' obedience he took advantage of the order which instructed that the ends of the cartridges should be torn off with the fingers instead of biting them, to give a final explanation - and test-to his men. A parade was ordered of the ninety men the skirmishers of the regiment, who would ordinarily be the only ones armed with a musket. He explained the drill, drawn up he said in deference to their scruples, and ordered them to accept the cartridges offered to them. Even though they were *cartridges of the old kind,* only five NCOs would even touch them, the eighty-five troopers refused. Smyth dismissed the parade and convened a Court of Enquiry, and this echoed the conclusions arrived at in Ambala that it was not so much a genuine fear of the cartridges as a fear of public opinion that influenced the men. The report was sent to the Commander-in-Chief for his decision. Incendiarism became a nightly occurrence, in more than one station.

MAY 1: The recruits of the 7th Oudh Irregular Infantry at Lucknow refused to accept their cartridges on the grounds that the older soldiers of the regiment had warned them that obnoxious grease had been used on the ends of each of them. Their officers explained that these were the old familiar, cartridges, but to no avail.

MAY 2: The entire regiment of the 7th Oudh I.I. refused the cartridges, saying that they must do as did the rest of the army.

MAY 3: Sir Henry Lawrence, the Chief Commissioner of Oude[Awadh] and commander of all troops in that province, was told that the 7th Oudh I.I. had determined to murder their officers and break into open mutiny. In the evening therefore he confronted them with all the European troops he could muster and in the pale moonlight an artilleryman's lighting his port-fire led to a general panic and the sepoys slipped away in the darkness until only 120 remained; these laid down their arms when ordered to do so, and returned to their lines that same night. A good account of these events is in Martin Gubbins. *The Mutinies in Oudh,* London. 1858. esp. p 10-13. The leaders of the 'mutineers' were then seized and imprisoned.

Sir Henry Lawrence

MAY 5: At long last (five weeks after the Mangal Pande affair) the decision of the Governor General as to the punishment to be given to the 34th Bengal N.I. was announced: they were to be disbanded and dismissed. There was much British criticism of what was seen as this excessive, leniency - see *Friend of India,* May 14 1857, p 459. The disbanded sepoys, stripped of their uniforms contemptuously trod under foot their caps and rejoiced, apparently, at their release.

MAY 6: On the orders of the Commander-in-Chief the eighty-five troopers of the 3rd Cavalry at Meerut were court-martialled, the court consisting exclusively of Native Officers, (each was subsequently murdered by mutineers) and were sentenced to be dismissed and to ten years' imprisonment.

MAY 8: General Hewitt, commanding the Meerut Division, confirmed the sentence although reducing it to five years only for eleven of the youngest troopers.

MAY 9: The 3rd Bengal Native Cavalry- were publicly punished at Meerut, for the refusal of the eighty-five skirmishers to accept cartridges: on a parade of the entire Brigade the eighty-five were stripped of their uniforms and fettered, arms and legs (this process apparently took some *hours)* and led off to gaol. The remainder of the regiment watched impassively but were clearly greatly shocked. That evening a native officer of the 3rd Cavalry told Lieutenant Hugh Gough that the regiment was determined to rescue their comrades, but neither Colonel Smyth, to whom this was reported, nor Brigadier Archdale Wilson, took this seriously and no precautions were taken.

All, apparently, was normal.

4

May 10-31, 1857

MAY 10: The Mutiny began in the evening, on this Sunday, at Meerut. In the hearts of the sepoys a vague but irresistible tear mingled with hatred and the thirst for vengeance, and impelled them to anticipate the doom which they imagined the English to be preparing for them; while stronger than all their passions was the sense of a brotherhood linking them with the rest of the army...' see T. Rice Holmes, *History of the Indian Mutiny,* London, 1904, p 89. To what extent the rising was pre-planned is still under dispute. See P.J.O.Taylor, *Companion to the 'Indian Mutiny' of 1857,* O.U.P. Delhi. 1996, pp 243-6. 'Nature of the Conflict', for anexhaustive review of the possibilities. Most commentators believe the Bengal army had indeed been planning a mutiny for some time, and that the date fixed for the outbreak was May 31st 1857, and that correspondence between regiments had established this plan. If this is accepted then the rising at Meerut was premature, and this would have undoubtedly handicapped its success, and prejudiced the outcome. Colonel G.W. Williams was subsequently appointed to investigate the rising at Meerut; he took a great deal of evidence and concluded the outbreak there was not the result of a preconceived plan but was almost spontaneous, given the mood of the Bengal army. See G.W. Williams, *Depositions taken at Meerut under the direction of Lt. Col. G.W.W.*, Allahabad, 1858. At 8pm the first telegraphic message *re* mutiny was sent (to Agra.) See Kate Moore, *The Nineteenth Century,* November 1903. If there was a signal for the rising it was the church bells of the Garrison Church calling Christians to evening service: but there is a distinct possibility that it began, almost by accident, as the result of one trooper breaking under the taunts of the courtesans of the *bazar* brothels: they were egging on the men to rescue their 85 comrades from the gaol. See P.J.O.Taylor, *Companion etc.* op.cit.. p 217. The 3rd Cavalry galloped to the gaol in wild triumph and released their comrades. The infantry regiments, the 11th and 20th BNI fell in on their parade ground under their native officers. When the British officers arrived they held the men steady for a brief period, but when Colonel Finnis of the 11th was shot down in the gathering dusk (by sepoys of the 20th), the mutiny had really begun. The 11lh reacted to the death of their Colonel by hustling their officers off the parade ground (although they refused to harm them); the 20th were by now shooting at even white face in sight; the 3rd Cavalry spread arson and murder throughout the cantonment. Those murdered by the mutineers on that first day were buried in the churchyard and most of their graves may still be seen. From the Burial register of St John's church:- '11 May 12/3 Mav Buried Colonel John Finnis, Capt John Taylor. Veterinary Surgeons Phillips and Dawson, Corporal Richard Mortimer, Gunner Wm Benson, Lt MacNabb, Charlotte Chambers wife of Capt Chambers. 3 unknown men,

Eliza Law aged 9, John Mackenzie Chelsea Pensioner, John Marks ditto. Amelia Courtney, 2 Heatherley children, Sophia Langdale 7, Louise Macdonald, 2 unknown women. Fife Major Murphy, Capt Macdonald. Lts Henderson and Pattle, Vincent Tre- gear, Eliza Dawson, 2 unknown men. On 17 May Pte Fred Kingsford and Capt Edward Fraser Sappers & Miners.

The mutineers marched the same night for Delhi, some thirty miles to the south-west; General Hewitt could have pursued them and cut them down ruthlessly, but he did nothing; he did not even send news to Delhi of the outbreak. There are those who believe the greater fault lies with the Brigadier (Archdale Wilson) than with Hewitt. For a detailed factual account of this first day, and an assessment of the role of the chief protagonists, see J.A.B.Palmer. *Mutiny Outbreak at Meerut in 1857* Cambridge. 1966; see also Kaye or Rice Holmes, *op.cit.*

MAY 11: The Meerut mutineers, ie the 11th and 20th BNI and 3rd BL Cavalry marched to Delhi, arriving in the early hours at the bridge of boats on the left bank of the Jumna [Yamuna]. The Palace of the Ring of Delhi, descendant of the Mughal Emperors. Bahadur Shah Zafar, was on their route into the city, and they immediately proclaimed him Emperor, possibly to his surprise and certainly to his embarrassment, as he had no funds with which to pay them and sustain the revolt. All Europeans they could find were murdered, regardless of gender or occupation. The 5th Light Fd Batt Foot Art, 38th, 54th & 74th BNI, ie the entire garrison, mutinied at Delhi.

The great Magazine was blown up by the seven British officers and warrant officers in charge, when it was clear that it could no longer be held. Up to 250 of the mutineers were killed in the explosion, and this act provoked, in retaliation, the massacre of British prisoners, including women and children, a few days later. A handful of British survivors retreated first to the Flagstaff tower and then to Kurnaul. The City and surrounding countryside were completely in the hands of the rebels.

The same day 600 of the Bengal Sappers and Miners set off to march from Roorki to Meerut.

A desperate telegram sent from Delhi before the telegraph office was broken into, to Ambala, alerted the government of the Punjab and allowed for swift action to be taken before the news of Meerut and Delhi actually became common knowledge. See Llewellyn. Alexander.*The Siege of Delhi,* London. 1977 Rotton, Rev.John. *Chaplain's Narrative of the Siege of Delhi,* London, 1858; Kaye & Malleson; Metcalfe, Charles, *Two Native Narratives of the Mutiny of Delhi,* London, 1898. The last-named contains the significant account of Mainodin Hussain.

One of the strangest aspects of the story of the 'Mutiny' is that there now occurred an inexplicable lull in affairs. Until the end of the month of May little of note occurred, except in the Punjab, and the civil officers had time to study and report on their districts, and the army officers likewise their regiments. True, further units mutinied and many murders were committed, and a number of regiments disarmed by the British, but the concerted action which might have been expected from a planned uprising was entirely absent. The only explanation for this phenomenon is that the outbreak was premature and had been planned by the sepoys for 31st May 1857.

MAY 12: News of the Meerut outbreak reached Muzaffarnagar, Moradabad, Saharanpur, Etawah, Aligarh etc, and caused great excitement.

Bahadur Shah, as Emperor, in the Dewan-i-Khas in

the Red Fort at Delhi; three of his sons applied to him for army commands.

With a few exceptions the British military authorities remained paralysed and unsure of what to do. 'The rebels had it all their own way', says the Rev. John Rotton.

A telegram also reached Lahore on this day, conveying an exaggerated account of the massacres at Meerut and Delhi; Sir John Lawrence, the Chief Commissioner, was absent at Rawalpindi, but the Judicial Commissioner, Mr Montgomery, assembled a Council of seven senior civil and military officers who unanimously decided urgent action was required. Montgomery proceeded to Mian Mir, the military station near to Lahore, and consulted with Brigadier Corbett as to the action to be taken. A 'conspiracy' was then revealed, apparently by a Sikh NCO in the Police Corps, to the effect that the entire body of sepoys at Mian Mir intended to mutiny and seize the Fort at Lahore, release all prisoners (c.2,000) in the gaol and massacre all Europeans. The Brigadier determined to disarm all Indian troops in the station on the following day, but to allay all suspicion of anything unusual the ball scheduled to be given by the officers of H.M.'s 81st went ahead, and lasted until 2 a.m. the following morning.

MAY 13: At a parade for all troops at Mian Mir, 2,500 soldiers of the 16th, 26th and 49th BNI and the 8th Cavalry were disarmed by 600 Europeans of HM's 81st Regiment supported by twelve guns loaded with grape and with portfires burning: the exercise all went smoothly and with no violence. Lahore Fort was also occupied by the British troops, and all sepoys were marched off to their own lines at Mian Mir. There is considerable doubt as to whether the sepoys' conspiracy to mutiny here actually existed: there is no firm evidence, and the story depends upon the accounts written by Frederick Cooper in *Crisis in the Punjab*. Lahore, 1858, and an 'anonymous gentleman', in *Blackwood's Magazine*, Edinburgh. Jan. 1858.

Meanwhile, having heard, the night before, of the events at Meerut, Brigadier Innes, commanding the station at Ferozepur, in the Punjab, ordered a general parade to test the temper of the troops: he considered them 'haughty'. At noon the news arrived of the occupation of Delhi, seventy three miles to the south-east, and at five pm the 45th and 57th BNI mutinied and tried to capture the magazine, but were checked by a detachment of HM's 61st Regiment; men of the 45th were scattered and many killed, but because of the negative and defensive action of Brigadier Innes they were able to burn the Church, the R.C. Chapel, two vacant hospitals, the mess-house of the 6F and sixteen bungalows in the cantonment. The 10th and 25th N.L.Cavalry remained loyal to its officers, as did 133 men of the 45th BNI and about half of the 57lh BNI. For his ineptitude in handling this affair, Innes was removed from the list of Brigadiers.

At Peshawar on the same day a Council of War consisting of General Reed, Brigadier Cotton, Brigadier Neville Chamberlain, Colonel Edwardes and Colonel Nicholson resolved that the troops in the hills should be concentrated at Jhelum the central point of the Punjab. HM's 24th a troop of Horse Artillery. HM's 27th the Guide Corps, the 16ln Irreg cavalary, the Kumaon Regt, the 1st Punjab Infantry a wing of the 2nd Punjab Cavalry, and half a company of Sappers were ordered to concentrate at Jhelum for the purpose of forming a Moveable Column, to quell mutiny wherever it might appear. In this column there were a considerable number of Sikhs and Gurkhas, considered loyal to Government.

MAY 14: General Anson, the personally brave and energetic, but totally inexperienced Commander-in-Chief left Simla, bound for Ambala to head the troops.

MAY 15: Anson reached Ambala and held a Council of War there. By a strange coincidence not one of the senior officers there present lived to see the recapture of Delhi which was the reason for the Council's meeting: Generals Anson and Barnard, Brigadier Halifax and Colonel Mowatt died of cholera, and Colonel Chester, the Adjutant General was killed in action. Little therefore is known of what transpired, but the march upon Delhi was held up for want of tents and carriage, according to a telegram sent by Anson to the Governor General in Calcutta. The 8th Lt.Cav. were disarmed at Mian Mir.

MAY 16: In Delhi, some forty-eight (the number is far from sure) Europeans were massacred: they had either been taken to the King's Palace or had gone there of their own accord to seek protection. The King was probably unable to restrain the sepoys, in particular the sowars of the 3rd Cavalry from Meerut. It is said the King's sons witnessed, even if they did not organise, the massacre.

In Meerut 400 of the 600 Sappers and Miners who had marched there from Roorki broke into open mutiny and after murdering their commandant. Captain Fraser, they made off towards Delhi: being pursued by the Carabineers: they lost forty seven men killed but the remainder fled and eventually reached Delhi. The 4th BNI were disarmed at Kangra and Hoshiarpur.

MAY 17: On this Sunday an event occurred in Calcutta which plight have had serious consequences and which certainly shook the complacency of Government. The 25th BNI, or at least some elements thereof, attempted to obtain ball ammunition from the 70th BNI stationed in Fort William, with a view it was said to slaughter the Europeans and loot the city their advances were indignantly repulsed by the 70th and the European officers informed of the plot. The European 53rd Regiment was brought in from Dum Dum and the 25lh BNI disarmed without resistance.

MAY 19: General Anson had at first taken a firm line with regard to the 'cartridge question', but on this day he issued at Ambala a General Order to the army withdrawing the use of the offending cartridge: in future 'balled ammunition shall be made up by each regiment for its own use'. The proclamation was received by the men of the Ambala School of Musketry with satisfaction, but they constituted only a small portion of the troops in cantonment. The incendiarism in Ambala which had started in March continued unabated, and every night more bungalows etc were targeted.

MAY 20: The 55th BNI displayed disaffection, amounting to mutiny at Mardan forty-five miles north-east of Peshawar. Their Colonel, Spottiswoode, was so ashamed he committed suicide. 120 men remained loyal, the others fled and were pursued by Nicholson with horse artillery and Punjab Infantry: 150 were captured and others were brought in by the hill tribes. The 10th Irreg.Cavalry refused to act against the 55th BNI and were consequently disarmed and disbanded. Forty men of the 55th were blown away from guns.

At Aligarh, between Delhi and Agra, and fifty miles north of the latter, the 9th BNI, which had remained steady and loyal to government, suddenly mutinied, and without harming their officers, broke open the Treasury and the gaol and then (the majority) marched to Delhi to join the King.

MAY 21: The 24th, 27th, 64th and 51st BNI with 5th BN Cavalry were disarmed without incident in the morning at Peshawar, in accordance with the orders of Brigadier Cotton. The order was not extended to the 21st BNI which was considered to be staunch (and subsequent events proved this to be so). At Cawnpore [Kanpur] the Europeans commenced their 'intrenchment'. Major General Sir Hugh Massy Wheeler decided to fortify the old Dragoon Hospital buildings; a mud wall, four feet high and pitifully inadequate, was thrown up around two brick structures, one thatched and the other properly roofed. All Christian women and children were ordered into these barracks, but the officers of the sepoy regiments continued to sleep in the lines of their men. Wheeler hoped that his own reputation with the sepoys would prevent an outbreak, or, at the worst, ensure the sepoys marched straight off to Delhi.

MAY 22: News of the mutiny at Aligarh on the 20th reached Mainpuri and caused great excitement; the garrison consisted of three companies of the 9th BNI. The magistrate, Power, sent the European women and children off to Agra, seventy miles distant, and prepared to defend the station. He was assisted by a cousin of the Raja, one Rao Bhowani Singh, and by a remarkably brave young officer of the 9th BNI, Lieutenant de Kantzow. The result was that the station was held by the Europeans and the mutineers having done some looting but failing in their attempt to open the Treasury, marched off to Delhi.

At Etawah another detachment of the 9th BNI mutinied and marched off to Delhi after plundering the Treasury'. They were assisted by the local raja; the magistrate, Hume, escaped in the dress of an Indian woman. Bulandshahr, near Meerut, was also lost temporarily to government by the mutiny of yet another detachment of the 9th BNI.

MAY 24: Part (100 troopers) of the Gwalior Irregular Cavalry of the Gwalior Contingent, which had previously given loyal service to Government, mutinied at Hattras and went off to Delhi: 123 men remained with their British officer,

Lieutenant Cockburn, and with the help of volunteers re-opened some of the roads around Agra.

General Anson, the Commander-in-Chief left Ambala for Delhi. The Muslim festival of Id passed off without incident in Lucknow although Sir Henry Lawrence had been very apprehensive.

MAY 25: The Lieutenant Governor of the NWP, J.R. Colvin, now attempted to halt the spread of the rebellion by declaring in the *Agra Gazette Extraordinary,* that rebel landholders, *taluqdars,* would forfeit their land and that it would be given to such as remained loyal to Government. He also issued a Proclamation: '*Soldiers engaged in the late disturbances, who are desirous of going to their own homes, and who give up their arms at the nearest government civil or military post, and retire quietly, shall be permitted to do so unmolested. Many faithful soldiers have been driven into resistance to government only because they were in the ranks and could not escape from them, and because they really thought their feelings of religion and honour injured by the measures of government. This feeling was wholly a mistake; but it acted on men's minds. A proclamation of the governor general now issued is perfectly explicit, and will remove all doubts on these points. Every evil-minded instigator in the disturbance, and those guilty of heinous crimes against private persons, shall be punished. All those who appear in arms against the government after this notification is known shall be treated as open enemies.*

Hume, the Magistrate, temporarily restored British authority in Etawah, with the aid of some Grenadiers from the Gwalior Contingent, but the fidelity of the latter was doubtful, and indeed the re-occupation did not last for long.

MAY 26: Colvin's Proclamation of 24 May was disapproved of by Canning in Calcutta, and a telegram was today sent to

Agra insisting on its withdrawal, on the grounds it offered means of escape to sepoys who had murdered their officers.

Further disaffection was noticed in the Gwalior Contingent.

MAY 27: General Anson, the Commander-in-Chief died of cholera at Kurnaul, on the march towards Delhi. Sir Henry Barnard assumed temporary command, Martial law was declared at Etawah.

Brigadier Archdale Wilson's Field Force at long last left Meerut for Delhi.

MAY 28: General Reed provisionally succeeded Anson, and set off from the Punjab to take command of the British force converging on Delhi.

In Rajputana the 15th and 30th BNI and 7th Lt Fd Batt. mutinied at Nasirabad, near Ajmer, and marched off to Delhi. The wing of the 1st Bombay Light Cavalry (Lancers) remained for the most part loyal to government (although eleven troopers joined the rebels), and charged the mutineers but were repulsed.

MAY 29: Mutinous conduct was now widespread at Lucknow in Oude [Awadh] and at other, smaller, stations. It was reported that some *taluqdars* were resuming possession of villages of which they had been deprived by the Land Settlement of 1856.

By now Europeans were being hunted and killed in many areas of the NW Provinces.

The 5th BNI and 4th Lt. Cav at Ambala were disarmed as mutiny was imminent.

MAY 30: The British force (about 700 men) from Meerut under Brigadier Wilson arrived at Ghaziuddinnagar on the

Hindun river about ten miles from Delhi, and were encamped (and mostly asleep) at four p.m. when they were suddenly attacked by heavy guns. A force of mutineers from Delhi, numbering perhaps 3,000 men of all arms, was defeated in the resulting battle, losing many-dead and five guns: they retreated within the walls of Delhi but were so reproached for their failure that they determined to fight again the next day.

That same evening the firing of the 9 O'clock gun gave the signal for the mutiny in Lucknow of a section of the 71st BNI. They were joined by the 13th BNI, the 48th BNI and the 7th Light Cavalry, although in each case some small numbers of the regiment remained loyal to the British, to a total of about 500 out of the 4,000 trained troops. Later that night the mutineers were attacked by Sir Henry Lawrence at the cantonment area of Mudkipur with four guns and a company of the H.M.'s 32nd regiment, and were dispersed, some thirty prisoners being taken.

The Bhurtpore [Bharatpur] troops who were garrisoning Muttra | Mathura] some thirty-five miles from Agra, mutinied and marched for Delhi: one result was that Colvin in Agra determined to disarm the 44th BNI and 67th BNI.

MAY 31: The more militant citizens of Lucknow now at tempted to join the mutineers, but finding that the latter had fled they returned to the city and commenced a disturbance there, but were dispersed by the police and some of the irregular infantry, and many killed and some taken prisoner and lodged with the mutineer prisoners in the Machhi Bhawan: a court martial sentenced these prisoners to death to the number of 40 and they were hanged in front of the Machhi Bhawan, an 18pdr gun loaded with grape overawing the massed onlookers.

Some mutineers from Delhi returned to the attack on the Hindun River but were again defeated by Wilson and

The West Gate of the Machhi Bhawan

driven back into the city: this battle was fought mainly as an artillery duel, and the rebels succeeded this time in saving their guns.

General Barnard left Kurnaul to command the army against Delhi.

On this day also the 28th BNI mutinied at Shahjehanpur and attacked the Christians in the church, the *26* survivors, including 8 women and 4 children, made for Mohamdi which they reached in (temporary) safety. At Bareilly the 18th BNI, 68th BNI. 15th Lt Fd Ban, 8th Irreg Cavalry, all mutinied; the artillery took the lead, followed by the 68th BNI, while the 18th BNI and the cavalry hesitated, and at one stage actually asked to be led against the mutineers. In the end the entire Brigade rose. Brigadier Sibbald was killed on the parade ground, some officers Hod to Nainital, others were killed by villagers while escaping. Of the British civilians, nine were murdered, although a number also escaped. The story that the English judges, Robertson and Raikes, were hanged after a trial by the new Viceroy of Bareilly, is described by Kaye as 'pure fiction': see Kave Vol III p 274. Khan Bahadur Khan a government pensioner took the lead and was proclaimed Viceroy under the King of Delhi.

Moradabad also was in a state of ferment.

At Agra the 44th BNI and 67th BNI regiments were disarmed, and sent to their homes on two months' furlough: the extraordinarily complex nature of the revolt is illustrated by the fact that these sepoys were attacked and robbed, by villagers, on their journey down the Jumna river.

5

June - July 1857

JUNE 1: Lieutenant Governor Colvin completed the disarmament of the 44th and 67th BNI at Agra.

The sepoys at Mathura shot their officers and marched for Delhi. At moradabad Mr. Cracroft Wilson anxiously waited for news from Bareilly where the Bareilly Bridge (all Indian troops) was stationed : at 2 a.m. he was wakened by a letter from the Nawab of Rampur advising him that there had been a mutiny and massacre at Bareilly and telling him to flee at once. Instead he called a meeting of the officers (British and Indian) of the 29th B.N.I, and telling them the position frankly, asked them to march to Meerut with the guns and Government treasure: they agreed, but the native officers and sepoys had no real intention of complying. The local people were roused to revolt by two local Nawabs who hoped to profit from the confusion: one. Abbas Ali tried to persuade his followers to murder Wilson, but this was not done. The treasure was abandoned to the sepoys: Wilson and the

Collector, Saunders, rode off to Meerut with the civil surgeon and their families, while the British officers of the 29th with their families, left for Nainital which was closer. The subordinate clerks, and other Eurasians and Christians were subsequently murdered or carried off to Delhi.

The news of the Bareilly uprising also reached Budaon, thirty miles away on the Ganges, and at first it appeared that the Treasury Guard (men of the 68th BNI from Bareilly) would not mutiny, but by the evening the sepoys had risen, the treasury was looted, the gaol opened and the town and district given over to plunder. All trace of British rule was effaced, and Khan Bahadur Khan was proclaimed ruler: the rural population, incensed by British land settlement 'interference,' was as anxious to rebel as were the sepoys, although they had little sympathy for the latter. See particularly William Edwards, Personal Adventures during the *Indian Rebellion*, London, 1858. The magistrate, William Edwards, succeeded in reaching Kanpur eventually.

JUNE 2: The majority of the 5th BNI regiment mutinied at Saharanpur; some sepoys remained loyal, and protected their officers and the civil authorities. The detachment of the 29th BNI also remained loyal, together with the 4th Cavalry, and with their help (and the arrival shortly afterwards of some Gurkhas) the British made a determined stand and kept Saharanpur and its district, including the important engineer cantonment of Roorki, in the hands of government. See in particular H. Dundas Robertson, *District Duties during the Revolt*, London, 1959. p 68 et seq. On more than one occasion the decision to mutiny or to remain loyal appeared to be the result of impulse, sometimes influenced by panic. Once taken, the decision was occasionally reversed, though, again, logic played little part.

JUNE 3: The 17th BNI mutinied at Azimgarh, 65 miles north of Banares [Varanasi] after wavering for some time; the imminent despatch of government treasure to the extent of six lakhs of rupees proved impossible for them to resist. They shot two officers but protected the others and sent them on in safety to Ghazipur. For the time being all British authority in the city was gone. In many ways Azimgarh is a typical since it changed hands more than once, as the fortunes of each side ebbed and flowed.

At Sitapur, 50 miles north of Lucknow, the 41st BNI and 9th and 10th Oude Irrcg. Inf. and 2nd Oude Military Police mutinied. At this place the Commissioner, George Christian, had put his faith in the Oude troops and had taken up a position which he thought fully defensible; in the event *all* the troops mutinied. Colonel Birch of the 41st eight other officers. Mr & Mrs Thornhill, and Christian and his wife and one child were all murdered together with many other Christians; a few, including Sir Mountstuart Jackson and his two sisters escaped, for the time being. The most complete account of the rising in Sitapur is given in George Hutchinson, *Narrative of the Mutinies in Oudh*, London. 1859. The 41st BNI soon became notorious as the most bloodthirsty and extreme of the mutineers, yet no plausible reason has ever been advanced for this.

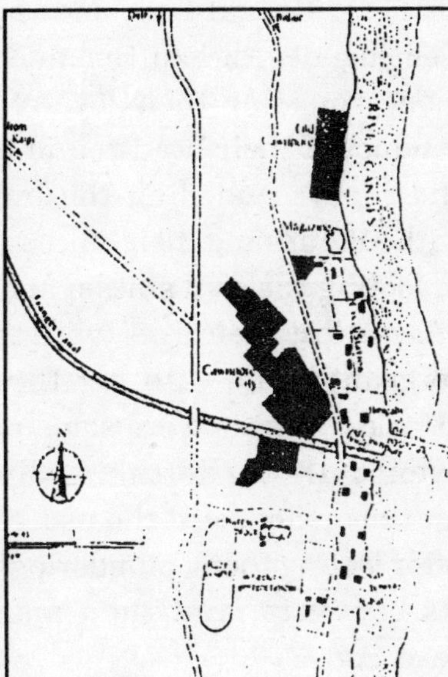

Cawnpore, Plan, 1857

Abbas Ali proclaimed himself ruler in Moradabad.

During the night a cashiered British officer (of the Bengal Fusiliers) fired on a patrol of the 2nd Cavalry in Cawnpore [Kanpur] and although no one was hurt it has often been considered that this was the 'spark that set fire to the dry tinder", that is. provoked the mutiny of the 2nd Native Cavalry on the following day. The officer claimed his rifle had gone off 'by accident' while he was drunk: troopers of the 2nd Cavalry are said to have muttered that one day soon their weapons also might be fired by accident.

JUNE 4: At Neemuch, about one hundred and fifty miles south of Nasirabad the entire force mutinied, viz 1st Lt Cav, 4th Tp 1st Brig Horse Art. 15th Lt Fd Batt, 72nd BNI, and a wing of the 1st Bengal Cav. and the 7th Regiment of the Gwalior Contingent. All had remained quiet until the 3rd June, the men protesting their loyalty, and their indignation at the conduct of their brethren in mutinous regiments. At 4 a.m. the sepoys guarding the impromptu fort mutinied, and, without harming their officers, filed out to join their comrades in looting the civil station and the cantonment. Although no officers lost their lives (with the exception of the murder of a sergeant's wife with her three children, no European was attacked), there were some narrow escapes, but all officers eventually made their way in safety to Udaipur. The mutineers followed the usual practice of burning bungalows after looting them, plundering the local Treasury and dividing its contents, and then marching on Delhi, via in this case, Agra.

At Mullaoh in northwest Oude [Awadh], a detachment of the 41st BNI and a detachment of the 4th Oudh Irregulars finally mutinied and the Deputy Commissioner, Mr Capper, who had behaved with great bravery at his lonely post, mounted his horse and rode to Lucknow, where he survived the siege of the Residency, although wounded.

Meanwhile at Banares [Varanasi] matters were rapidly coming to a head. The Indian troops consisted of the 37th BNI, the 13th Irreg. Cav. and the regiment of Loodianah Sikhs. The civil officers, Tucker and Gubbins, had preserved calm for the most part, but it was known that the 37th in particular was likely to rise. The British troops numbered only 250 (H.M.'s 10th, some Madras Fusiliers and thirty Artillery). The situation was complicated by the fact that the Brigadier, Ponsonby, was far from well, and that there had just arrived in Benares one Colonel James Neill. a Madras officer who had very decided views. Kaye describes him thus:*'Leading the way' to future conquests, he came to strike and to destroy. He was one of those who wisely thought from the first, that to strike promptly and to strike vigorously would be to strike mercifully; and he went to work before him with a stern resolution not to spare.'*

The immediate effect of this officer's conduct was to provoke a mutiny (partial) among the Sikhs, an event almost unique since the Sikhs practically without exception sided with the British elsewhere. The 37th were disarmed but in the panic that followed shots were fired and men killed. The Irregulars mutinied, and in the belief that the Sikhs had done so or were about to do so the British artillery opened fired on them and dispersed them. Ponsonby gave over command to Neill, but at what exact time is not known, although it is crucial to the understanding of the event. The detailed story is best read in Kaye. Vol II, p 222 et seq.

At Mohamdi in Oude, J.G.Thomason was the Deputy Commissioner, and his assistant was Captain Patrick Orr; the European population had been increased by the arrival of refugees from Shahjehanpur. The troops (from the Oude Irregular Force) rose in mutiny, sacked the Treasury, and released the prisoners from the gaol. Because apparently of the influence of Captain Orr, who was well known to the men the Europeans were suffered to depart unharmed, and they left in the evening, hoping eventually to reach Lucknow.

At Cawnpore [Kanpur] where mutiny had been long expected by Major-General Sir Hugh Massy Wheeler (although he had also anticipated that the mutineers would immediately depart for Delhi), the 2nd Lt Cav. the Ist, the 74th and 56th BNI rose in revolt. The most succinct and readable account is to be found in Mowbray Thomson's *The Story of Cawnpore*. London. 1859.

The first boatloads of Europeans left Fatehgarh to float down the Ganges, to 'safety', as they thought, at Cawnpore. See F.R.Cosens & C.L.Wallace, Fatehgarh and the Mutiny' Lucknow, 1933, reprint Karachi, 1978.

JUNE 5: At Aurangabad near Mohamdi in Oude[Awadh] the European refugees from the latter place were ambushed and murdered, with the exception of Captain Orr whom the troops allowed to depart to join his wife who was already in hiding.

One company of the 12th BNI at Jhansi, where there were no British troops, and where local feeling was already very anti-British in view of the way that the Rani Lakshmibai, had been treated, led by a havildar and cheered on by some gunners, marched straight into the Star Fort, and announced their intention of holding it. Their commanding officer, Captain Dunlop, rushed to the parade ground, but was assured by the remaining companies of the regiment that they would not mutiny, but would stand by their officers; the cavalry, the 14th Irreg. Cavalry, also protested their loyalty.

The 53rd BNI joined the mutiny at Cawnpore [Kanpur] possibly provoked to do so by the action of Lt Ashe

(Artillery) who fired upon them. Wheeler called all Europeans into his 'intrenchment' a pathetically inadequate defensive position based upon two unoccupied barrack buildings: a determined attack could not have been resisted, but the mutineers contented themselves for the most part to keeping up an almost continuous artillery barrage.

At Jaunpur, some forty miles from Benares a wing of the Ludhiana Sikhs at first had made demonstrations of fidelity on hearing of the revolt of the 37th BNI, but then news reached the men that the headquarters of their own regiment had been fired on by European troops and they at once rose in revolt. Lieutenant Mara their officer commanding was shot, as was Cuppage the joint-magistrate. The treasury was plundered and all the bungalows in the civil station, and the local people joined in the insurrection and the looting. The remaining Europeans fled to Benares, and the Sikh soldiers went off in the direction of Oude | Awadh].

The Rani of Jhansi

JUNE 6: At Jhansi a parade of the troops produced a second protestation of loyalty, but Captain Dunlop was shot by his own men that morning, on the way back from the post office, and it would seem that the events of the previous day were simply preparations for the 6th. The Rani, who may or may not have been aware of the plans of the mutineers, escorted by some new levies went in procession towards the cantonment. This, or the call of the muezzin, was the signal: all the infantry and cavalry now mutinied. They shot three officers and a sergeant-major while some officers and their families occupied the larger. Jhansi, Fort, and were led by the Political Officer, Captain Skene and succeeded in the first instance in repulsing the attack of the sepoys.

Generals Barnard and Wilson joined forces at Bhagput for the advance to Delhi.

The 6th BNI (part) mutinied at Allahabad, although on the previous day it had been paraded and given the thanks of Government for its unswerving loyalty: nearly all its officers were murdered, including some sixteen year old Ensigns just arrived from England. One effect of this uprising was the temporary break in government communication with Agra.

The Hurrianah Battalion was reported to have mutinied at Hansi ditto the Bhurtpore levies at Bhurtpore [Bharatpur].

Today saw the beginning of the siege of Wheeler's intrenchment at Cawnpore[Kanpur]. The Nana Sahib had apparently been supporting the Europeans but he now sent a somewhat quixotic message to Wheeler telling him that he intended to attack him. He is said to have persuaded the mutineers not to go to Delhi, which was their first intention, until the Europeans in Cawnpore had been destroyed. He promised each sepoy a gold anklet if he would join him. He was now proclaimed Peishwa the title he had so badly wanted and which had been denied him by the British. The siege of the intrenchment was not pushed home with any great determination, although the British defences were pitifully inadequate: it is said the mutineers preferred to take their ease in the bazar.

At Azimgarh the 4th Cov. 9th Bengal Artillery joined their comrades of the 17th BNI mnutiny.

The Nawab of Rampur who remained stead-fastly loyal to the British throughout, visited Moradabad to take charge.

JUNE 7: At Jhansi the Europeans in the Fort realising that they could not hold out sent three of their number to treat with the Rani; she handed them over to the Rissaldar of the Irregular Cavalry who had them all killed. Further attacks on the Fort however were again repulsed.

At Jullundur [Jallandhar] in the Punjab there were stationed HM's 8th Regiment and some British Artillery as well as the 6th Bengal Lt Cav and the 36th and 61st BNI. The sepoys could easily have been disarmed in May, had resolute action been taken as elsewhere in the Punjab, but the station commander, Brigadier Johnstone given wildly conflicting advice. had subsided into inaction. This day the three Indian regiments mutinied, having first fired the bungalow of the Colonel of HM's 8th, Colonel Hartley, as a signal to their comrades. They then marched off for Delhi, but killed only one officer, Adjutant Bagshawe. On the way they collected another regiment of the BNI, the 3rd, which had paradoxically not only been staunch to this date but had actually assisted in the despatch of the Siege in Train from Phillour to Delhi. The military authorities here, as at Meerut, were strongly criticised for their failure to pursue and punish the mutineers. Too late the men of HM's 8th Regiment were sent after the sepoys but returned having made no contact.

The Maulvi Liaquat Ali moved to Allahabad from Cawnpore and attempted to take charge of the city. He appointed officials, and had some semblance of power for a short time, but he was not accepted as leader by many Muslims, nor by the Hindus.

At Faizabad in Oude[Awadh] the troops were all Indian: the 22nd BNI, the 6th Oudh Irregular Infantry, a squadron of the 15th Irregular Cavalry and a Horse Battery of Artillery. The local *taluqdars* also were ripe for revolt, having suffered consi-derable material losses as a result of the British annexation of Oude [Awadh] in 1856. Only Raja Man Singh appeared to be friendly to the British cause, and this was the result of his personal feeling for a British officer. Captain Alexander Orr who had been instrumental in releasing him from prison. Reluctantly Man Singh accepted the task of protecting the wives and children of European officers of the station, and they were received into his fort of Shahganj on this evening. The same night the sepoys rose in revolt but did not murder their officers; instead they gave them four boats, and some money and told them to be off. But at the same time they sent a message to the 17th BNI at Azimgarh requesting them to intercept the boats on the river and to kill the occupants! The 17th subsequently did so. and although a few European fugitives did eventually reach Gorakhpur or Danapur in safety, the majority perished, at the hands of sepoys or villagers.

The British contingent from Meerut marched into Alipur, just north of Delhi, and effected a junction with the Commander-in-Chief Barnard, who had brought his forces from Ambala.

JUNE 8: At Jhansi events reached a climax, although the facts in the case are still in dispute: one version is that the Rani sent messengers to the Fort demanding a parley, and promising that if the Europeans laid down their arms they would be escorted to another station; Skene and the others agreed to the terms, walked out of the fort, but were then massacred in a garden known as the Jokan Bagh: all, perhaps 60, were killed, men women and children. There would appear to have been no atrocities, mutilations, violations etc as were afterwards reported. The complicity of the Rani is still in dispute.

At 1 a.m. the combined British force set out from Alipur on the final stretch of their march towards Delhi. At dawn they came under fire, some six miles from the city, at Badli-ki-Serai, on the Grand Trunk Road, and there then took place one of the most significant of all battles of the 'Mutiny'. It was hard fought, and took the form, at first, of a major artillery duel, but superior tactics eventually caused the rebels to retire precipitately within the walls of the city, and Barnard occupied the Ridge to the north-west of Delhi, and overlooking the city. The area is now the campus of Delhi University. The 'Siege of Delhi' now began, although at no time was the city fully invested: the British always held communication with the Punjab and the north-west and the north-east, while the rebels had unrestricted access via the south and east. For details see Kaye. or Alexander Llewellyn. *The Siege of Delhi*, London, 1977.

JUNE 9: Early in the morning the 1st Regiment of Military Police mutinied at Sultanpur in Oude(Awadh) between Faizabad and Allahabad. Colonel Fisher, commander of the 15th Irregular Cavalry, rode down to their lines in an attempt to recall them to duty, but was shot and mortally wounded by a policeman, whereupon his own men shot the second-in-command. Captain Gibbings; Lieutenant Tucker escaped and was sheltered by Raja Rustam Shah in his fort on the river Gomti; other Europeans were murdered in the town although they had sent their families in safety to Allahabad.

At Futtehpore [Fatehpur] on the Grand Trunk Road

between Allahabad and Cawnpore, the Europeans, civilians, were driven from the city by rebels: all fled (with the exception of the judge. Robert Tucker who refused to leave and was shot down after killing many of his assailants) and reached Banda in safety. Until Havelock and his column passed through this place in July, communications between Calcutta and Agra and the Punjab were effectively cut. An excellent account of this affair is to be found in J.W. Sherer's *Havelock's March on Cawnpore*, London, 1910.

The cavalry of the Malwa Contingent, who were recruited from much the same areas and castes as the Bengal Army, mutinied some fourteen miles from Neemuch in Central India, to which place they had been sent by Colonel Durand: they murdered their two officers. Captain Brodie and Lieutenant Hunt and then returned to their cantonment station, Mehidpur, marching some eighty miles in two days, and attempted to seduce the artillery and infantry of the Contingent, but without success. They then joined the (rebel) Neemuch Brigade. See Khushhalial Srivastava. T*he Revolt of 1857 in Central India-Malwa*, Bombay. 1966.

At Dariabad on the road between Faizabad and Lucknow in Oude[Awadh], the 5th Oudh Irregular Infantry mutinied, apparently overcome by the temptation of there being no fewer than 300,000 silver rupees in the local treasury; their commander. Captain W.H. Hawes, attempted to have it taken into Lucknow. but this precipitated the mutiny. Haves and the other officers, military and civilian, and their families, all managed to escape: most were then to take part in the siege of the Lucknow Residency, where Hawes was wounded but survived.

About an hour before noon on this day. the mutineer regiments from Jullundur [Jalandhar] entered the city of Ludhiana on their way south to Delhi, anxious for food, supplies and plunder: there were no troops to oppose them and they were assisted in their looting by many of the local people, notably the Kabuli refugees, the Kashmiris and the Muslims. Rioting continued unchecked until nightfall. Had the mutineers taken the fort and the Treasury, and held the city against government, the British would have been hard pressed to have reconquered Delhi, but the mutineers chose instead to continue their march.

The right wing of the 12th BNI and the left wing of the 14th Irregular Cavalry, and a detachmem of Bengal artillery (the complementary half of the mutinied force at Jhansi) were stationed at Nowgong some 200 miles to the east; when the news of the mutiny at Jhansi and the murder of Captain Dunlop and Ensign Taylor arrived there was naturally great excitement. At sunset three Sikhs of the 12th BNI came to the front on parade and shot the havildar-major. When the officers arrived it was too late to halt the mutiny, and they attempted to flee, accompanied by their families and eighty-seven faithful sepoys, some survived thanks to the assistance of the Rani of Chatarpur and the Nawab of Banda, but the majority perished, killed by bandits or villagers or pursuing sepoys.

At Saloni in the Faizabad Division of Oude [Awadh] the 1st Oudh Irregulars, commanded by Captain Thomson, mutinied but their officers, together with Captain L. Barrow (later to become Chief Commissioner of Oudh) and their families escaped and took refuge in the fort of a *taluqdar*. Raja Hanmant Singh of Kala Kankar.

At Sikrora in the Bahraich Division of Oude[Awadh] the troops mutinied and their officers fled to Balrampur where the *taluqdar*. Raja Dirg Bejai Singh had promised a safe refuge for them and their families. One officer, Lieutenant Bonham of the Artillery, refused to leave and bravely attempted to assert authority had he not had to deal also with cavalry and infantry mutineers he might have succeeded. His own men gave him money and a horse and good advice as to a safe route and he managed to reach Lucknow in safety. See John Bonham. *Oude in 1857*. London, 1928.

JUNE 10: The Commissioner at Bahraich, Charles Wingfield, had arrived at Gonda, bringing the news that the troops at Faizabad had mutinied and that those at Sikrora were on the verge of rebelling also. Today the troops at Gonda also mutinied, that is the main body of the 3rd Oudh Irregulars. Wingfield and the officers from Gonda fled to Balrampur where the Raja protected them all, nineteen Europeans in all, and sent them on to Gorakhpur and safety.

At the same time the three Europeans at Bahraich, Cunliffe, Jordan and Clarke attempted to escape, disguised, but were discovered when crossing the Gogra river and shot down.

At Rohtak the 60th BNI mutinied, and marched at once for Delhi, although they did not harm their officers they none the less became violent assailants of the British before the city.

The 1st Irreg Oudh Infantry mutinied at Pershadipur.

Some European refugees from Fatehgarh had taken to boats on the Ganges when the troops mutinied and today they reached Bithur, twelve miles from Cawnpore [Kanpur] but were fired on by Nana Sahib's troops. Of these Europeans who first took to the boats at Fatehgarh and sailed down to Kanpur in the first week of June 1857, over one hundred were dragged before the Nana and ordered to be killed (some depositions say it was his brother Bala Rao who insisted on their death and actually gave the order). For a list of these refugees see P.J.O.Taylor. *A Companion to the 'Indian Mutiny' of 1857,* OUP, Delhi. 1996. p 124. At Multan the 69th BNI and 62nd BNI were disarmed, but not banded.

JUNE 11: Brigadier General James Neill arrived at Allahabad. The Sikhs of Lieutenant Brasyer had remained staunch to the British and they and the remaining Europeans had retired to the Fort and held out until the arrival of Neill and the Madras Fusiliers a few days later altered the position. The story of Allahabad at this time makes remarkable reading: Disease, drunkenness and insubordination among the Europeans and Sikhs and their indiscriminate looting of the property of both friend and foe added to the hatred already felt there for the English, and Neill's policy of destruction of suburbs and 'making a severe example by laying the city under the heaviest possible contribution, to save it from destruction also must have aggravated this hatred. For a detailed account of the events in Allahabad at this time See R. Montgomery Martin, *The Indian Empire,* Vol II. London (n.d.) p 292-303.

There was an outbreak of rebellion at Jalaun, in Jhansi territory.

The Jhansi mutineers left for Delhi, much to the relief of the Rani who, though now threatened by her neighbours, was able to raise her own forces to deal with the crisis.

JUNE 12: The massacre by Nana Sahib of 130 Europeans from Fatehgarh took place at Bithur. Although there were no European survivors to tell the tale, there are a number of accounts by witnesses. See *the Companion* op. cit.

The garrison at Lalitpur, consisting of three hundred men of the 6th Infantry, Gwalior Contingent mutinied and looted the treasury. Their officers fled to the protection of the Raja of Banpur who was in reality. the leader of the rebels!

On this occasion he protected them, although keeping them in confinement.

JUNE 13: Considerable disaffection, which might be described as partial mutiny took place among the Ist Irreg, Cavalry of the Nizam's Contingent at Aurangabad, under the command of Captain H.D.Abbott. The latter had no reason to doubt the lovalty of the corps until the news of the revolt in the NW Provinces began to arrive. This caused much agitation among the Muslim sowars in the regiment, and they apparently persuaded many of the Hindus to join them in declaring that they would not march against the rebels in the north (rumours had been spreading that they were to be led against the mutinous regiments of the Bengal Army), nor would they fight against their King, ie the King of Delhi.

At Hamirpur, between Cawnpore [Kanpur] and Banda, the small detachment of the 56th BNI mutinied; they looted the treasury but did not share its contents, but kept them to be given to Nana Sahib: all the Europeans but one junior officer perished.

The disarmament of the 47th BNI at Mirzapore had been intended but not carried out and the regiment assisted in the pacification of the district.

A Press Gagging Act was issued by Government at Calcutta, and was very unpopular, although censorship was to be imposed for one year only; Lord Canning in particular lost much popularity as a result of this action.

Dinkar Rao

JUNE 14: The 43th and 57th BNI and the H.Q. of the 32nd BNI, and the 2nd Native Cavalry were disarmed at Barrackpore, and in nearby Calcutta there was a disgraceful panic among many of the Europeans who had heard rumours that the sepoys from Barrackpore would march upon the city.

Most significantly the Gwalior Contingent mutinied today and murdered seven of its officers and their families at Morar the cantonment of Gwalior. Those who avoided the massacre, like Mrs Coopland the widow of the chaplain, escaped to Agra, assisted, to the best of his power by Scindia Maharaja of Gwalior and his minister Dinkar Rao.

There was also an outbreak at Banda: the troops there were a detachment of the 56th BNI and when they mutinied they looted the treasury and went off to join their comrades. The Nawab, who had previously been helpful and protective of Europeans continued the practice for the time being, giving shelter to army officers and their families, civilians also from Hamirpur and Futtehpore (Fatehpur), but soon he was to proclaim his own rule and issue a proclamation which in effect accepted the end of the British raj.

Allahabad by now was in total disorder, the Europeans being in small numbers only were shut up in the foil awaiting further reinforcements from Benares, and the city was in complete confusion, none attracting the loyalty of all citizens, although Liaquat All the Maulvi, held partial sway over certain Muslims factions.

JUNE 15: At Calcutta the deposed King of Awadh Wajid Ali Shah, and his chief councillors were suspected (probably quite unfairly) of intriguing with the mutineers and were imprisoned in Fort William.

The Bareilly Brigade reached Moradabad en route for Delhi: they were commanded by Bakht Khan, a Subedar and soon to be made Commander-in-Chief of all the rebel forces at Delhi. The rebel leader Walidad Khan at Malagarh today asked Bahadur Shah Zafar King of Delhi, if the Bareilly Brigade could be given to him to establish a power base in Rohilkhand but he received no answer.

At Aurangabad apparently by this date matters had considerably changed for the Hindus of the Hyderabad Contingent had separated themselves from the die-hard Muslims who were bent on mutiny and indeed many of the Muslims, under *Rissaldar* Abdul Rhyman Khan, also expressed regret for their action and said they were now willing to obey orders. Abbott was instructed to arrest the ringleaders, try them by court-martial and carry the sentence into execution: a moveable column under General woodburn was he was told, on its way to help in the coercion. On the regiment being paraded under menace of guns, some men refused to stay, and when they mounted they were fired upon and a few were killed, and about a dozen or so were cut down by the dragoons. One sowar stepped forward and fired his pistol at Abbott but it misfired and he was arrested, tried by drumhead court-martial and hanged the next morning. Thirty or forty of the cavalrymen were put on trial together with a *subadar* of the 2nd Infantry Hyderabad Contingent and some *golandauzes*. The affair ended with two men blown from guns, seven shot by dragoons 'several' hung, 30-40 transported, 100 disbanded and turned out of the station. 50-60 flogged or otherwise punished. There was no further mutiny among the Hyderabad Contingent. Indeed, the mutiny and rebellion in India, may now be said to be confined to the area north of the Narbada river.

JUNE 16: Maulvi Liaquat Ali fled from Allahabad: had he been supported by all factions he might well have established his rule in the city, at least until the British reinforcements from Calcutta came up country in overwhelming numbers.

The Nawab's rule was proclaimed at Farruckabad/

Fatehgarh: he had previously enjoyed the title and a pension but no power: to what extent he was now a willing rebel has always been disputed.

The Nagpur Irreg Cav were disarmed at Nagpur. The latter was a large and populous city, with much anti-British feeling in view of the way their ruling family had been treated: only the presence of troops from the Madras army prevented an outbreak here.

JUNE 18: At Fatehgarh the 10th BNI previously loyal, eventually broke out into mutiny: they were taunted by the 41st BNI and could not resist their share of the contents of the treasury.

Mewati and Pathan villages in Allahabad district were attacked and destroyed by the British, on Brigadier General Neill's orders: the destruction and the executions that followed were indiscriminate, the guilty and the innocent perishing alike. Neill himself did not say that they were found guilty of murders. He executed vengance on '*all who had taken an active part in the Mutiny, and when we know how these things were done we may well doubt if there was any proof of that... Neill is one of those people who have been elevated into a hero on the strength of a feminine sort of violence there was not much more in him...*If can never forgive Neill for his very bloody work. See Sir George Campbell, *Memories of my Indian Career*, London. 1893. pp 281-2.

The 3rd Regiment of the Gwalior Contingent mutinied at Sipri, and the three Europeans in the station fled to Augur.

JUNE 19: William Tayler, Commissioner at Patna the chief city of Bihar. arrested four leading Maulvis and disarmed the citizens: he was convinced that the danger to British power came from the Muslims who he believed, were intriguing throughout Northern India against the government: but he had quarrelled with Halliday, the Lieutenant Governor of Bengal: the men were incompatible, and Halliday took the excuse of Tayler's order to his subordinates to concentrate at Patna the resources in men and money of the province, to remove him from office for his 'ill-juded and faint-hearted order', which had, so Halliday averred spread alarm in every direction. Although disgraced at this time, Tayler was to some extent vindicated many years after the Mutiny by the discovery of widespread Muslim plots, at this time, against British rule, *See* William Tayler, *Thirty-eight Years in India*, 2 vols, London 1881/2.

An engagement took place at Delhi: a strong force of rebels from the city, including the newly-arrived Nasirabad mutineers, attacked the British position one hour before sunset and the action continued some hours after darkness fell; although technically defeated (they retired back within the city walls) the mutineers inflicted severe losses on the British force - twenty killed and seventy-seven wounded - who could not be replaced. More particularly they inflicted a blow to British morale, many of the senior officers despairing of ever being able to retake Delhi which was being constantly reinforced by newly mutinied troops. The engagement is also significant for a 'serious accident': by reason of the darkness British guns actually fired into the ranks of British soldiers.

JUNE 22: In continuation of the process of rendering suspect sepoy units harmless the 39th BN Cavalry were disarmed at Jhelum.

JUNE 23: Another severe battle took place outside the walls of Delhi. This was the centenary anniversary of the Battle of Plassey when Clive may be said to have established British rule in India, and there was a prophecy in wide circulation that the British Raj was to last just a hundred years. The day had been looked forward to with anxiety by the British on the Ridge at Delhi, and with exultation by the rebels within the city. A considerable force issued from the city and occupied the Subzi Mundi a large suburb, and attacked the Ridge near Hindu Rao's house. The battle lasted eleven hours, from 6p.m. to 5a.m. the next morning, before the rebels were compelled to retreat again within the walls of the city. The British lost 38 men killed and 118 wounded, the rebels were estimated to have lost 400 killed and over 300 wounded. From this time an advanced picket was stationed in the Subzi Mundi by the British, between a *serai* and a Hindu temple which came to be known as the Sammy House.

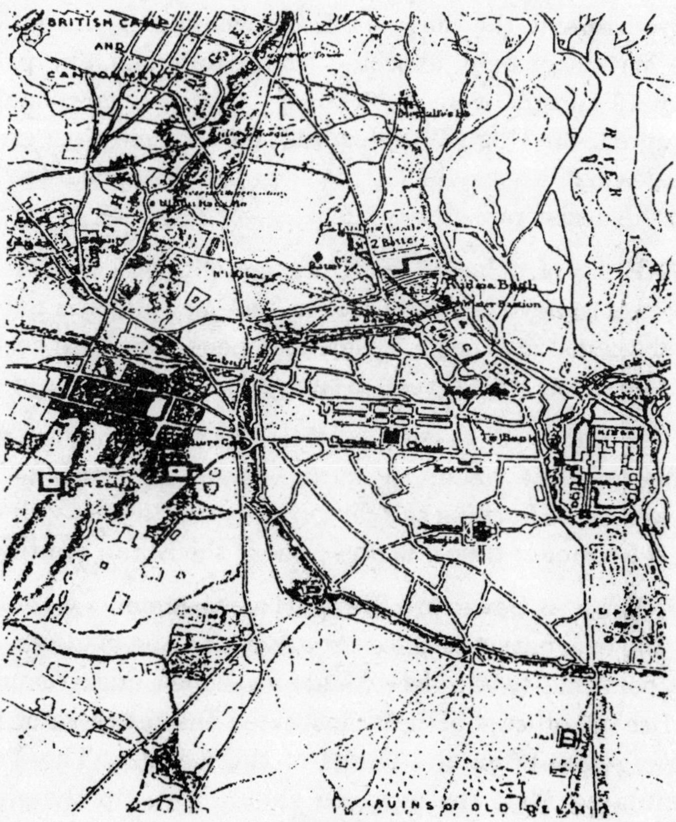

Delhi in 1857

JUNE 24: Those still alive in the Entrenchment in Cawnpore [Kanpur] had been on half rations now for some time, that is half a pint of pea-soup and two or three *chapaties* each per day; even on this meagre diet there was very little food left. It was at this time that there stumbled into the entrenchment, after dark, 'with a white wand' Mrs Greenway the elderly widow of a wealthy merchant of Cawnpore held prisoner by the Nana Sahib. She bore a message from him, to the effect that "All soldiers and others unconnected with the acts of Lord Dalhousie, who will lay down their arms and give themselves up, shall be spared and sent to Allahabad'. The offer led to furious debate among the British in the entrenchment, the younger officers wishing to hold out until the arrival of help, expected from Allahabad, the private soldiers and the women declaring that the terms should be accepted. Sir Hugh Wheeler was so overcome with grief at the death of his son during the siege that he appears to have left the decision to others.

JUNE 25: Mrs Jacobi, the Eurasian wife of a watchmaker appears to have been the second emissary of Nana Sahib to the besieged in Wheeler's Entrenchment. She bore back the message that they agreed to surrender on the terms offered.

Contingent troops mutinied at Malthone in Central India, and the Neemuch mutineers, on their way to Agra sacked Deoli burning the cantonment and taking with them the 24-pounder time gun and some of the Kotah Contingent.

JUNE 26: At Cawnpore [Kanpur] arrangements were made for the evacuation of the entrenchment to be made the next day boats had to be collected and provisioned, and a committee of British officers actually inspected the progress of these arrangements on the banks of the Ganges. The Treaty stipulated That the garrison should give up their guns, ammunition and treasure; should be allowed to carry their muskets and sixty rounds of ammunition with them: that the Nana should provide carriage for the sick, wounded, women and children, to the river's bank, where boats would be in readiness to convey all to Allahabad.

The 33rd and 35th BNI were disarmed at Phillour, in the Punjab.

JUNE 27: The entrenchment at Cawnpore [Kanpur] was duly evacuated by the garrison which by now probably amounted to no more than 350 persons of whom the majority were women and children and other non-combatants; by 8a.m. they had reached the Ganges some mile or so away. The boats were there waiting at a place usually identified as Satichaura Ghat, but more accurately named the Fisherman's Temple. Embarkation began, when suddenly there was a bugle call, the boatmen of the 28 boats leapt from them having first fired the thatch in many cases, and heavy musketry fire began, to be followed by artillery salvoes opened up on the Europeans: they had been trapped in an elaborate ambush. This was the second of the "Cawnpore Massacres" (see June 12). All the men were killed save four who managed to swim down river to safety: the Nana ordered the women who had survived the first attack to be made prisoner: they were taken first to Savada House and then to the Bibigurh. For details see W.J. Shepherd. *A Personal Narrative of the Outbreak and Massacre at Cawnpore*, Lucknow. 1886. Reprint. New Delhi. 1980 Capt. Mowbray Thomson, *The Story of Cawnpore,* London, 1859 (The author was one of the four survivors of the Satichaura Ghat massacre); see also Andrew Ward. Our Bones are Scattered, *the Cawnpore Massacres in the Indian Mutiny of 1857*, London. 1996: (the author is an acknowledged expert on the affairs of Kanpur in 1857-58 which he has meticulously researched over a long period of time).

The first news of the Mutiny reached England: accompanied by much rumour dispensed as fact, leading to many untrue or exaggerated atrocity stories the truth was sufficiently horrendous without fanciful addition.

JUNE 28: Fatehgarh Fort, in which the remaining Europeans had taken refuge was besieged by the mutineers, belonging to the 10th and 41st BNI. There is a full account of the uprising at Fatehgarh/Futtehghur in the London *Times*. 3 November. 1857. *See also* F.R.Cosens & C.L. Wallace. *Fatehgarh and the Mutiny*. Lucknow 1933, reprint Karachi 1978.

In Bundelkhand the populace was almost entirely anti-British at this time although some of the rulers, notably the Nawab of Banda demonstrated sympathy for government, and the regiments of the BNI did not actively mutiny for some weeks: the state of feeling was however demonstrated by the Nagode gaol being broken into, and the murder of some European fugitives.

JUNE 30: Chinhat (or Chinhut) In the Pargana and Tehsil of Lucknow a village on the metalled road from Lucknow to Faizabad, at a distance of about six miles from the former: it was the scene on this day of a decisive battle between the British, led in person by Sir Henry Lawrence, and the mutineers. Strictly speaking the battle actually took place at Ishmaelganj a hamlet close to Chinhat. Lawrence himself sent a message to Colonel Neill at Allahabad for onward transmission to the Governor General: '*Lucknow 30th June. Went out this morning eight miles to meet the enemy, and were defeated through misconduct, chiefly of artillery and cavalry, many of whom deserted. Enemy followed us up, and we have been besieged for four hours. Shall likely be surrounded to-night. Enemy very bold and our Europeans very low...unless we are relieved in fifteen or twenty days,* *we shall hardly be able to maintain our ground.'* See Gubbins *'An Account of the Mutinies in Oudh etc'* pp181 *et seq.* The rebel victors was decisive and led to the Lucknow Residency being surrounded and besieged. One result was that the Kingdom of Oude[Awadh] successfully defied British power for a further nine months.

Bulandshahr not far from Delhi, was captured by Walidad Khan.

The 4th Irregular Cavalry mutinied at Muzuffarnagar.

The Europeans at Saugor [Sagar], anticipating mutiny and despairing of early reinforcement, entrenched themselves in the fort and awaited attack.

JULY 1: At Saugur [Sagar) in Central India, the Brigadier commanding troops, Sage, had anticipated the mutiny of the sepoys, seduced by the Raja of Banpur, who by now had openly rebelled. Sage withdrew his small European force of sixty artillerymen, together with other Christian men and women, into the mud fort. He had supplies and medical stores for six months and a sufficiency of guns and ammunition. The 42nd BNl and the 3rd Irregular Cavalry today mutinied as expected; they plundered the bazars and the bungalows of the officers. The 31st BNI however held aloof, professing loyalty.

The Residency at INDORE

The Governor General's Agent for Central India was Colonel H.M. Durand, a man of considerable ability and prestige: he was stationed at the Residency at Indore, the capital of the dominions of Maharaja Holkar. The latter always protested his inno cence in the affairs of this day, when his own personal troops attacked the Residency and drove Durand and the other Europe ans out of Indore.

At Mhow the 1st Light Cavalry and the 23rd BNI, who were in communication with Holkar's troops mutinied: they shot dead Colonel Platt the C.O and Captain Fagan, the Adjutant, of the 23rd; the cavalry troopers likewise killed their commandant Major Harris. The mutineers then marched off to Indore and subsequently made their way to Delhi. Captain Hungerford in charge of a mixed battery of artillery was thus left in charge, and for a time assumed the role of Governor General's Agent.

At Hatrass, twenty two miles from Aligarh, north of Agra the 1st Cavalry of the Gwalior Contingent mutinied lowing no ill-feeling towards their officers, but simply telling them they must go.

The real siege of Lucknow Residency began, with the rebels surrounding the compound and opening fire with artillery and musketry.

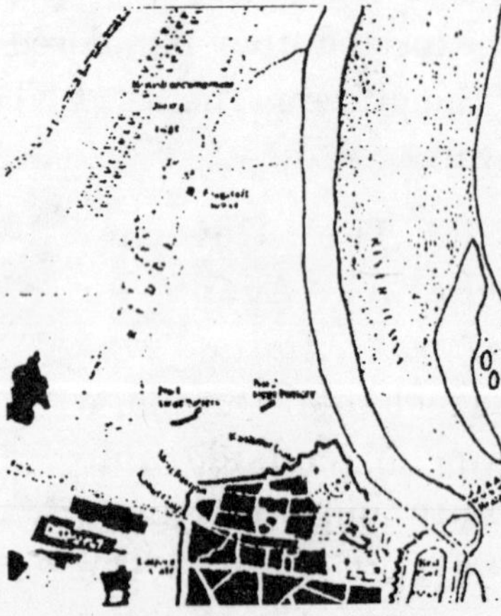

Delhi before the Assault

The Nana Sahib's rule was proclaimed at Hamirpur.

Neemuch rebels were reported to be at Fatehpur Sikri, close to Agra.

Bakht Khan arrived at Delhi with the Bareilly Brigade: there was much rejoicing: in the city bands played a selection of military airs -eluding, it is said, *'God Save the Queen!'*. It was reported thus: *The longing eyes of the rebel Delhi garrison were gladdened* and those of the besiegers mortified, by the sight of the Rohilkund mutineers, who were watched by friends and foes crossing the Jumna in boats (the bridge being broken) and marching into one of the seven gates of the city in millitary array, with infantry cavalry and artillery, and some hundred cartloads of treasure.

JULY 2: At Mhow [Mau] the 2nd Coy 6th BN Artillery mutinied. This left no loyal Indian troops at British disposal at this station.

Pearson's Battery and the 2nd Cavalry commanded by Burlton mutinied near Agra, at a place called Sansi seven miles beyond Hatrass: they used no violence towards their officers (who retired to Agra) but quietly told them they were no longer required and asked them to leave.

In Delhi Bakht Khan was declared the Commander-in-Chief of the King of Delhi's army.

JULY 3 : A large contingent of the King's army came out of Delhi and took up their position to the south of the British camp on the Ridge. Clearly another attack was planned so a British force, before dawn, was sent to intercept them; an exchange of artillery fire appeared to result in the rebels' retirement, and the British force sat down to a leisurely breakfast, but was suddenly attacked from dense woodland on the flank and many infantry soldiers were killed (and elephants panicked and escaped into the surrounding countryside); despite this apparent success the rebels again withdrew under heavy shelling into the city.

There was a strange event at Damoh in the Sagar and Narbada Territories: the garrison consisted of two companies of the 42nd BNI (which had already mutinied), but this contingent remained loyal to government and refused to join their comrades or to surrender the treasure they were guarding: their attitude was due entirely to the management, and bravery, of their Subadar-Major and a certain Havildar, Ranjit Singh.

Throughout north India a report (10 weeks premature) circulated that the British had reoccupied Delhi: this certainly had the effect of causing waverers to come down on the side of the British.

A so-called 'Mussulman Conspiracy' was discovered at Patna; how genuine it was has still to be established. The repressive conduct of Mr Tayler the Commissioner, and a Major Holmes (commanding the 12th Irregular Cavalry at Segowlie) had caused much alarm and opposition among the mainly Muslim population of Patna (over 300,000 inhabitants); Holmes had, without authority or justification declared 'martial law' from Gorakpur to Patna. At 8pm some 200 men, armed with flags, music and guns, broke into the premises of a Roman Catholic Mission, and destroyed some property but stole nothing and injured no one, but subsequently a Dr Lyell, assistant to the Opium Agent, was shot, in circumstances that have never been explained.

JULY 4: At Patna thirty men, accused of having been involved in the incident of the night before, were arrested and put on trial. Fourteen were condemned to death and executed the same day, including a book-seller, Peer Ali said to have been the one who had shot Dr Lyell: his guilt was doubtful. Tayler's attitude, and behaviour while still in power, is reminiscent of that of Colonel James Neill, ie repress rebellion with terror, avoiding the niceties of justice.

A massacre took place at Rampore on the Ganges of a further party of European fugitives fleeing from Fatehgarh. See Lt. Colonel F.R. Cosens. and C.L Wallace! *Fatehgarh and the Mutiny*, Lucknow. 1933. Reprint Karachi. 1978.

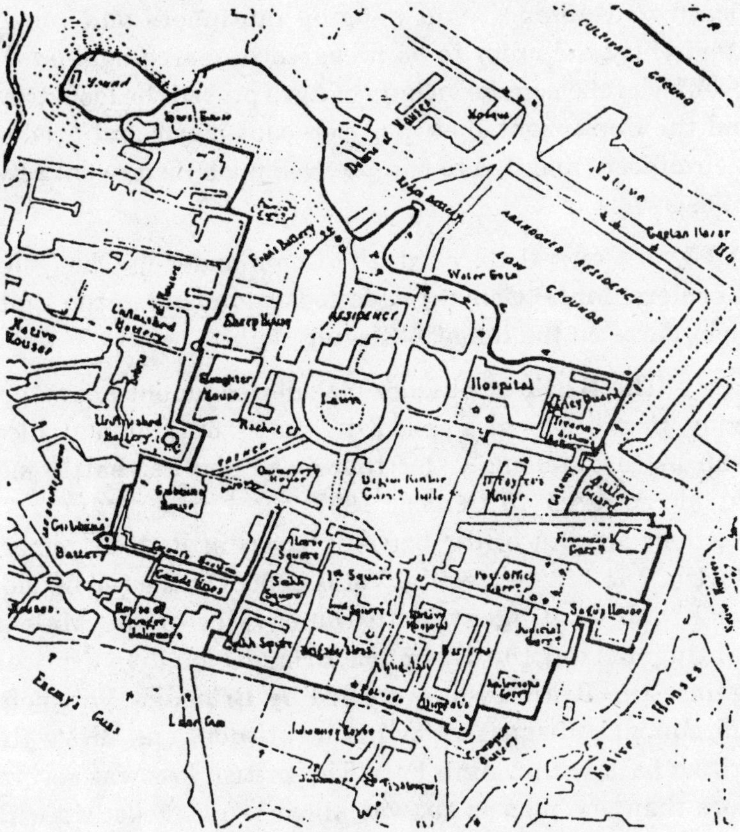

The Lucknow Residency

Sir Henry Lawrence died of wounds in Lucknow Residency: incredibly he had been struck, in the same room, a second time, by a cannon-ball fired from an identical howitzer. He was succeeded as leader of the garrison by Brigadier John Inglis.

At Agra the Kotah Contingent, long believed to be free from contagion finally mutinied. It consisted of 700 men in all, cavalry, infantry and a battery of six guns, and had been used successfully in collecting revenue, burning disaffected villages, and hanging mutineers and rebels. Apparently the order to be prepared to march against the Neemuch rebels in the vicinity of Agra proved the last straw, and the Contingent shot their sergeant-major and fired on their officers and fled to join the Neemuch men twenty-two miles away.

JULY 5: General Barnard, the Commander-in-Chief died of cholera; Major General Reed took command of the Delhi Field Force on the Ridge, besieging Delhi.

The Battle of Sussiah [Sasia] was fought near Agra today. Sometimes also called the Battle of Shahganj. also, even more confusingly (for there was another battle just outside Agra on 10 October 1857) the Battle of Agra. An excellent account of the battle is given in R. Montgomery Martin, *The Indian Empire,* Vol II p360. On the rebels' side the Kotah Contingent, with the cavalry of the Malwa. Contingent and the Neemuch Brigade fought very well against the British who were led by Brigadier Polwhele, subsequently dismissed for his ineptitude, and drove the British back within Agra Fort. The British loss was severe, more than one man in six was killed ie 141, together with some thirty Europeans subsequently killed in Agra during the disgraceful panic in which the fort gates were shut and no attempt was made by the British to rescue their co-religionists and fellow-countrymen. The rebel loss was estimated as 'exceeding 500'. Fortunately for the British the rebels now headed for Delhi to join the King's forces.

JULY 6: A Proclamation was issued in the city of Delhi:*'To all Hindoos and Mussulmans, Citizens and Servants of Hindostan, (he Officers of the Army now at Delhi and Meerut send Greetings.'It is well known that in these days all the English have entertained these evil designs, first to* *destroy the religion of the whole Hindostani army and then to make the people Christians by compulsion. Therefore we, solely on account of our religion, have combined with the people, and have not spared alive one infidel, and have re-established the Delhi dynasty on these terms, and thus act in obedience to orders and receive double pay. Hundreds of guns and a large amount of treasure have fallen into our hands: therefore it is fitting that whoever of the soldiers and people dislike turning Christians should unite with one heart and act courageously, not leaving the seed of these infidels remaining. For any quantity of supplies delivered to the army the owners are to take the receipts of the officers: and they will receive double payment from the Imperial Government. Whoever shall in these times exhibit cowardice. or credulously believe the promises of those impostors the English, shall very shortly be put to shame for such a deed, and rubbing the hands of sorrow, shall receive for their fidelity the reward the ruler of Lucknow got. It is further necessary that all Hindoos and Mussulmans unite in this struggle, and, following the instructions of some respectable people, keep themselves secure, so that good order may be maintained, the poorer classes kept contented, and they themselves be exalted to rank and dignity: also, that all, so far as it is possible, copy this proclamation, and dispatch it everywhere, so that all true Hindoos and Mussulmans may be alive and watchful, and fix in some conspicuous place (but prudently to avoid detection), and strike a blow with a sword before giving circulation to it. The first pay of the soldiers of Delhi will be 30r. per month for a trooper: and 10r. for a foot-man. Nearly 100,000 men are ready, and there are 13 flags of the English regiments and about 14 standards from different parts now raised aloft for our religion, for God, and the conqueror, and it is the intention of Cawnpore to root out the seed of the Devil. This is what we of the army here wish.'* Not to be outdone the Nana Sahib, temporarily in power at

Cawnpore[Kanpur], also issued a proclamation: *'It has been ascertained from a traveller who has lately arrived at Cawnpore from Calcutta, that previously to the distribution of the cartridges for the purpose of taking away the religion and caste of the people of Hindostan, a council was held, at which it was resolved that, as this was a matter of religion, it would be necessary to employ 7,000 or 8,000 Europeans, and to kill 50,000 Hindostanees, and then all Hindostan would be converted to Christianity. A petition to this effect was sent to Queen Victoria and the opinion of the council was adopted. A second council was then held, to which the English merchants were admitted, and it was agreed that, to assist in carrving out the work, the same number of European soldiers should be allowed as there were Hindostanee Sepoys, lest, in the event of any great commotion arising, the former should be beaten. When this petition was perused in England, 35,000 European troops were embarked in ships with the utmost rapidity and despatched to India. Intelligence of their despatch was received, in Calcutta, and the gentlemen of Calcutta issued orders for the distribution of cartridges. Their real object was to make Christians of the army under the idea that when this was done there would be no delay in Christianizing the people generally. In the cartridges the fat of swine and cows was used. This fact was ascertained from Bengalees who were employed in making the cartridges: one of these men was put to death and the rest were imprisoned. Here they were carrying out their plans. Then the Ambassador of the Sultan of Constantinople at the Court of London sent information to the Sultan that 35,000 English troops were to be despatched to India to make Christians of that country. The Sultan sent a firman to the Pasha of Egypt to the effect that he was colluding with Queen Victoria: that this was not a time for compromise: that from what his ambassador sent it appeared that 35,000 English soldiers had been despatched to India to make Christians of the people and soldiers of that country: that there was still time to put a stop to this: that if he was guilty of any neglect in the matter, what kind of a face would he be able to show to God: that day would one day be his, since, if the English succeeded in making Christians of the people of Hindostan, they would attempt the same in his country. On the receipt of this firman of the Sultan, the Pasha, before the arrival of the English troops, made his arrangements and collected his troops at Alexandria - for that is the road to India - and on the arrival of the English army the troops of the Pasha of Egypt began firing on them with cannon from all sides, and destroyed and sank the ships so that not a single Englishman of them remained. The English at Calcutta, after issuing the order for biting the cartridges and the breaking-out of this now spreading mutiny and rebellion, were looking for assistance from the army coming from London: but God by the exercise of His Almighty power, settled their business there, When the intelligence of the destruction of the army of London was received the Governor General felt great grief and beat his head. At the beginning of the night murder and robbery were contemplated: in the morning the body had no head, nor the head any covering! In one revolution the sky became of the same colour: neither Nadir nor Nadir's Government remained. This paper has been printed by order of Nana Sahib, 13th zeiroe. and add 1273. Higree, 8.' quoted in* Mowbray Thomson, *"The'Story of Cawnpore, London. 1859. pp 142-6.*

JULY 7: The 14th BNI mutinied at Jhelum in the Punjab, but it was a very different affair from the usual: because the regiment had been giving signs of discontent the British had decided to disarm it, but the force sent against it was beaten back with many casualties by a most spirited defence first of the Quarter Guard of the regiment and then of a village lying behind its lines. A British gun was captured and turned against the retreating British troops.

Meanwhile the 58th BNI were successfully and quietly disarmed at Rawalpindi.

Major-General Havelock's Column at long last left Allahabad, en route for Cawnpore [Kanpur]: there were rumours of Wheeler's death and the evacuation of the entrenchment, but nothing was known for certain; the troops believed they would be in time to relieve both Cawnpore and Lucknow.

At Saugur [Sagar] a desperate fight took place between the 42nd BNI and the 31st BNI, the latter having remained loyal to the British; the 42nd were having the better of it as they had two guns, so the 31st asked Brigadier Sage in the fort to send them assistance: he promised to do so in the morning and this fixed the 31st in their resolve and disheartened the 42nd so much that they fled, pursued by the loyal sepoys. The latter consisted of all but 40 of the 31st, 50 of the 42nd and about 120 troopers from the 3rd Irregulars.

JULY 9: At Jhelum the fight was resumed but the mutineers now fled: very few ultimately escaped; some had been killed in the battle, others drowned in the Jhelum. and some were captured either by the police or by the Cashmeri authorities who handed them back to the British by whom they were blown away from mins.

The 46th BNI and the 9th Lt Cavalry mutinied at Sealkote [Sialkot] upon the news of the disarming of their comrades at Jhelum; a summons also had come to them from the King at Delhi requiring them to go to his assistance. There were no British troops in Sialkot and the Europeans made their way if they could, to the comparative safety of an old fort once the stronghold of the Sikh chief Tej Singh. Many Europeans, including women and children, were however murdered by the mutineers. See Captain Gregory Rich. *The Mutiny in Sialkot,* Sialkot, 1924.

The British abandoned Sehore twenty miles from Bhopal, and the headquarters of the Bhopal Contingent, because their presence there embarrassed the Begum: to the latter was made over command of the Contingent, then in a state bordering on mutiny; she had the greatest difficulty in controlling them, but remained throughout faithful to her pledge to the British.

At Amritsar the 59th BN Cavalry were successfully disarmed.

At Burhanpur, twelve miles from Asirgarh (a famous fort between the Tapti and Narbada rivers) a company of the 6th Regiment of the Gwalior Contingent mutinied and marched on Asirgarh, but there it, and the remainder of the regiment were successfully disarmed without bloodshed by two companies of the 19th Bombay N.I. and some of the Bhil Corps, thus opening the road to the advance of a British column into Central India.

JULY 11: Some of the Europeans who had avoided the Rampur massacre, in the second boat party from Fatehgarh, arrived at Bithur and suffered the same fate as the first: all but three of the men were killed and the women taken to join their compatriots in the Bibigurh.

JULY 12: The 46th BNI and the 9th Bengal Cavalry had mutinied at Sialkot on 9 July and after looting the cantonment had left the town the same night. General Nicholson caught up with them today on the banks of the river Ravi where they were endeavouring to cross at a ford known as Trimmoo Ghaut [Trimmu Ghat]. The mutineers were cut up and more than 400 killed, while many fugitives were brought in (and executed) by

Sir Colin Campbell

local villagers in the succeeding days. On the 15th it was discovered that about 300 had taken up a position on a large island in the middle of the Ravi: they were attacked and routed, many bayoneted and others drowned as they sought to cross the river. Some 200 of the original party of mutineers sought shelter over the border in the territories of the Maharaja of Jammu. but were handed over and either executed or sentenced to transportation after drum-head court-martial. The most detailed account of this 'battle' is given in Ball Vol I p 565.

Havelock still on his way from Allahabad to Cawnpore defeated the mutineers at Futtehpur[Fatehpur]; it was in this battle that Nana Sahib's brother, Bala Rao was badly wounded, and returned full of anger to Cawnpore.

General Sir Colin Campbell newly appointed as Commander-in-Chief left England for India.

At Ambala the 5th BNI which had been disarmed on 29 May mutinied and dispersed.

JULY 14: A severe battle took place outside Delhi, and although the rebels were beaten and driven back within the city walls, the result was far from satisfactory for the British. Mutineers had sallied forth in great numbers and attacked the batteries on the Hindu Rao Ridge: their loss was estimated at 1000 men. the British losing 15 killed and 200 wounded. But the rebels had left six guns exposed which the British failed to bring back and which were recovered by the rebels, and among the casualties was the Adjutant General Brigadier Chamberlain who was badly wounded and put *hors de combat* indefinitely: ironically this was possibly to the advantage of the British for he not only hazarded his own life, with considerable personal bravery, but he also was inclined to be reckless of the lives of British soldiers, and in the struggle before Delhi, numbers were likely to be decisive.

On this date it was estimated that there were 2200 British troops, and 500 Punjabis, while the rebel force in the city of Delhi was computed to be 80,000 armed men, of whom more than half were trained soldiers.

General Havelock

JULY 15: Havelock and the Allahabad Column were advanc-5 on Kanpur and had already beaten the forces of Nana Sahib Fatehpur. They now had to fight two actions in one day to continue the advance. '*Early on the 15th, we marched on towards Aong. where the General had been led to suppose he should me with considerable resistance. His information was perfectly correct the village was occupied in strength. The enemy had intrenched themselves across the road, not indeed in a very formidable manner, but the village offered great cover in the walled gardens, thickly grown with trees, which flanked it on either side. From this shelter, a steady fire of musketry was kept up for a considerable time. It was in this engagement that the enemy's cavalry made more than one attempt to get round our force and cut off the baggage. Once or twice, they regularly charged, but as soon as the bullets of the baggage guard began to fly amongst them, they pulled up and galloped away in quite a ludicrous fashion. After a struggle of some little endurance, the village of Aoung was taken, and as it was supposed the enemy -would try and injure the bridge over the Pandoo Nuddee, the General pushed on. The rebels had placed two heavy guns on the bank on the opposite side of the Pandoo, one a 12-pounder, and the other an old carronade, I think, of large calibre. These were fired straight down the high road, but Enfield riflemen were sent on through the fields to the river bank, and from that position, very soon dislodged the gunners, and the whole body then made off* *leaving the guns. Some miserable attempts had made to blow up the bridge, but quite ineffectual in their nature, and our troops marched across with perfect ease, and occupied* the opposite bank.......*The battle of Aoung was fought early in the forenoon of the 15th, and the Pandoo Nuddee was forced to the best of my recollection, by about eleven o'clock the same day. There was therefore ample time for news of the repulse, and the steady* advance *of the British troops to have reached Cawnpore early in the afternoon. There is every reason therefore to suppose, that the fate of the unhappy captives was immediately made the subject of discussion. The decision arrived at is now know and execrated throughout the civilized world. It was decided that the captives should be put to death.*

The order was carried into execution about sun-down. There were four gentlemen, three of them of the Futtehgarh party, who by some mischance, or for some especial reason, had been reserved from the fate which had already fallen upon their male companions. These were first taken out of the Beebeegurh and murdered on the high road. Then the general massacre commenced. It seems probable, that vollies (sic) were first fired into the doors and windows, and then that executioners were sent in to do the rest with swords. If the work was any thing like completed, it must have taken a considerable time. At length, the doors were closed, and night fell upon what had happened. The hotel, where the Nana had his quarters, was within fifty yards of this house, and I am credibly informed that he ordered a nautch and passed the evening with singing and dancing.' John Y. Shercr, Havelock's March on Cawnpore. A civilian's notes, Edinburgh c. 1910. Incidentally, Major Renaud associated in many men's minds with the excesses of Colonel Neill was killed here: the battle was continued at Pandu Nadi. This evening there took place one of the most notorious of all events of the "Mutiny", ie the 'Massacre of the Ladies" in the Bibigurh at Cawnpore.

'On Bala Rao's return to Kanpur from the field of battle, wounded on the right shoulder by a musket ball, a council was held at Noor Mahomed's Hotel, at which a large number are said to have assembled, and over which the Nana presided.....They are said to have been unanimous in one fearful resolve, and that was the death of the unoffending and innocent women and children, and the few gentlemen whose lives had hitherto been spared. Two reasons were advanced in favour of this brutal resolve: the one that it would probably prevent the further approach of the British: the second, that many rebels even now determined to forsake a losing cause and return to their old allegiance, and knowing full well that many amongst the unfortun*ate prisoners could recognize the leaders, and give important evidence against them, being intimately acquainted with nearly all those implicated in rebel proceedings, and felt that it was positively necessary to destroy all European evidence, as only chance of evading the condign punishment their crimes richly merited. Hence was the fate of these unhappy captives to be sealed in blood, and all were to perish in one common lot.'*W.J. Shepherd. *Personal Narrative, etc.,* Lucknow 1886. p 116.

JULY 16: At Cawnpore [Kanpur] the victims of the Bibigurh masacre (c. 200 European women and children) were thrown into a to dry well not all it was said, were dead. Havelock continued on his march and fought the first battle of Cawnpore. a not very significant action, since the Nana had clearly decided to evacuate the city. Before he did so he ordered all Bengali babus to be arrested on grounds no more than that they could speak English.

JULY 17: Havelock entered Cawnpore, and the Nana Sahib retreated to Bithur and was again defeated in a pitched battle.

General Reed resigned his command on grounds of ill-health,and handed over at Delhi to Archdale Wilson.

Colonel Millar with the Nagpore Moveable Column, marched towards Jabalpur; his troops were from the Madras army, and he was instructed to assist the civil authorities on his march but not to divide his force nor to sit in garrison.

The Neemuch Brigade (rebel) arrived in Delhi yet another morale-boosting addition to the rebel force, but which presented problems as the King of Delhi was short of fund to pay his army.

JULY 18: As British forces, from the Bombay and Madras Armies unaffected by the mutiny of the Bengal army, came up from the south and east, so more and more action took place in Central India, in the Sagar and Narbada Territories and in Bundelkhand. The Raja of Shargarh in correspondence with the Raja of Banpur had now openly rebelled, and from being kind to the Europeans he now ill-treated them on even opportunity. But his actions were still extraordinary: he fired a salute in honour of the "recapture" of Delhi by the British, but on the same day sent British refugees as prisoners to a guard under his brother Diwan Lachman Singh: the latter attacked British troops at Benaika was defeated, lost a gun and was severely wounded; the prisoners were then sent to Papit confined in a cowshed and insulted in every way possible.

JULY 20: To date the besiegers of the Lucknow Residency had confined their activities to keeping up a constant fire of musket and cannon, doing a great deal of damage to the Residency compound (which measured thirty-seven acres in extent) and killing a few of the garrison each day. But today they mounted a serious general attack; they sprang a mine intended to destroy the Redan Battery, but they had badly miscalculated the distance and the explosion was well short. Not realising this error, there being much smoke to hinder vision, the sepoys fixed bayonets and charged at what they thought would be the breach, and were met by a galling fire from muskets and camion, and many were killed; other parts of the perimeter were also attacked but no breach was made and the rebels eventually retired having lost perhaps 1000 men: the British loss was fourteen killed and twelve wounded. The affair lasted from 9 a.m. to 4p.m.

JULY 22: The 42nd BNI from Saugur [Sagar] arrived at Kalpi, on the river Jumna[Yamuna] to the southwest of Cawnpore. This place was to be of considerable significance to the rebels as for many months it served as their headquarters and arsenal.

JULY 24: The 12th Irregular Cavalry mutinied at Segowlie [Sagauli]. Their commanding officer, Major Holmes (he who had delared martial law) and his wife were out driving in the evening when six of the cavalry troopers stopped the carriage and headed them both. They then also murdered the surgeon and his wife and child and a Mr Bennet the postmaster, and after plundering arid burning the station the regiment left.

JULY 25: Havelock intent now on relieving Lucknow crossed

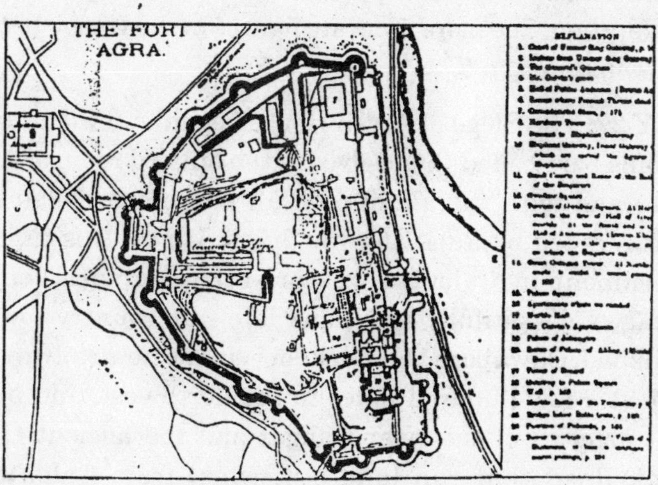

the Ganges into Oude [Awadh] into what was to prove very hostile-territory. His force was inadequate for the task he had been given; he was short of nearly everything, but the absence of cavalry was to be of particular concern. His little army consisted of artillery, ten guns imperfectly equipped and manned, Infantry the reminants of HM's 64th, 84th, 78th the Madras Fusiliers, and Brasyers Sikhs, cavalry some sixty volunteers: in all no more 1000 effectives.

At Dinapore [Danapur] the 7th, 8th, 40th BNI mutinied. They had long been held in check by the understanding and conciliatory policy of Major General Lloyd, the latter's attitude was in complete contrast to that of the Comissioner William Tayler at Patna some three miles away. In the end the ties with their brethren in other, mutinied, regiments. allied to their sympathy for a local landowner, Raja Kunwar Singh, proved too much and they rose in rebellion. The majority set out for Arrah to the west, where it was known there was considerable money in the treasury.

JULY 26: Reputedly 6000 persons were now sheltering in Agra Fort of whom 2000 were children. This is probably an exaggeration. See more accurate figures in the Impey Letters, the *Companion,* p 5.

JULY 27: The Siege of Arrah House began. A few European civilians barricaded themselves in the billiard room of Arrah House and with the aid of 50 Sikh policemen defied 2000 mutineers led by Raja Kunwar Singh. Up till this time the government in Calcutta was pro-occupied with sending military aid - pitifully small and late - up country towards Allahabad. Cawnpore and Lucknow via the new railway that ran just a few hundred miles to the northwest, and by the great arteries of the river Ganges and the ancient Grand Trunk Road that ran (and still runs) from Calcutta to

Peshawar on the N.W. Frontier. It is just as well for the British the Europeans in Arrah did what they did. Without their stand, Bihar would have fallen to the rebels: the road from Calcutta, whence came all British reinforcement to the area most affected by mutiny/ rebellion ie the North-west Provinces from the Punjab to Allahabad, would have been cut. See L. G.Sieveking. *A Turning point in the Indian Mutiny,* London, 1910.

JULY 28: Most of the Christians from Fatehgarh and Farruckabad had already been killed, at Rampore or Bithur or in the Bibigurh at Cawnpore, but a few mainly Eurasians, had been taken prisoner and were today murdered in what came to be known as the 'Parade Ground Massacre' at Farruckabad. This was the killing often men and twenty-three women and children at Fatehgarh on the orders of the Nawab but at the instigation of the Bigga Begum: the latter it is thought was trying to ensure the death of all Christians, including her rival the notorious Bonny Byrne. *See* F.R. Cosens and C.L. Wallace, *Fatehgarh and the Mutiny,* Lucknow, 1933.

Azimgarh once again changed hands and was evacuated by the British.

JULY 29: Havelock defeated the Oude rebels, mainly *taluqdaris*' men at the battles of Unao and Busheratganj but could never follow up any victory as he had no cavalry; his force grew gradually weaker from casualties and disease.

JULY 30: Some commotion was noticed in the lines of the disarmed 26th BN1 at Mian Mir the military station adjoining Lahore. It is said by some to have been no more than the reaction to a dust-storm; at all events the commanding officer, Major Spencer and the havildar-major were both murdered, in unclear circumstances, whereupon the regiment panicked, and under cover of the dust-storm which was still raging they fled.

The 8th BNI mutinied at Hazaribagh influenced by the news of the mutiny at Dinapore and the rebellion of Kunwar Singh: they drove their officers and the civil authorities from the city but did not otherwise harm them.

Captain Dunbar an officer of HM's 10th Foot, stationed at Dinapore was sent, on 29 July to relieve Arrah House which was being attacked by Kunwar Singh and the mutinous regiments from Dinapore. The attempt, by 410 men including 70 Sikhs, was a disastrous failure, the troops being ambushed this night only a mile or so from Arrah; the panic was so great that many of the British casualties resulted from fire from their own comrades. Dunbar and six other officers were killed with 184 men. Many also were wounded. For the failure of this expedition. Major General Lloyd was blamed, and subsequently dismissed from his command. *See* Martin Vol II p.403.

JULY 31: The 26th BNI fled in panic to the banks of the Ravi; Mr F. Cooper was a Deputy Commissioner of the Punjab, based at Amritsar and although a civilian was responsible for the 'extermination', on this day of the disarmed 26th BNI at Ujnalla in particularly inhumane and unpleasant circumstances, for which he was praised and supported by his superiors but roundly condemned by many in the House of Commons when the news reached London. He wrote a book, to vindicate his conduct which he considered 'prompt, spirited and thorough. *See* Frederick Henry Cooper, *Crisis in the Punjab from 10th May until the Fall of Delhi.* Lahore. 1858.

Large rebel forces from Mhow and Indore arrived today at Gwalior leaving Maharaja Scindia helpless to prevent their onward march towards Agra.

The Ramgarh Infantry mutinied at Ranchi and Duranda in Chota Nagpur: both cities fell into the hands of the rebels, but with the aid of the Raja of Ramgarh and a few-loyal sepoys and troopers the British were able to recover Hazaribagh.

The British siege army before Delhi by now numbered 6918 effectives and 1116 sick and wounded, but it was clear that the only reinforcements that could be expected would be the Moveable Column from the Punjab, and that the British force could only decline in strength as disease and casualties multiplied.

Kolapur: This was the scene of the only mutiny to take place in the Bombay Army. Kolapur was a town and state south of Satara and north of Belgaum. On this day a part (140 men) of the 27th Bombay N.I. mutinied, killed three young officers, looted the *bazar* and the regimental quarter-guard, but were overpowered by a small force of troopers of the Southern Maratha Horse from Satara, led by Lieutenant Kerr. The regiment was disarmed, 63 sepoys executed, 66 transported, 18 imprisoned and 14 acquitted. The mutiny may well have been linked to an attempt to restore the House of Sivaji at Satara. For a ftill account see R. Montgomery Martin. *The Indian Empire,* Vol II.

At Muzaffarpur in Bihar there took place an incident which was becoming quite common in that Province, that is to say that the military rebelled, the Hindu landholders might join in the rebellion, but the majority Muslim, of the population, preferred to remain with government. A detachment of Holmes's Irregulars mutinied here but were unable to loot the treasury because the *nujeebs* and the populace stood up against them. As a result, British authority was in abevance for no more than twenty-four hours.

6

August 1857

AUGUST 1: The 63rd BNI and the 11th Irregular Cavalry were disarmed at Berhampore where of course the 19th BNI had been among the first to show signs of dissent, on 26 February. It could hardly be supposed that these two regiments could now avoid being influenced by the recent events at Dinapore and it had been decided herefore to disarm them; fortuitously for the British. HM's 90th Regiment were passing through on their way up country and they were used to effect the disarmament which was done without bloodshed and before any positive mutinous action had taken place.

There was a further skirmish outside the walls of Delhi, but both those inside and outside knew now that an assault not long be delayed.

AUGUST 2: Mhow a station near Indore. was relieved by the British: Colonel Durand arrived there with Brigadier Stuart's column of Bombay army units.

Major Vincent Eyre was on his way from Calcutta, 'up-country' with a European battery of artillery. He had reached Dinapore on 25 July the day the three Sepoy regiments there successfully rebelled and joined Kunwar Singh. Eyre had offered his services to Major-General Lloyd, but as they were not required he moved on upstream to Buxar where he learned the news that the sepoys were *en route* to Arrah. Leaving part of his little force to protect Ghazipur. he collected all the men he could, including a contingent of 154 men of the 5th Fusiliers under Captain L'Estrange whom he persuaded to join him, and marched to the relief of the little garrison of Arrah. Had he failed he would undoubtedly have been in considerable trouble as he had no orders to do anything but proceed up-river to Allahabad. As it was he managed to defeat Kunwar Singh and his sepoys near Arrah, and to relieve the little garrison of Arrah House.

AUGUST 3: Arrah House having been relieved by Eyre, condign punishment was handed out by court martial to all who had given aid to the mutineers. Eyre then marched towards Jagdishpur in pursuit of Raja Kunwar Singh.

AUGUST 5: Havelock again defeated the rebels at Bashiratganj but it was another hollow victory since the rebels still outnumbered him by many thousands.

Kunwar Singh was reported to have proclaimed himself King of Shahabad, but he now headed westwards to aid the rebellion in Oude [Awadh] and Bundelkhand.

In Chota Nagpur, sepoys of the Ramgarh battalion, stationed at Parulia and Chaibasa mutinied and robbed the treasury and released all the prisoners from the gaol: the European civilians, few in number, fell back on Raniganj.

AUGUST 8: The remainder of the 59th BNI was disarmed at Amritsar.

Nicholson arrived, in advance of his Punjab Moveable Column, at Delhi his presence did much to improve the morale of the British troops on the Ridge.

Khan Bahaur Khan's forces from Bareilly were reported as advancing on Naini Tal.

The gunpowder factory in Delhi was blown up almost certainly by accident, but it caused many casualties and led to a shortage of powder for the defenders of the city.

AUGUST 10: A second outbreak of mutiny took place at Nasirabad: a trooper of the 1st Bombay Lancers suddenly mounted his charger and galloped in front of his regiment calling them to mutiny: they refused and pursued him whereupon he fled to the lines of the 12th Bombay NI who gave him shelter. Brigadier Macan ordered the 12th to turn out but only a few obeyed but they were then overawed by artillery and HM's 83rd regiment and disarmed: their muskets were found to be loaded. The ringleaders were then hanged or sentenced to be transported and the 12th given back their arms on their expressing contrition: thereafter they gave loyal service to the British. This incident shows that it is not entirely true to say that the Bombay Army was untainted by rebellion.

Further severe engagements outside Delhi took place.

AUGUST 11: The King of Delhi required chiefs to contribute money to the cause: he had a large army to pay and his own treasury was empty, so he sent his emissaries throughout northern India: some chiefs responded with promises, a few with cash, but the majority made no reply.

Eyre burned Kunwar Singh's palace at Jagdishpur near Arrah.

AUGUST 12: There was also a second outbreak of mutiny at Neemuch and events took place not unlike those at

Nasirabad two days earlier: again Bombay troops were involved, but mutiny was nipped in the bud and the ringleaders arrested by the commanding officer Colonel Jackson.

Havelock defeated the Oude rebels in a Third Battle of Bashiratganj just to the south of Lucknow.

At Deogarh, in the Santhal districts, much nearer to Calcutta two companies of the 32nd BNI suddenly mutinied and killed all their officers.

AUGUST 13: Despite his victories Havelock was forced by the weakness of his force to withdraw back to Cawnpore, an act which the rebels naturally seized upon as a great victory. Thus apart from the beleaguered garrison of the Residency at Lucknow there were no British at all in Oude.

At the same time the British abandoned Gorakpur to the east of Oude.

By now it was clear that popular support for the mutiny/rebellion varied dramatically from district to district. In Central India Colonel Durand reported today to the Governor General in Calcutta in the following terms: *Bundelkhand is in insurrection along the line from Jhansi by Chanderi to Saugur, and the Shahgarh Raja is said to have joined: but in the north the mass of Bundelkhand, though perturbed, has not broken out,and Rewah is staunch and as actively friendly as several of the Bundelkhand Chiefs under Major Ellis.* It is worth perhaps summarising the position in other areas on this date. In Oude [Awadh] virtually the entire province was in the hands of the rebels; they were aided by the sepoys of mutinied regiments but by no means dependent upon them since they had considerable popular support. The 37 acre site of the Lucknow Residency still held out for the British, and the pathetic little column of Havelock although undefeated had been driven back over the Ganges, the rebels closing in behind them. In Rohilkhand, the rebels were in total control save in the area round Saharunpur and the foothills of the Himalayas. Around Delhi the British controlled only a corridor leading north towards the Punjab; on the Ridge they were finalising plans for a desperate assault on the city, an assault which the commander, Archdale Wilson, had grave fears might fail. In the Punjab itself British authority was supported in the many by the people, although there were sporadic outbursts of rebellion, from spoy regiments recruited from Oude and Bengal, known as *porbeahs.* or men from the east. In Lower Bengal there were occasional violent outbreaks, but they were unco-ordinated and limited to individual army units: the mass of the population appeared to prefer the security of British rule. In Chota Nagpur the British were far from popular but the proximity of troops from the Madras army overawed the majority. In Rajputana all remained relatively quiet: nearly all the Indian Princes adhered to government. In the Doab (the area between the Ganges and Jumna rivers) which included Fatehgarh and Cawnpore. British Authority was limited to the latter city. Agra was not itself beieged in the sense of being surrounded by enemies, but it was virtually cut off by hostile territory, and in the months to come was to be further isolated as the Gwalior Contingent moved towards active anti-British action. Calcutta, the seat of government, was denied communication with much of North India by the cutting of the telegraphic links, and at this time the Governor General Canning, can have had only an imperfect understanding of the progress of the rebellion and its suppression: communication with the Punjab for example was now possible only via Bombay!

The new Commander-in-Chief Sir Campbell arrived in Calcutta.

AUGUST 14: At Bhagalpur in eastern Bihar the 5th

Irregular Cavalry mutinied: they then pressed on towards Baosi where they hoped to seduce the 32nd BNI.

The many body of the Punjab Moveable Column arrived at the Ridge before Delhi: these were to be the last British reinforcements, and everyone knew that henceforth the Delhi Field Force could only get weaker.

Kunwar Singh still accompanied by the main body of the Dinapore mutineers, arrived at Sasseram heading westwards.

AUGUST 15-18: More severe engagements took place outside Delhi, but they were on a small scale: the rebels continuously probed and reconnoitred, and allowed the British no peace, and curtailed also the drawing up of plans for assaulting the city. There were murmurs within the British camp at Wilson's delay in attacking the city.

AUGUST 16: At Baosi in eastern Bihar the mutinied 5th Irregular Cavalry was received by the 32nd BNI with bullets and bayonets: the Colonel of the 32nd, Burney. an excellent linguist, had convinced his regiment, for the time being, that the mutineers had been defeated at Arrah and Jagdishpur, and that if they mutinied they would have no safe line of retreat either to the west or the east.

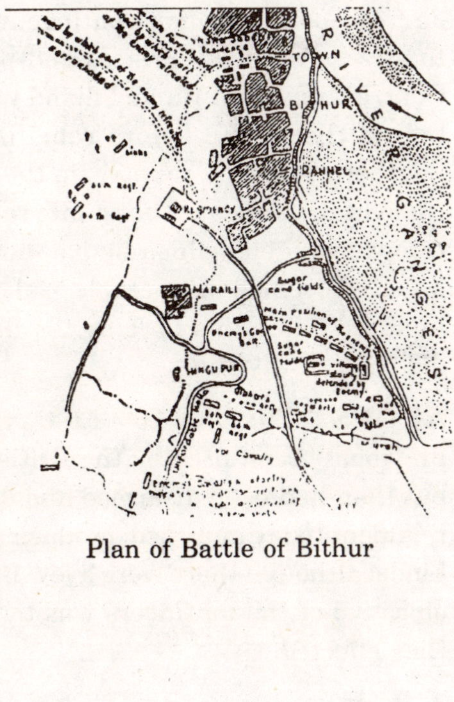

Plan of Battle of Bithur

Havelock defeated Nana Sahib's forces at Bithur. some twelve miles north of Cawnpore, but it was a pyrrhic victory. The rebel-numbered over four thousand, mainly sepoys, and they fought with great spirit, even crossing bayonets with the British soldiers but eventually retreated. Havelock lost twelve men from sunstroke and had sixty, battle casualties, and his men totally exausted returned to Cawnpore the next day.

AUGUST 17: Sir Colin Campbell took over as C in C. His information as to the military position was far from complete since communication up-country was cut, and rumour often took place of fact. It was believed that the British force before Delhi was more besieged than besieging; Agra and its garrison was known to be isolated; of Lucknow it was known only that a small British force, defeated in the field, was shut up in an indepensible enclosure; Havelock had been forced back on Cawnpore: Gwalior Contingent was thought to be about to attack Agra: the Princes and petty rulers of Rajputana. Central India and Bundelkhand were believed to be merely biding their time before rebelling: ominously, even the Southern Maratha country, in the Bombay Presidency, was thought to be about to burst into rebellion. Even had he fresh troops available (which he had not) the immense distances involved seemed insuperable. Calcútta to Allahabad is eight hundred miles, and for only the first 120 miles to Raniganj did the railway run.

AUGUST 19: The 10th Lt Cavalry at Ferozepur had previously been used by the British against the mutineers, but then had been disarmed and dismounted. A part of this regiment today mutinied, producing secreted arms of various kinds: although there were a few British casualties the main objective of the mutineers was to flee the station, and this they effected.

Kunwar Singh reached Akbarpur, still apparently heading south or westwards: his force consisted of upwards of one thousand men four elephants and fourteen camels and many horses but no ammunition. At the same time his brother Amar Singh at the head of some of Kunwar Singh's men was on the Grand Trunk Road in Bihar between Sasseram and Dehri on the Soane river, threatening to burn the latter town.

AUGUST 20: Kunwar Singh was at Rohtasgarh, crossing the Soane river to head westwards.

There was a fierce attack on the Lucknow Residency, where the ranks of the besieged garrison were thinning rapidly: heaviest cannonade yet, particularly on what was called the Cawnpore Battery: there were three hours of continuous firing; Deprat's House fell in and an attempt was made to burn down the Baillie Guard Gate. See P.J.O. Taylor. *A Feeding of Quiet Power,* p114.

AUGUST 21: The Jodhpur Legion mutinied at Anadra which lies at the base of the hill on which the hill station of Mount Abu is situated, in Rajputana. The mutineers then attacked their commanding officer. Captain Hall, and some European invalid soldiers on Mount Abu, but were driven off and marched off to join their comrades at Erinpura.

AUGUST 22: The entire Jodhpur Legion, infantry, artillery and cavalry, mutinied at Erinpura. The adjutant. Lt Conolly displayed considerable coolness but was eventually taken prisoner, although 'protected' by forty-five loyal troopers.

AUGUST 23: Conolly was released by the mutineers and rode into Erinpura with three loyal troopers, the mutineers now headed for Ajmer. The Raja of Jodhpur then sent his own personal army to stop them: the Raja's troops dug in at a place called Pali.

AUGUST 24: The British in Agra were still apprehensive of an attack by the Gwalior Contingent, only seventy miles away, so little offensive activity was undertaken, but today Major Montgomery and Lieutenant de Kantzow defeated rebel cavalry and *ghazis* at Aligarh thus clearing the road to Meerut.

AUGUST 25: Prince Firoz Shah, *Shahzada,* and nephew of the King of Delhi was placed on the *musnud* at Mandsaur, some twenty-four miiles from Neemuch in Rajputana: he assumed the title of Humayun Shah.

A large rebel force, including eighteen guns, left Delhi with the avowed intention of intercepting the Siege Train known to be on its way from Ferozepur with only a slender escort. Nicholson defeated them and captured all their guns in the battle of Najafgarh near Delhi; this battle is remarkable in having been won with scarcely any British casualties until the very last minute when it was found that a few sepoys had hidden themselves in the village of Nugli, where they fought with gallantry and desperation, inflicting one hundred dead and wounded on the British; many of the latter are said to have acquired considerable amounts of loot, in the form of bags of rupees left by the rebels.

A Mansion House meeting in London established the Indian Mutiny Relief Fund.

AUGUST 26: The green flag of revolt was raised at Mandsaur. The town was fortified and thirteen guns mounted on the walls, and many men flocked there to join Firoz Shah.

AUGUST 28: The 51st BNL already disarmed, were subjected to a search for hidden arms and broke into open mutiny at Peshawar.

AUGUST 29: The pursuit of the unarmed 51st BNI was conducted with the utmost ferocity by General Cotton, the fusillade beginning at Peshawar and extending to Jamrud in the Khyber Pass; either in the pursuit or after drumhead court-martial more than 700 of the 51st were killed, virtually in cold blood.

Still moving away from his home base in Shahabad Kunwar Singh arrived at Ramgarh, whose Raja had remained loyal to the British, and plundered Ghorawal.

AUGUST 31: A body of four hundred mercenaries, acting apparently under the orders of the (Maratha dominated) Durbar seized the very strong fort of Dhar some thirty miles west of Indore and for two months defied the British.

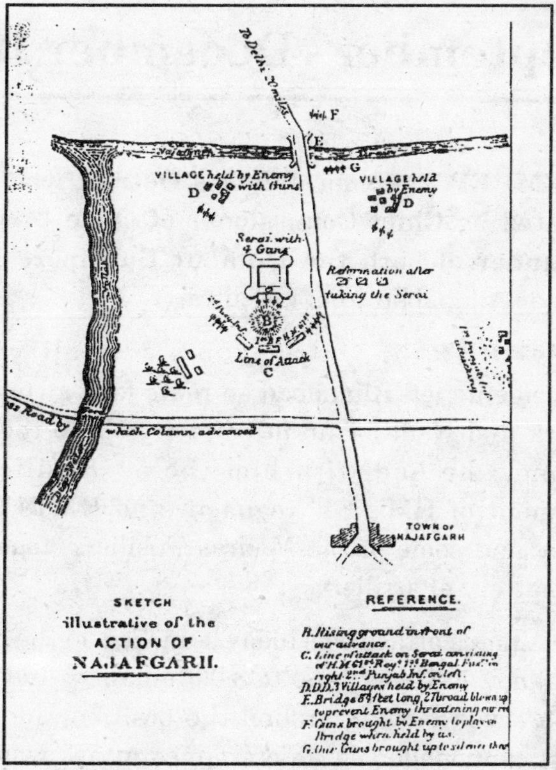

Battle of Najafgarh

7

September - December 1857

SEPTEMBER 2: General James Outram who had been nominated as Chief Comissioner of Oude [Awadh] and Commander of both the Dinapur Cawnpore Divisions arrived at Allahabad from Calcutta.

SEPTEMBER 5: Outram and a small column of reinforcements left Allahabad en route for Cawnpore to join Havelock and Neill for an attempt to relieve the Lucknow Residency: he had with him the 5th Fusiliers and a detachment of HM's 64th regiment and HMTs 90th Light Infantry and some of the Madras Fusiliers, together with Eyre's battery of artillery.

A fierce attack was today launched on the garrison of the Lucknow Residency: up to 8.000 infantry and 500 horse were observed moving around the position, and after the severest cannonade yet, a determined attack was launched particularly upon Gubbins's Post: two mines were exploded but again the distance had been miscalculated. The attack was bravely pushed home but was beaten back by the defenders; Lieutenant James Graham committed suicide by throwing himself off a high building in the Residency, an eventhat caused the garrison great depression.

SEPTEMBER 7: Kunwar Singh still moving westwards closed the road to Rewah the ruler of which State was a relation his whom he hoped to recruit to the rebel cause.

The Indore rebels, ie a considerable force of contingent troops, and including also the 23rd BNI. were at Gwalior and today threw off restraint of Maharaja Scindia and marched north. They captured the town of Dholpore. only thirty four miles from Agra and this caused great anxiety in the latter place where the fort was still held by the British.

The British siege army on the Ridge before Delhi had now reached its maximum, a total of 13,000 men.

SEPTEMBER 8: The mutineers of the Jodhpur Legion defeated the Raja of Jodhpur's army, which came out of its entrenchment to do battle at Awah; the commander of the Raja's army. Anar Singh, fought and died bravely; the mutineers remained at Awah until 10 October when they marched towards Delhi.

Kunwar Singh had by now moved through Mirzapur and was reported to have arrived at Rewah.

Maharaja Jung Bahadur's Gurkhas, from Nepal, today arrived at Jaunpur, anxious to assist the British, in theory, but even more anxious for loot.

SEPTEMBER 9: John Russell Colvin the Lt Governor of the N.W.Provinces died at Agra, and was succeeded as chief civil officer by Mr E.A. Reade who at once recommended to the Governor General that Agra be placed under military control for the time being, ie under the command of Colonel Cotton.

SEPTEMBER 11: The British assault upon the city of Delhi having been finally decided upon, massive cannonading commenced.

Outram making steady progress on the road to Cawnpore learned from spies that a strong party of rebels from Oude [Awadh], up to four hundred strong with four guns, had crossed the Ganges behind him and intended to sever his communications with Allahabad. He therefore despatched Major Eyre with two hundred troops and he defeated the rebels at Koondun Puttee [Kundanpati] on the Grand Trunk Road.

SEPTEMBER 14: The British assault on Delhi began. 'A little after midnight we fell in as quietly as possible on the left of our tents; by the light of a lantern the orders for the assault were then read to the men. They were to the following purport: Any officer or man who might be wounded was to be left where he fell; no one was to step from the ranks to help him as we had no men to spare: if the assault were successful held be taken up by the *doolies* and carried to the rear or to wherever he could best receive medical assistance: if we failed, wounded and sound alike should be prepared to bear the worst. There was to be no plundering, but all prize taken was to be put into a common stock for fair division after all was over. No prisoners were to be made as we had no one to guard them, and care was to be taken that no women and children were injured. To this the men at once answered; No fear sir! The officers now pledged their honours on their swords to abide by these orders, and the men then promised to follow their example'. The main assault was made via the Kashmir Gate. So many British casualties were incurred (4493 of whom 1254 were killed) that Archdale

Wilson seriously considered a retreat. Brigadier General Nicholson was mortally wounded. The battle that followed, mainly street fighting, was to last seven days.

SEPTEMBER 15: At long last Outram joined Havelock and Neill at Cawnpore: he was technically now in charge of the column that was to march to the relief of Lucknow. but he waived his nght to command, allowing Havelock to have the honour of rescuing the British garrison.

SEPTEMBER 16: The 50th BNI were stationed at Nagode which lies between Rewah and Allahabad, and had displayed no mutinous tendencies at all to this date. The news came that Kunwar Singh was in Rewah territory and the regiment was told that it would be used against him. They accordingly marched out of Nagode apparently delighted at the thought of action, but after two miles halted and quietly told their officers they were no longer wanted and had better go, which, seeing no option, they did. They and their families were safely escorted to Mirzapur and the regiment returned to Nagode which they plundered and burnt subsequently ravaging the district.

In Jubbulpore [Jabalpur] the British discovered a conspiracy between the sepoys of the 52nd BNI and the pensioned Gond Raja. Shankar Sa and his son Raghunath Sa, and these two men were arrested.

SEPTEMBER 17: In the Saugar and Narbada Territories affairs remained confused: the area abounded in rebels or potential rebels. As an example: Major Jenkins marched from Darnoh with a force of about five hundred men. Madras and Bombay armies, for the purpose of collecting grain from certain rebel villages. He arrived at Narsinghar and found that the fort, a strong stone built place with a wet ditch was occupied by about 250 matchlockmen. Shahgarh rebels. He brought his guns into position to throw shrapnel, but before he commenced firing the enemy retreated, attempting to ford the swiftly flowing river Sunar. Many of the rebels were killed in their panic flight and thirteen were captured and hanged in Narsinghar.

SEPTEMBER 18: At Jubbulpore [Jabalpur] the 52nd BNI mutinied at 10p.m. that night, on the news that Raja Shankar Sa and his son had been executed, having being fired from a gun. On the raja's death his widow seized Ramgarh and took part in several-skirmishes; at length being closely pursued she dismounted from her horse and plunged a sword into her own bosom: she was taken into the English camp where she died.

There was considerable minor activity in the Jubbulpore district during the next few days, the rebels being partly from the 52nd BNI but also from the supporters of local rajas.

An abortive attack by General Lawrence on the Jodhpur rebels at Awah was made, the British being forced to withdraw, and losing considerable face, as a result of the strength of the rebel position.

The Nagode mutiny continued.

SEPTEMBER 19 : At Deoghar and Rampurhat, just to the west of Berhampur in Bengal, the 32nd BNI were showing signs that they were intending to mutiny.

Havelock and Outram set out for Lucknow from Cawnpore.

SEPTEMBER 20: After fierce street fighting Delhi finally fell to the British, when the Burn Bastion was captured. Many of the mutineers marched away out of the city, led by Bakht Khan who had been their Commander-in-Chief. It is possible that Bakht Khan tried to persuade the King of Delhi,

Bahadur Shah Zafar to leave with him and the soldiery, to carry on the fight from another centre. If so, he failed, for the King simply moved out of Delhi towards the southern outskirts, and took refuge in the tomb of his ancestor. Humayun.

Note : It had been generally believed that the fall of Delhi would mean the end of the rebellion, but this was not the case; at most it prevented the Punjab from rising in revolt. One positive result was that the mutinous sepoys were no longer cooped up in the but were spread in numerous detachments throughout the country, spreading rather than containing the rebellion.

Although women and children appear to have, been spared in Delhi there was much indiscriminate slaughter by the British, neither friend nor foe was safe. Many British and Sikh soldiers found liquor stores and were drunken and out of hand. See A. Llewellyn.*The Siege of Delhi.* London, 1977, and N.K. Nigam.*Delhi in 1857,* Chapter V. The City of the Dead, Delhi 1957.

The British still had reservations about the role to be played by the allies from Nepal, but to some extent re-assurance came today, for after marching fifty miles in two days Jaunpur to Azimgarh and then to Mandori, the Gurkhas defeated the rebels there, in a spirited charge on to a well fortified position. inflicting over two hundred casualties and forcing the rebels to flee.

SEPEMBER 21: The controversial Captain Hodson of Hodson's, claimed to have captured the King of Delhi, Bahadur Shah Zafar at Humayun's Tomb: he certainly set out to do so with General Archdale Wilson's permission (Wilson declared afterwards that he had never expected to see Hodson alive again) but there has always been doubt about the account which Hodson himself gave of the event. The unpublished statement of a certain Capt Maisey, Judge Advocate General's office, says: 'It is clear that the King of Delhi gave himself up, and was not captured by Captain Hodson who was apparently obsessed with the complex everything for his own. Actually brought in by Rajab Ali (Meer Munshi or head of native intelligence) plus an escort. Rajab Ali met Hodson on the way back to Delhi'. The King was placed under guard in a small room in the Red Fort.

Because of the mutiny of a part of the 52nd BNI at Jabalpur the British disarmed the remainder of the regiment and abandoned Damoh: it was handed over to a friendly raja. Kour Shamleju and the Panna troops, and the British of the Nagpore Moveable Column then concentrated on Jabalpur.

Muhammad Hasan claiming to be the *Nazim* or official ruler in the name of the King of Oude entered Gorakhpur, a place which, like nearby Azimghar changed hands frequently at this time: if British troops or their Gurkha allies were in the vicinity then the cities were held for Government, when there were no such troops present, the rebels contested with each other, and with loyal zamindars. for control.

SEPTEMBER 22: There is equal controversy and conflict of evidence in Hodson's conduct on this day. That he killed the three Mughal Princes, with his own hand, is not in doubt. They were Mirza Mogul and Mirza Abubakr sons of Bahadur Shah, and Mirza Khair Sultan, a grandson, but while some applauded his action many, before and since, have condemned it: it is unlikely that he was, as he claimed, in danger of losing his own life from the crowd pressing round. He caused each prince to strip down to his underclothes and then shot each one deliberately from close range. The Princes, when captured by Hodson said with a jaunty air, 'Of course there will be a proper investigation into our conduct in the proper court. Their bodies were taken back into Delhi and thrown down for the dogs and vultures to devour. and no opposition was encountered.

SEPTEMBER 23: Outram and Havelock with their small British column captured the Alambagh. a walled garden and mnsion some four miles to the south of Lucknow on the Cawnpore road. This was to act as a British military base for the next six months.

SEPTEMBER 25: Generals Outram and Havelock finally relieved the Lucknow Residency, although more accurately it should be said that it reinforced the British garrison: the area held by the British was extended and made considerably more secure, but no evacuation either of the garrison or of the numerous women and children was possible. Colonel Neill and Lt. Col. Tyller were both killed, together with 600 other British casualties.

SEPTEMBER 27: Another column of Gurkhas from Jaunpur marched against Mubarakpur and captured the place and its raja. Iradat Khan, who was promptly hanged.

SEPTEMBER 28: The highly tenuous nature of the hold of the British on the Cawnpore district is illustrated by the fact that the *thanah* or police post, of Bithur. only twelve miles from Cawnpore was attacked by the 42nd BNI aided by the Raja of Sheorajpur.

A military column, numbering 2500 troops and headed by Colonel Greathed had been despatched from Delhi to work south and westwards against the rebels. Today Greathed defeated a considerable body of rebels at Bulandshahr the home town of one of the most implacable of the enemies of the British, Walidad Khan, some half way between Delhi and Agra. The rebel force included the 12th BNI and the 14th

Irregular Cavalry and a large body of *burkundazes* Walidad Khan's Fort of Malaghar was destroyed.

SEPTEMBER 29: Kunwar Singh reached Banda. in Central India, and was able to link up with the forces of Nana Sahib led now by Tatya Tope, and eventually with the Gwahor Contingent. It was reported that he was accompanied by 1800 of the Danapur mutineers.

Yet another party of Gurkhas, this time operating out of Azimgarh, marched upon Atrowlia, the stronghold of Beni Madho. and although the latter escaped his fortress was demolished.

OCTOBER 2: The position in Central India remained very confused: where government could deploy even a few loyal troops or police it remained in charge; in their absence the mutineers or local rebels moved in. A good example is the town and fort of Rehli in the Sagar District: the Deputy Commissioner of the latter place determined to secure Rehli and sent against it a body of police and a hundred sepoys of the 31st BNI; before they arrived a loyal inhabitant, Girdhari Naik had captured the fort and made himself *killadar* in the name of the British government.

A Muslim governor, Muhammad Husain still ruled Gorakhpur for the King of Delhi: the presence of rebels so far eastwards was of much concern to Calcutta; the Governor General feared that communications to the northwest might be cut off. This may well have influenced his decision to accept the help of Jung Bahadur and his Gurkhas.

OCTOBER 3: Four hundred and eight officers and men of Peel's Naval Brigade arrived at Allahabad: they were from H.M.S. Shannon, a Royal Navy frigate which had arrived at Calcutta from Hong Kong. Their services had been offered to Canning because of the severe shortage of trained artillerymen available to the British in India at this time. They took with them ten eight inch, sixty-eight pounder guns from the ship, together with lesser guns and mortars and rocket tubes.

Rebels from Delhi arrived at Hathras twenty two miles south of Aligarh on the road to Agra.

OCTOBER 5: Walidad Khan, driven from Bulandshahr, reached Bareilly with 500 followers; his welcome was far from universal as there was already another rebel power in control there.

Greathed's Column marching southwards towards Agra expected opposition at Aligarh, but the rebels evacuated the town, were pursued and some two hundred and fifty cut down by cavalry, for the loss of only two wounded.

OCTOBER 7: Captain Rattray of Rattray's Sikhs, had been worsted by a body of six hundred rebels, including the 5th Irregular Cavalry, at Gaya in Bihar, but today he avenged the disaster by defeating the rebels at Akbarpur,

Queen Victoria proclaimed 7 October a Day of Humiliation, so both we and our people may humble overselves before Almighty God in order to obtain pardon of our sing and send up prayers to the Divine Majesty for imploring His blessing and assistance on our arms for the restoration of tranquillity.

OCTOBER 8: Ali Bahadur the Nawad of Banda attacked the fortress of Ajaigarh, whose Rani, like the Nawab himself had been faithful to the British. Thus the position in Bundelkhand, as in so many areas, was confused: much of the fighting was between rivals taking the opportunity of the weakness of government to assert by force of arms their ancient claims to land or sovereignty. See Tapti Roy, *Politics of a Popular Uprising, Bundelkhund in 1857,* Delhi 1994.

OCTOBER 9: Greathed was at Bijegarh. still forty-eight miles from Agra whence he received many imploring messages to hurry, for the British shut up in the Fort at Agra daily expected attack from the, Indore rebels coming up from the south.

The 32nd BNI two companies, mutinied at Deoghar. not far to the west from Berhampore and this further confused the position in Bihar. Of the 32nd many dispersed after the usual looting spree but a number remained together as a military unit, and at the end of October very nearly captured the Commander-in-Chief Sir Colin Campbell, on the Grand trunk Road, as he made his way with very little escort up country from Calcutta. Captain Rattray went in pursuit of the mutinied 32nd.

OCTOBER 10: After a forced march Greathed and his Column arrived on the parade ground outside Agra Fort, and were eating breakfast at ten-thirty when they were attacked, in a complete surprise, by the rebels of the Mhow and Indore Brigades. Neither of the British commanding officers - Greathed or Cotton was present when the attack started, and somewhat fortuitously. it was repulsed, and some 2000 of the rebels reported killed. After this so-called Battle of Agra there followed a grossly unfair punishment, by burning of a number of villages around Agra for failing to warn Agra. Ironically the peasants had also failed to tell the Mhow and Indore rebels of the arrival'of Greathed's Column, so, apparently, the surprise on the parade ground was on both sides. There are numerous accounts of the battle, the most succinct being in R. Montgomery Martin, *The Indian Empire,* Vol II. London 1858.

The territory to the north of the Ganges at Allahabad and Benares was becoming increasingly disturbed - and complicated - A rebel, described as an 'adventurer' and calling himself Nazim of Sultanpur. Mehndi Hasan was reported today as enlisting men at Hasanpur: he was eventuly to command an army estimated at 15000 men. His activities led directly to the formation of General Franks's Column charged by the Governor General to protect Benares at all costs and to prevent the rebels crossing the Ganges into Bihar.

Central India was largely in turmoil and many men were flocking to join the standard of the Shahzada Firoz Shah; Bhopawar and Sirdarpur the latter being the headquarters of the Malwa Bhil Corps were attacked and plundered by his men. although the Bhils showed spirited resistance so long as their ammunition lasted.

OCTOBER 12: Troops of the Madras Army at Mirzapur moved out on the road to Rewah. where the Raja had long since decided to throw in his lot with the British, although at times surrounded by rebels: his resolve was reinforced by the Political Agent, Lieutenant Willoughby Osborne, who behaved with considerable courage throughout.

OCTOBER 13: In Central India at Rehli the mutineers of the 52nd BNI plus local rebels attacked the fort but were repulsed, the sepoys of the 31st BNI remaining loyal: the place now continued in British possession and assisted Sir Hugh Rose eventually his advance towards Garhakota.

Two Shahzadas Mirza Bakhtawar Shah and Mirza Mendu sons of the King of Delhi were tried by the British and shot beside the Jumna.

OCTOBER 15: The Gwalior Contingent, which had mutinied 14 June, but had been held in check by Scindia. Maharaja of Gwalior (by various pretences, eg waiting for the end of the rainy season etc), finally decided to join the rebels: the deciding factor was probably Scidia's unfeigned joy on hearing that Delhi had fallen to the British.

There was also today an outbreak at Kotah in Rajputana where the Maharao's troops mutinied, This is the name given to the personal troops/levies of the ruler of Kotah [Kota] to distinguish them from the Kotah Contingent.(see 5 July 1857). It was a formidable force consisting of four regiments of infantry, ten troops of cavalry, some 300 artillerymen, and 3,500 armed police. The Maharao warned the Political Agent. Major C Burton, that he could no longer rely on these troops, and Burton and his two young sons were indeed murdered by them, after putting up a spirited and lonely defence. The British subsequently signified their opinion that the ruler had not fully performed his duty to Major Burton, and *reduced his salute from seventeen to thirteen guns!*

OCTOBER 22: The Durbar at Dhar was known to be intriguing with the rebels, so the British at Mhow determined to march on the place, under the command of Brigadier Stuart. The rebels were driven back inside the fort which was then invested.

OCTOBER 23: The British were repulsed at Jiran, ten miles from Neemuch in Rajputana; their small force of four hundred men mainly Bombay troops, with two guns and a mortar, were insufficient to deal with the rebels who had come from Mandsaur and were led by a *Shahzada:* strangely enough the rebels evacuated Jiran that same night, possibly believing that a larger British force was on its way from Neemuch.

OCTOBER 26: Greathed and Hope Grant arrived at Cawnpore.

Van Cortlandt an officer who had served under Ranjit Singh in the Punjab before its annexation, had by now totally subdued the districts, notably Rohtak to the northwest of Delhi.

OCTOBER 28: Sir Colin Campbell, the Commander-in-Chief started from Calcutta for the scene of operations.

OCTOBER 29: Tatya Tope had now taken command of the Gwalior Contingent, and with it arrived at Jalaun en route for Cawnpore.

OCTOBER 31: Dhar about to be assaulted, was found to have been quietly evacuated during the night and was thus captured by the British, with units of the Bombay army and the assistance of the Hyderabad Contingent Field Force. The local population appeared to be very happy at the restoration of government authority.

NOVEMBER 2: A severe action was fought at Kajwa which is about twenty-five miles northwest of Fatehpur, between Cawnpore and Allahabad; The rebels numbered over two thousand and included many of the mutineers from Danapur plus others from the Banda area. The British column headed by Col Powell (killed) and Captain Peel and his Naval Brigade, were on their way up country to Cawnpore. following the Commander-in-Chief. Most of these columns or detachments reached their destination without seeing the enemy, but this one, numbering five hundred men in all, had to deal with a considerable body of rebels. Powell attacked them in the village of Kajwa, and although he succeeded in driving them off and capturing their three guns, there were heavy casualties on both sides: Powell was himself killed (Peel took over command) and the British suffered ninety-five killed and wounded; the rebels were estimated to have lost some three hundred men.

NOVEMBER 3: Campbell reached Cawnpore, and despite the threat from the forces of Tatya Tope approaching from the west, he determined to deal first with the relief of the Residency at Lucknow to the northeast. The garrison there were considerably heartened by the news of the fall of Delhi;

they extended the position they occupied and turned to the offensive on occasion: this had the effect of reducing the value of the enemy's mining operations which had continued unabated.

NOVEMBER 6: Captain Rattray caught up with the 32nd BNI at Dhanchua in Bihar; the battle was hard fought and inconclusive, but the mutineers retreated under cover of darkness.

NOVEMBER 7: The Gwalior Contingent and the 40th BNI with Kunwar Singh, joined up and began the advance on Cawnpore.

NOVEMBER 8: Four thousand rebels, who had previously ocupicd the fort of Jiran advanced on Neemuch and took possesion of the station and cantonment but were unable to dislodge the small British force in its entrenchment (after a fifteen day iege the rebels evacuated the town and fell back).

The Malwa Contingent mutinied at Mehidpur which was attacked by a body of the Mandsaur rebels including many *vilaities:* the Malwa cavalry had already mutinied, now the infantry either went over to the enemy or deserted. Mehidpur was infamous for the firing by the rebels of the hospital which was full of sick and wounded men. The rebels objective was to capture the guns of Mehidpur and other ordnance stores, badly needed for their projected assault upon the entrenched British in Ncemuch.

NOVEMBER 9: Thomas Kavanagh, a clerk in one of the civil offices, volunteered to slip out of the Residency at Lucknow with details of the garrison and his insider knowledge of the approaches to the Residency, and make his way to the Commander-in-Chief; Outram reluctantly accepted the offer which, to his surprise, was successful and the information taken to Campbell proved valuable. Kavanagh was awarded the Victoria Cross, and given an appointment as an Assistant Commissioner.

The Europeans were by now wholly besieged in the fort of Neemuch.

Campbell crossed the Ganges into Oude [Awadh], and hastened to the Alambagh still in British hands and rapidly being built up as a base for the assault on Lucknow.

NOVEMBER 11: Rebels were reported to have continued to enter the district of Allahabad in some numbers. As a result the British were obliged to leave considerable parties of troops at intervals to guard the line of communication with Calcutta.

NOVEMBER 12: The total number of fighting men available to Campbell was now three thousand four hundred, and after inspecting them on his arrival at Banni south of Lucknow he ordered the advance, and moving forward towards the Alambagh he captured Jellalabad Fort and with only minor opposition he brought his army to the cover of the Alambagh.

Major Orr and three hundred of the Hyderabad Contingent cavalry caught up with the Mandsaur rebels and recaptured the guns taken from Mehidpur: they also killed a hundred of the rebels (who fought extremely well) and captured seventy-four, all of whom were shot the same day after court-martial.

NOVEMBER 13: Campbell made his last plans for the assault on Lucknow. With the men he found in the Alambagh, and with the final reinforcements coming in from Cawnpore he now had close on five thousand men of all arms, including 450 of the Naval Brigade and Artillery, twelve heavy guns, ten mortars and twenty-seven light field guns.

NOVEMBER 14: Campbell advanced to the attack, on a

circuitous route via the Dilkusha and the Martiniere both of which were captured and became forward bases for the campaign. The rebels made two determined efforts to turn

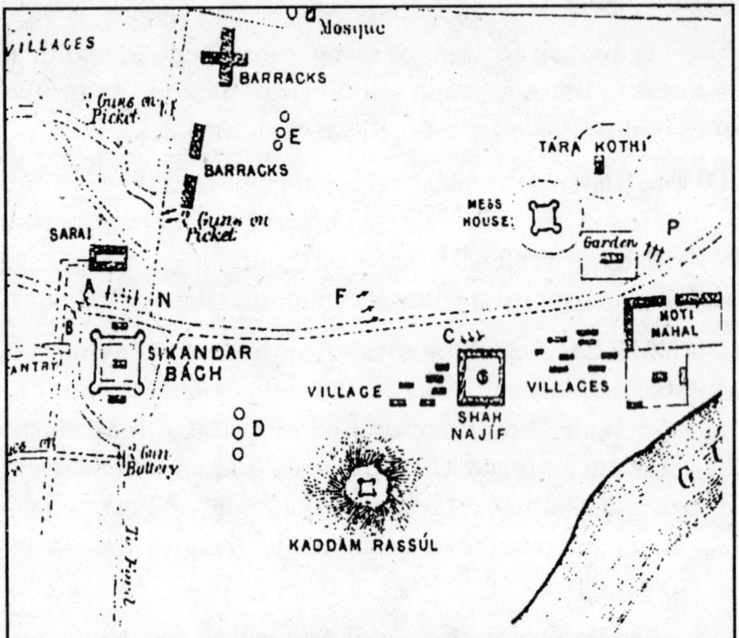

Lucknow. November 1857

the British position but were driven back with heavy loss, and the canal was crossed. The army then bivouacked for the night,the men sleeping with their arms by their sides, ready for immediate action.

NOVEMBER 15: In Lucknow the Dilkusha was fortified and the day spent preparing for the final assault.

NOVEMBER 16: The British moved to the attack in Lucknow choosing to follow the line of the river Gumti rather than run the risk of severe street fighting. Their first major obstacle was the Sikander-bagh. a high-walled enclosure some 150 yards square, with towers at the angles. It was captured only after a desperate battle, in which quarter was neither sought nor given, and in the end the entire rebel force within the enclosure over two thousand men, were killed; it is said that only four escaped. This was followed by the taking of the Shah Najif a very strong position indeed; it was effected by good fortune as well as gallantry. Brigadier Adrian Hope finding a narrow fissure that would just admit a storming party, one man at a time, to enter and take the garrison from the rear. The British then again bivouacked for the night.

The area to the west of Delhi was still far from pacified. No sooner had Brigadier Shower's column returned, apparently successful, to Delhi, when Jajhar and Riwari were again occupied by rebels, this time by the men of the Jodhpur Legion who had beaten the troops of the Raja of Jodhpur who had remained loyal to government. Colonel Gerrard was sent out with a column numbering over two thousand men of all arms, and today met the rebels, led by Sannand Khan, brother of the Nawab of Jajhar at the village of Narnul; the country people were all it is quite clear, well-disposed to the rebels. It was a very hard-fought battle. Gerrard was killed, but the rebels were killed or dispersed, leaving eight guns in the hands of the British, together with the fort of Narnul and their camp and all its contents.

NOVEMBER 17: The major fighting having taken place on the previous day Sir Colin Campbell was able to enter the Lucknow Residency.

What remained of the Jodhpur Legion fled to the southeast from Narnul towards the dominions of the Raja of Alwar.

NOVEMBER 18: Despite the apparent turn in the tide of the rebellion, mutinies still continued. Today the Wing of the 34th BNI mutinied at Chittagong; the sepoys plundered the treasury, released the prisoners from the gaol burnt down their own lines, fired the magazine and then left the station, taking with them three elephants on which they piled stolen government property; they harmed no Europeans, and the only man to suffer at their hands was a native gaoler who was killed when he protested at their proceedings. They then made off to the hills in a northwesterly direction.

NOVEMBER 22: The detachments of the 73rd BNI numbering three hundred and fifty sepoys, mutinied at Dacca, when they saw that an attempt was to be made to disarm them. They were successfully dispersed by a composite force of sailors and volunteers under the command of Lieutenant Lewis of the Bengal Navy, forty-one sepoys were killed before the remainder broke and fled: they found a temporary refuge in Bhutan. Pursued throughout December and January the survivors eventually escaped into northeastern Oude [Awadh] where the majority perished miserably. Also involved in the mutiny was the 4th Coy 9th Bn Bengal Artillery.

NOVEMBER 23: The British completed the evacuation of the Residency at Lucknow. Campbell achieved this, without a single casualty to the garrison or to the women and children, by carrying out a fierce bombardment on the Kaiserbagh which was breached in three places: the rebels assumed an assault there would take place but this had been only a diversion. The Residency was left deserted, although it was some twelve hours before the besiegers realised this fact and entered the grounds. Campbell decided to leave Outram, and a comparatively large force of four thousand men at the Alambagh; the rebels naturally saw the British withdrawal from Lucknow as a great victory.

In Central India a decisive battle took place at Mandsaur, which was Prince Firoz Shah's power base, and from which the rebels had been intending to launch a final attack on Neemuch. In many ways this battle was as significant as any to the east or lortheast, for it effectively restored British power in an area crucial to the containment of the rebellion: had Central India been totally overrun, the way would have been open to an extension of the conflict into the southern Maratha country, which was ripe for rebellion. See Sir George le Grand Jacob, *Western India before and during the Mutinies,* London, 1871. The battle itself was hard fought between on the one side Brigadier Stuart's Column, containing Bombay Army troops and Hyderabad Contingent cavalry, in addition to British regiments and cavalry and on the other many thousands of determined rebels, in which there was a high proportion of the *vilaitie* followers of Firoz Shah. Their defeat owed much to the skilful use of guns and cavalry by the British. At the end of the day the rebels retreated back into Mandsaur where they still held the fort, and into the village of Goraria.

Communication between the northwest and Calcutta on the one hand, and Bombay and the south on the other was still cut by the activities of rebels on the Deccan or Mirzapur road: this area, to the north of the Narbada river, was infested by two gangs whose activities were little better than *dacoitie.* Today saw the defeat of one of these bands - two hundred men led by Dalganjan Singh. and the capture and hanging of the latter.

NOVEMBER 24: Stuart defeated the final Bundela rebel force at Goraria near Mandsaur: although some two hundred *vilaities* surrendered under a flag of truce, most of the rebels were killed.

General Havelock died, of dysentery, and was buried in the Alambagh grounds: he had learned, before his death, of his promotion to Major General and his knighthood (subsequently changed to a baronetcy that his son might inherit the title).

NOVEMBER 25: The rebels evacuated Mandsaur and dispersed in all directions; one party appeared before Partabgarh but the raja there attacked and killed eighty of them and the remainder fled across the Chambal river. The main body of the rebels retreated to Nangarh, where they are said 'to have broken up their standards, saying their gods had forsaken them' As most were Muslim followers of Firoz Shah this story appears unlikely. The standards that appeared in numbers at the battle of Mandsaur had nearly all been green, ie Muslim.

NOVEMBER 27: At about 1 lam Campbell and three thousand of his army set out for Cawnpore from the Alambagh. He had with him also the women, children, sick and wounded, numbering in all about two thousand, and the treasure which had been rescued from the Residency. That same evening he encamped at Banni Bridge. Although the sound of distant cannonading could be distinctly heard no news had come from General Windham whom Campbell had left in charge at Cawnpore.

The Gwalior Contingent, now led by Tatya Tope, had been slowly approaching Cawnpore since leaving Kalpi on 9 November: their plan was to attack only when they knew Campbell was fully engaged in relieving 'Lucknow' Windham had taken up a position beyond and to the west of the town, and had been reinforced by some troops coming up country to join the Commander-in-Chief notably the Madras Brigade. Contrary to the orders he had received from Campbell. Windham now advanced and attacked some of the Gwalior Contingent, and captured three guns, but then fell back into Cawnpore. The superioriry of the rebels in artillery was most marked, and as the British fell back so the rebel attack grew in confidence. They came forward in overwhelming, and highly disciplined, numbers.

NOVEMBER 28: General Windham was comprehensively defeated by the Gwalior Contingent in the second battle of Cawnpore. The city was occupied by the rebels who took possession of the baggage of all British troops who were with Campbell and also took, or burnt, all the stores that had been prepared for the use of the refugees from the Lucknow Residency. Fortunetely for the British, Tatya Tope did not succeed in driving Windham from the entrenchment, nor did he manage to break the bridge of boats which was Cawnpore's only connection with the Oude side of the Ganges whence Colin Campbell could come to Windham's assistance. For a full account of the attack of the Gwalior Contingent see Malleson, *History of the Indian Mutiny.* Vol II. pp 226-257. Campbell crossed the bridge of boats with his staff, a few hours ahead of the main body of his army, on the evening of this day.

Muhammad Hasan still held Gorakpur.

NOVEMBER 29: Campbel's army from Lucknow had encamped on the Oude side of the Ganges, whence the heavy guns of the Naval Brigade could give cover to the bridge of boats. At 3 p.m. the army began to cross *via* this bridge into Cawnpore a process that lasted until 6 pm on the next day. The position occupied Tatya Tope and his considerable force was very strong. A good account is given in *Blackwood's magazine*. October 1858: *Their left was posted among the wooded high grounds interesected with nullas and thickly sprinkled with ruined bungalows and Public buildings, which lie between the town of Kanhpur and the Ganges. Their centre occupied the (own itself which was of great extent, and* *traversed only by narrow winding streets, singularly susceptible of defence. The portion of it facing the intrenchment was uncovered: but from the camp of our army it was separated by the Ganges canal......Their right stretched out behind this canal into the plain.* They numbered twenty-five thousand men. with forty guns: the number of trained soldiers did not exceed fourteen thousand.

NOVEMBER 30: By this evening every man woman and child from the Lucknow garrison had crossed the Ganges into Cawnpore, Campbell spent the next three days perfecting arrangements for their onward transmission to Allahabad; communications with the latter were now restored.

Eldest son of Bahadur

The rebel leader Debi Singh Guntia was active in the Jabalpur area, effectively cutting British connection with Bombay and the south: today he burned the *thanah* of Shahpura and when pursued by cavalry escaped over the river Narbada. He had a considerable force, estimated at 1500 men.

DECEMBER 3: Campbell despatched all the women and children and the sick ex Lucknow Residency to Allahabad, and prepared to attack the Gwalior Contingent. The latter had not been idle, and each day cannonaded the British entrenchment, or attempted to break the bridge of boats, on one occasion using fire boats floated downstream.

The Nazim of the Nawab of Fatehgarh reached Etawa with a large force: although he achieved little, this movement demonstrated the volatility of the situation in the Doab, ie the land between the Jumna and the Ganesh.

DECEMBER 4: The detachments of the 11th Irregular Cavalry at Madariganj and Jalpagori mutinied to the east of Bihar below Darjiling and went off, spreading alarm throughout the district They then headed for Dinajpur where there was an unusually large sum of money (ten lakhs of rupees) in the treasury, but veered away when they heard it was defended and entered Nepal.

DECEMBER 6: Of the rebel forces confronting the British in Cawnpore something like seven thousand were from the Gwalior Contingent, a fine body of extremely well trained and armed men being particularly strong in artillery. In addition there were an equal number of trained sepoys who had attached themselves, after mutinying, to the Nana Sahib or to Kunwar Singh: the remainder of the rebel force consisted of the adherents of the Rani of Jansi and other minor rulers and landholders. The British force consisted of about five thousand infantry, six hundred cavalry and thirty-five guns, the whole divided into four brigades, the Brigadiers being Greathed. Adrian Hope. Inglis (who had commanded in the Lucknow Residency), and Walpole Peel commanded the Naval Brigade whose heavy

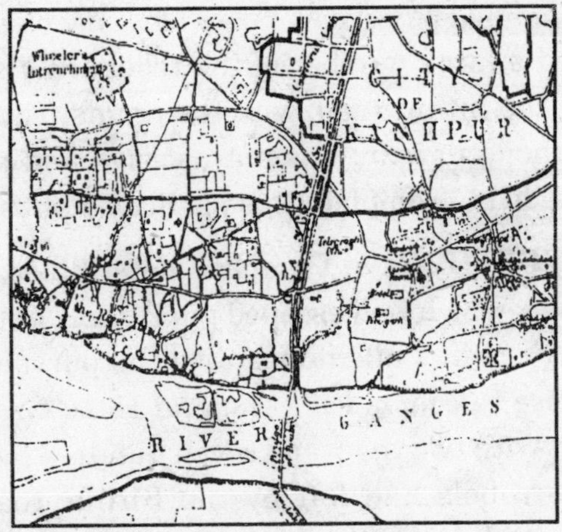

Cawnpore, December 1857

guns were to be of importance. Windham was given command of the intrenchment, ie virtually the reserve. The Third Battle of Cawnpore, as it came to be called, began at 9 am on this day and by a turning movement on the enemy's right, Campbell defeated Tatya Tope at the head of 25.000 rebels. Within a few hours the rebel camp was captured and occupied, and the Gwalior contingent pursued along the Kalpi road to the fourteenth milestone. The rebel's centre and left were thus cut off, shut up in Cawnpore city, with only one line of retreat, the road to Bithur. If General Mansfield, Campbell's Chief of Staff had fully obeyed his instructions the rebels would have been unable to escape by this route, but he remained passive at a position known as the Subadar's Tank and a large number of the rebel army succeeded in leaving on the Bithur road, with their guns. Thus the British victory although great, was not decisive and a further battle was needed to complete this particular phase of the campaign.

DECEMBER 8: Campbell determined to pursue the rebel army which had escaped via Bithur, but gave his troops one day's rest, while he planned the pursuit with the officer he chose to comand it - General Hope Grant. Hope Grant set out with two thousand seven hundred men at 1pm. Although the rebels had left by the Bithur road, it was guessed, correctly, they would be heading into Oude[Awadhj and for this they would have to cross the Ganges, probably at the Serai ferry, three miles from Sheorajpur.

DECEMBER 9: Hope Grant arrived at Sheorajpur just before daylight, and learnt, from a captured trooper, that the rebels were still on the right bank of the river but were about to embark their guns for the crossing. The British force defeated the rebels at Serai Ghat, in an action where artillery and the irregular cavalry played the major role: fifteen rebel guns, belonging to the Gwalior Contingent were captured. The result of this battle, and that at Cawnpore on the 6th was that the rebel army, and possisibly their best ever chance of succeeding in the rebellion, was effectively crushed: they had lost thirty-two guns, thousands killed and been forced to give up a strong position and all their warlike stores. The two parts of the rebel army which fled away never again came together: one was driven to Kalpi, the other, without its guns was at Bithur and unable to cross into Oude. The British casualities totalled ninety-nine, including thirteen killed. That Campbell now remained comparatively inactive was the result of his almost complete lack of transport: he had to wait until 23 December before the carriage that had taken the ladies etc to Allahabad returned and was available to him.

Brigadier Seaton left Delhi with a considerable force, escorting a convoy of grain and stores to Cawnpore: he learnt that the rebels had congreagated in large numbers at Aligarh through which he would have to pass.

DECEMBER 14: Brigadier Seaton operating from Delhi, defeated the rebels at Khasganj south of Aligarh.

The British entered Indore.

Debi Singh Guntia was captured and hanged and his small army dispersed: this resulted in the pacification of the Bargi district (near Jabalpur) which had been one of the very few areas south of the Narbada river to have been affected by the mutiny: communications with Bombay were henceforth uninterrupted.

DECEMBER 15: Stuart's Brigade in Central India, having defeated the rebels at Mandsaur and relieved the siege of Neemuch today entered Indore and camped in the Residency grounds. Three of Holkar's regiments were disarmed at Indore without opposition: some of the mutineers were hanged here and some blown from guns.

DECEMBER 17: Seaton, continuing his march southwards defeated another party of rebels at the battle of Pattiali, notable for the death of the *Hakim,* he reditary commander-in-chief of the Nawab of Farruckabad, killed by Hodson. The rebels were now in full flight from the district, falling back on Fatehgarh or trying to cross the Ganges into Oude.

DECEMBER 18: Brigadier Walpole was despatched by Campbell to sweep the area towards Etawa which was known

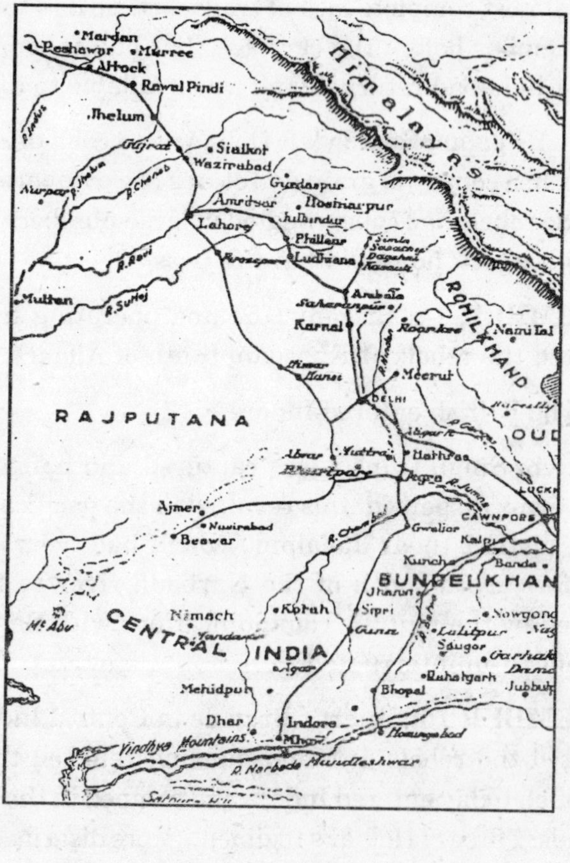

to be in rebel hands and to make a junction with Seaton at Mainpuri thence marching to Fatehgarh to support Campbell's attack on that place: that was the plan, although it did not work out quite like that.

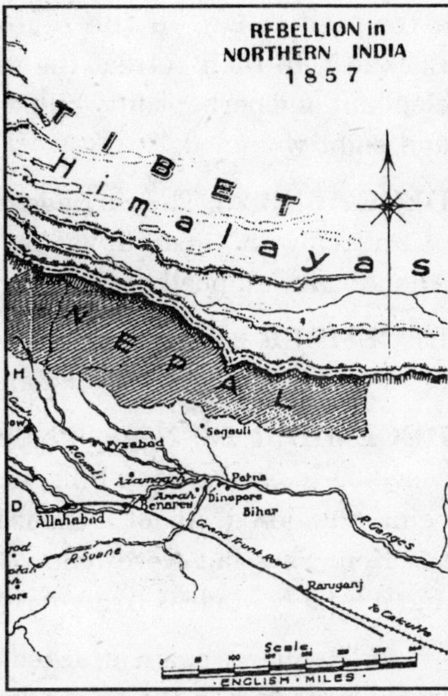

The detachment of the 34th Regiment, which had mutinied at Chittagong, was finally tracked down and defeated by the sepoys of the Silhet Light Infantry, which had remained loyal, at the Battle of Latu. The survivors fled into the hilly jungle where they perished within the next few weeks.

DECEMBER 19: Mainpuri was recaptured or, more accurately, re-occupied by the British.

In London the Government announced to the Honourable East India Company that it intended to make a change in the Company's powers: both political parties apparently agreed that the Company by maladministration was responsible for the Mutiny.

DECEMBER 22: An attempt was made today, led by the Maulvi Ahmad Shah (the 'Maulvi of Fyzabad'). to cut off Outram and his troops in the Alambagh from Cawnpore. A large force, possibly 4000 rebels, marched out of Lucknow intending to entrench themselves at Banni. but were defeated by Outram who sent out over 1000 troops, who in turn attempted to cut off the rebel party from returning to Lucknow. In their retreat the rebels lost four guns and an elephant and perhaps fifty killed: Outram reported two dead and eight wounded.

DECEMBER 23: The carriage necessary for the movement of an army in those days having today returned from Allahabad, Campbell prepared to march.

DECEMBER 24: Campbell left Cawnpore with the bulk of his army, heading north for Fatehgarh.

DECEMBER 26: Near Jabalpur there was still active rebellion in the Katangi hills, numerous villages near Koni being plundered. About a thousand rebels made a stand in the Koni Pass but were today dispersed by Colonel Millar and a largely Madras Army force.

Rehli was again attacked by the mutineers and rebels from Garharkoa in the Sagar district, but they were driven off.

DECEMBER 27: Raja Tej Singh of Mainpuri was defeated by Seaton in the Battle of Mainpuri and fled towards Lucknow.

DECEMBER 28: Lieutenant Osborne the Political Agent at Rewah was able to persuade the young Raja not only to remain loyal to the British but to take active steps against the rebels. Today he reconquered Myhere [Maihar] a fortified town and fort. from the Bundela rebels.

DECEMBER 29: Walpole marched via Akbarpur to Etawa without hindrance. Etawa was wrecked and what remained of it was held by rebels, but on the approach of the British column the majority evacuated the place. A few men however occupied a covered, square, loop-holed enclosure, evidently intending to die rather than surrender. After some hours a mine was exploded on the roof and the building collapsed on top of them.

DECEMBER 30: In Chota Nagpur the tide of rebellion turned with the defeat by Captain Wood of the main body of the rebels near Sambhalpur, in the southerly district. Wood led a composite force of Madras infantry, Nagpur Irregular Cavalry and loyal Ramgarh infantry. The situation was complicated because inter tribal rivalries and general lawlessness were as much in evidence as rebellion against the government. Thus mutinous sepoys from the Ramgarh battalion might be mixed up with the followers of rebel landowners, and the latter might be as much concerned with fighting each other as opposing the British. See Gautam Bhadra, Four Rebels of 1857', in *Subaltern Studies,* Vol IV, Delhi, 1985.

Captain Hodson rode through enemy held country to convey to Campbell, who had now reached Miran-ka-serai, the news of Seaton's progress.

DECEMBER 31: The Honourable East India Company protested in London against the proposed legislation for India, but by now it was clear that the change would be enacted.

The rebels in the Doab, including the main body of the defeated army from Cawnpore. was driven steadily northwards by Campbell, Seaton and Walpole. They converged upon Fatehgarh inlarge numbers, and their leaders realised that if they destroyed the suspension bridge over the Kali Nadi riven Campbell would be effectively cut off from Fatehgarh. So today they attempted to destroy the bridge, and although they did some damage they left the piers and the main chains intact.

8

January - March 1858

JANUARY 1: Khan Bahadur Khan who ruled in Bareilly, still, nominally, in the name of the King of Delhi, had not given up hope of conquering Naini Tal where many Europeans had taken refuge. Today he sent a thousand insurgents, with two guns to attack Haldwani on the road to Naini Tal from the plains, but they were repulsed by a few Gurkhas. They nevertheless effectively besieged Naini Tal by cutting off its supplies, and some four thousand rebels with two guns were reported to be on the road to the plains below.

Campbell sent Hope's Brigade, some guns of the Naval Brigade, and some engineers and sappers to the Kali Nadi with orders to drive away the enemy and to repair the suspension bridge if it were found to be damaged. The rebels fled on the approach of the Bitish and in twelve hours the bridge was sufficiently repaired to crossed with care.

JANUARY 2: Campbell came up to the suspension bridge

this morning, and as he did so the rebels mounted a spirited attack on it, and on him. He ordered Adrian Hope to hold the bridge at all costs but not to attack the enemy; HM 53rd regiment were accordingly ordered to cross the river and engage the enemy th brisk musketry fire: this they did but against orders then charged the toll-house and the village in which the rebels had taken up position. The charge was a complete success, the rebels being driven from the village and followed up by cavalry they were completely routed. Nevertheless Campbell was angry at the diobedience of his orders, and "pitched into it well", but was constantly interrupted by the Irish soldiery who kept calling out, three cheers for the Commander-in-Chief boys!' until he gave up and went away laughing. This was the Battle of the Kalindi, in some ways one of the most decisive of the campaign, for the rebels did not stop even when they reached Fatehgarh but streamed away into Rohilkhand. leaving behind their guns and most of their stores. Lieutenant Roberts (later to be Field Marshal and Commander-in-Chief) won the V.C. at the village, called Khudaganj.

JANUARY 3: Campbell arrived at Fatehgarh blew open the gate of the fort and occupied it: the stores found there were found to be of great value. Retribution upon the leaders of the rebels captured in the town was particularly unpleasant, and was universally condemned; the newly appointed magistrate Power, was suspended from duty as a result of the acts, amounting to atrocities, which he committed.

JANUARY 4: Walpole's and Seaton's Columns arrived in Fatehgarh and the army thus concentrated amounted to over ten housand men well equipped with camp stores and transport. Campbell felt himself to be in an excellent position now to march into Rohilkhand and put down the rebellion there: a cold weather (January to March) campaign would, he considered, be sufficient. He wanted to leave the reduction of Oude [Awadh] until after the hot weather and the rains is until October of 1858, but was overruled by the Governor General. Canning insisted upon Oude being dealt with first, his argument, a political not a military one, was that Rohilkhand had long been ruled by the British, and that it would be in the nature of a police operation to reconquer it. whereas Oude had so recently been annexed that it was in reality a foreign state that required conquest without the delay that would give heart to its government. Reluctantly therefore Campbell turned to review his strategy. Oude [Awadh| certainly presented by far the greatest threat to the British. The Gwalior Contingent was supposed to be at Kalpi but it had been sorely discouraged by the battle on 6 December, and would be well aware of the British forces under Generals Rose and Whitlock moving up through Central India and Bundelkhand. Cawnpore was guarded by a brigade under Inglis; communications with Allahabad were preserved by a Madras Brigade under Carthew, and another brigade under Franks protected the line with Benares and beyond. True. Rohilkhand appeared the easier and more obious task, but-it could wait: Khan Bahadur Khan in Bareilly apparently had his hands full maintaining his position and was unlikely to show any ambition to move out of Rohilkhand. Campbell feinted towards the north in an attempt to deceive Khan Bahadur Khan, but he then left Fatehgarh under the command of seaton with a comparatively weak brigade which he estimated, correctly would be enough to hold the place. While waiting for the arrival of the siege train from Agra. Campbell now planned the final assault on Lucknow and the former Kingdom of Oude [Awadh].

In Rajputana the troops from Bombay that the British civil authorities had asked for had begun to arrive: they were to converge upon Nasirabad and to be known as the

Nasirabad Field Force. Today, on their way, a small British column led by Colonel Raines attacked and captured Rowah.

JANUARY 6: The British were by now receiving significant reinforcements, from England and elsewhere, and as a result ceased to be on the defensive in many areas. Major General Sir Hugh Rose may be said to have begun his Central India campaign today. The general plan of operations provided for the advance of three columns, one of which, coming from Mhow [Mau] under Rose, would sweep the country from that place to Kalpi on the Jumna, relieving Sagar and recapturing Jhansi; at the same time a Madras Force, under General Whitlock. was to cross Bundelkhand from Jabalpur to Banda; a Bombay Column under Major General Roberts was to operate in Rajputana. Rose's Central India Field Force consisted of two brigades Brigadier C.S. Stuart's First Brigade assembling at Mhow and Brigadier C. Stewards Second Brigade at Sehore twenty miles west of Bhopal.

In another, political, decision, Canning had accepted the offer of Maharaja Jung Bahadur of Nepal to bring his army into India in support of the British. This Gurkha army defeated the rebels at Gorakhpur, and drove them out after they had lost seven guns and about two hundred killed: the disheartened survivors crossed the Rapti and escaped: British civil administration was at once re-established in this district.

JANUARY 7: The trial of Bahadur Shah Zafar King of Delhi and last of the Moguls began in the Red Fort in Delhi: it was to last until 9 March, and was a farcical 'show-trial' from the start. Bahadur Shah had already been promised that his life was not at stake, nor that of his Queen Zinat Mahal or his somewhat obnoxious young son, Jumma Bakht. In fact it was more like a court of enquiry than a trial. The defendant tried to ignore both his accusers and judges: when he said anything it was obstructive or with some justification, he would make a simple statement that he denied the court the right to try him. His brief defence, such as it was, was to the effect that he had been perfectly helpless in the hands of the mutineers; that he had opposed them as long as he was able, by closing the gateway under the palace windowns: by giving warning to the European commandant of the Palace guards; and by sending an express to the Lieutenant Governor at Agra stating what had occurred: all of which he was admitted to have done. The detail of the trial is not so interesting as are the palace papers that lay neglected in Government store, for over 60 years, neither consulted nor even catalogued. They were put into 200 bundles, not in date order, virtually unsorted, and certainly not indexed. The papers were taken from Bahadur Shah's palace immediately upon its occupation by the British in September 1857: it was clearly expected that they would be of significance at his trial, but were hardly looked at let alone referred to. The fact is that where one looks for records of great ilitical events, of regal decisions that were to decide the fate of nations and peoples, of armies and princes, of proclamations and promulgations. of decrees and judgements - one finds only hundreds, perhaps thousands, of petty petitions and grumbles, and complaints - above all of not being paid. Perhaps that is why they mouldered so long in a dusty office store. Eventually someone with a conscience, or nothing else to do. had them published: in 1921 the Imperial Record Department, in Calcutta, printed them '*Press-List of Mutiny Papers 1857*'. They make most interesting reading. Another matter of interest that invites further search concerns the chief British prosecutor, Major Harriott of the 3rd Bengal Native Cavalry and deputy judge advocate general. He had also presided over the General Court Martial in Meerut of which no report was made public, which had condemned the eighty-five troopers of the 3rd Cavalry to lengthy terms of imprisoment and had thus sparked the outbreak of the mutiny. It is however reported that every one of the Native Officers who comprised this court was later murdered by the mutineers. Harriott left India in 1858 and died suddenly at Southampton, on landing from the mail-packet in March 1859: it was stated in the newspapers that £ 30,000 was found in his luggage, and that he left property to a nephew to the amount of £ 100,000.

JANUARY 12: Believing that Outram had considerably weakened his force by sending an escort for a convoy to Cawnpore the rebels again attacked the Alambagh this time in what was intended to be overwhelming force. The presence of British troops within the Kingdom of Awadh was an offence to the Begum Hazrat Mahal who frequently upbraided her forces for their lack of bravery in not driving the foreigners from the country even threatening that if they did not attack the British she would make terms herself with them. Stung by her reproaches the army did mount a major attack on the well-fortified Alambagh on this day. This attack was in great force, perhaps thirty thousand men, in two bodies, attacking simultaneously the right and the left of the Alambagh position: they were allowed to come somewhat nearer, and were then received with such a powerful fire of artillery, and musketry, as to drive them back at some speed. Twice they attacked, twice they were repulsed: they then attacked the centre of the Alambagh position but were driven off again by a very heavy and concentrated artillery fire.

JANUARY 19: Raines column was reinforced by other Bombay army troops until it numbered almost two thousand troops of all arms, and today, after a five day siege, the fortified town of Awah was assaulted and captured by the British, the majority of the garrison escaping under cover of darkness, and of a great storm. Twenty-four sepoy prisoners were taken, and shot after court martial. The defences were found to be of immense strength, consisting of a double line, the inner one being of strong masonry, loop-holed. After blowing up these defences and punishing local rebel Thakurs the British proceeded to Nasirabad.

JANUARY 23: The rebels were reported as mustering again in great numbers at Kalpi.

JANUARY 24: Rose arrived with his second brigade before the great fortress of Rahatgarh. This place was the key to the western entrance to Sagar and Bundelkhand. the former of which was partially, and the latter completely in the hands of the rebels. The fortress is at one end of a long high hill, surrounded by other hills, *nullahs* and dense jungle, the sides fall steeply to the river Bina or to precipitous rocks: the only access was on the eastern side by a steep and narrow road. The British found the fort garrisoned by *vilaiiti* and Pathans under the command of Nawab Muhammad Fazal Khan, a man of energy and courage, (and a relative of the Regent of Bhopal) who. having failed in his attempt to usurp the power of the Regent, had become a chief leader of the rebels. The *Shahzada* Prince Firoz Shah was also reported to be in the fortress, (this is possible as he was soon to seen in Jhansi) and the Raja of Banpur with a considerable force was not far away.

At Sehore the mutineers of the late Bhopal Contingent were tried by Court-martial: 195 were executed 274 dismissed and 228 re-enlisted: of the last named many were Sikhs and they formed the nucleus of what became the 1st Regiment. Central India Horse.

JANUARY 26: Rose mounted his first attack on Rahatgarh. He had to cut roads through the thick jungle to enable the guns to take up a position in front of the east curtain of the fort which had been selected as the most favourable for a breach to be made. At the same time other forces attacked the north side of the fortress from the town.

JANUARY 27: Brigadier Adrian Hope, in a move designed to deceive the Rohilkhand rebels had been sent northwards to give impression that the British, would be coming that way. Twelve miles north of Fatehgarh he came across a large body of rebels and defeated them in a battle determined largely by artillery but in which the cavalry on both sides fought well. This was the battle of Shamshabad although, more accurately, it should be called the battle of Sutia. McDowell, Hodson's second-in-command, was mortally wounded, and Hodson himself wounded twice. The rebels were pursued for ten miles, and those who escaped recrossed the Ganges into Rohilkhand leaving four guns in British hands.

JANUARY 28 : At 8am the heavy guns opened fire on the east curtain of the fortress of Rahatgarh and it was clear that a breach could soon be made: at the same time two bodies of rebels (one led by the Raja of Banpur) crossed the river Bina and advanced to the attack but were driven off by the dragoons, and fled to the village of Chandrapur whence they had attacked (but not captured) a convoy of supplies being sent to the British by Sindhia.

The Honourable East India Company delivered a petition to Parliament in London against Government proceedings, which they claimed to be unjustified and unlawful.

JANUARY 29: At 4am it was reported that some of the garrison was attempting a sortie from the fortress of Rahatgarh, by the main gateway: twenty-five out of fifty were killed. Judging by the stillness in the fort that its garrison was escaping or attempting to escape, the British entered by the incomplete breach and found only a few rebels, who were killed. The main body had fled during the dead of the night by an ancient sally port and a hole dug under the parapet to the southwest, from which ropes were hanging by which they had let themselves down a virtual precipice. They were pursued and forty of them killed: eighty prisoners were taken of whom twenty-four were executed, including Muhammad Fazal Khan who was hanged over the gate of the fort together with another seventeen members of the garrison. The British found many women and children in the fort, but these were released unharmed: they also found a year's food supply and a vast quantity of warlike stores.

JANUARY 31: Those who had escaped from Rahatgarh together with those at Chandrapur now assembled at Barodia. a strong village some twelve miles from Rahatgarh: their intention appeared to be to cut off supplies to the British, and if possible to re-capture the fortress. The rebels set an ambush for Rose and force, but alter a lengthy and hard fought action in which the *vilaities* and Pathans fought with great courage and determination the rebels eventually fled, abandoning their camp and bagage. Rose marched back to Rahatgarh. The rebels had five hundred casualties including their able commander Anant Singh. and Raja of Banpur was wounded. The British lost four dead and seventeen wounded. The effect of the rebels' defeat at Barodia was dramatic: British communications with the west and Sagar were now completely unobstructed and three strong places, Kursi, Krulassa and Nariaoli and their districts which had been in rebel hands for the last eight months were now abandoned by them.

FEBRUARY 2: Walpole reached Mainpuri having cleared the country of rebels between Cawnpore and Etawa.

FEBRUARY 3: Walpole's and Seaton's Columns met at Bewar fifteen miles from Mainpuri on the Fatehgarh road, too late to assist in the attack on the latter place.

Rose marched into Saugar which had been beleaguered for seven months. The Europeans, confined in the fort since 29 June and numbering 173 men, 67 women and 130 children, were thus liberated but it appeared that the entire population of the town and surrounding country were equally pleased to welcome the British force. The Bundelkhand, Shahgarh, Saugar and Narbada District rebels still held the forts of Sanoda and Garharkota to the east

FEBRUARY 4: Campbell returned to Cawnpore from Fatehgarh.

The Gwalior Contingent although defeated by Campbell at Cawnpore had retreated only as far as Kalpi some fifty miles to the southeast, and presented an ever-present menance to the British on their eastern flank. Until General Rose coming up country with the Central India Force could tackle this major body of rebels they had a good opportunity to exploit their strength and position. They certainly feinted with an advance on Cawnpore and Colonel Maxwell was sent from thence with a small column of infantry to check them his camp was at Bhogneepore only ten miles from Kalpi, and today he was in action against a superior force at a village called Chowra and killed eighty of the enemy before they withdrew back to Kalpi. The British casualties numbered only five wounded, one of whom was Lieutenant Mowbray Thomson one of the few survivors of the Satichaura Ghat massacre.

FEBRUARY 5: There was an action at Ayodhya in Oude between the rebels and a party of Jung Bahadur's Gurkhas, who were now well into Indian territory in support of the British.

FEBRUARY 7: Major General G. Whitlock with the Madras column arrived at Jabalpur and found there the Nagpore Moveable Column which had been operating in the southern Narbada territory under Colonel Millar. Whitlock was both slow and excessively cautious in all that he did, and although his orders were co-operate with Rose in the attack on Jhansi and to move through the eastern part of Bundelkhand suppressing the revolt there he failed to provide anything like the expected assistance.

FEBRUARY 8: Rose sent a detachment of the Hyderabad Contingent to capture the fort of Sanoda and to make the ford over the river Bias practicable for the siege artillery he intended use against Garharkota: the latter was garrisoned by sepoys of 52nd BNI and other mutinied regiments.

FEBRUARY 9: Campbell and Canning met at Allahabad. Exactly what they said to each other, or what was decided was not recorded. It may well be that Campbell was urged to act with greater speed against the rebels, particularly in Oude: his reputation. even among the common soldiers who knew he had their best interests at heart, was one of excessive caution. Sir Colin Campbell was also known as 'Sir Crawling Camel. The Delhi and Meerut Divisions were placed under the Punjab government.

FEBRUARY 10: Nana Sahib was reported to be Naubatganj in western Oude.

Colonel McCausland with a small force of Gurkhas and two field guns, repulsed a body of 5000 Bareilly rebels under Khali Khan at Sunda in the Kumaon district.

FEBRUARY 11: A great convoy of European women and

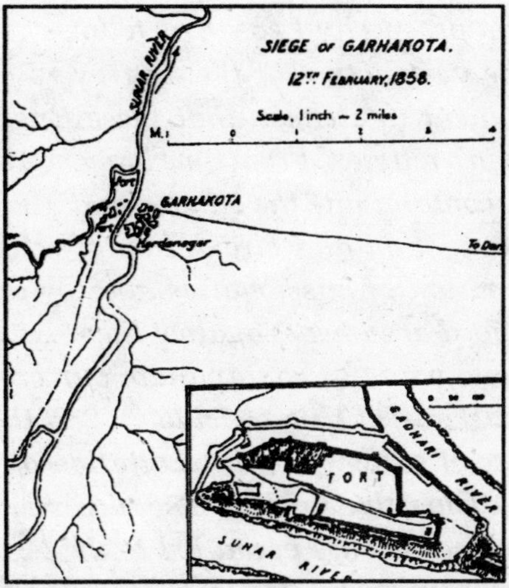

children today left Agra. the majority heading for Bombay by the newly opened road.

Rose arrived before Garharkota and invested the fort, which was of exceptional strength, built of stone with an inner wall 29 feet high and 15 feet thick.

FEBRUARY 12: The sepoys at Garharkota came out bravely to do battle with General Rose but were driven back into the fort, and apparently lost heart, for at 10pm the whole garrison fled by the gate on the south side and then turned northwards in the direction of Shargarh leaving all their cattle and stores and their thirteen guns loaded. See *Revolt in Central India, 1857-59,* Simla,1908. Produced by the Intelligence Branch Army HQ India. Cavalry pursued the sepoys and cut up about one hundred of the 52nd BNI.

Kunwar Singh reported as arriving at Ayodhya on the eastern border of Oude.

The British Prime Minister Lord Palmerston brought in the India Bill No l. After a long debate the Government majority six days later was 318 to 173.

FEBRUARY 14: The Rani of Jhansi issued a proclamation against the British: *'Victory of Religion' : To God only belongs the World, and the command of it rests with Him....Oh Rajas Be you religious, virtuous, benevolent and brave, and the protectors of your own and of the religion of others: desiring* *you prosperity I speak as follows.... God has created you for the destruction of the destroyers of your creed:....but it is evident to all men that these English are perverters of all men's religion. From time immemorial have they endeavoured to contaminate the Hindoo and Mahomedan religions by the production and circulation of religious books through the medium of missionaries. and by extirpating such books as afford arguments against them ..... Various endeavours they have made to contaminate our creed. 1st. The forcible re-marriage of Hindoo widows. 2nd the abolition of the ancient rite of suttee. 3rd the exaltation of those who may embrace the Christian faith, so also succession to the thrones of Hindoo princes is only permitted to the legitimate sons the adopted sons are prohibited from succession, while the Shastra gives him the same privileges as the legitimate heir: these are the stratagems by which the Europeans deprive us of our thrones and wealth, for instance I refer to Nagpore and Lucknow....They have forced the prisoners to eat their bread.....they powdered bones and mixed with flour sugar etc and exposed it for sale.... they ordered the Brahmins and others attached to the army to bite greased cartridges..... and in spite ommenced blowing from guns those in any regiments who refused to use the cartridges..... I conjure the Hindoos in the name of Gunga. Tollsee (Tulsi) and Salikram and the Mahomedans by the name of God and the Koran and entreat them to join us i destroying the English, for their mutual welfare.....Let not* this *opportunity pass away. Know oh people.* YOU *will never have such another.....This letter calling for the joint alliance of Hindoo and Mahomedan is published by Moulvie Syud Kootub Shah at the Bahaduree Press in the city of Bareilly.'* Full text in FSUP Vol III p 225.

Jung Bahadur and his Gurkhas started from Gorakhpur today, heading westwards to assist Campbell in the reduction of Oude [Awadh|.

FEBRUARY 15: The fourth attack on the Alambagh. led apparently by the Maulvi Ahmadullah Shah in person, though comparatively weak, and desultory, lasted longer than the earlier attacks and was pressed home with greater conviction, with the result that posts much closer to the British position were occupied: thence they could attack with greater suddenness. Again however they were defeated.

FEBRUARY 17: Whitlock at long last marched from Jabalpur. He was accompanied by Major Erskine Commissioner of the Division who frequently asked him to turn aside to destroy rebel strongholds such as Ramnagar. Mardangarh and Ramgarh but he refused to divide his force or turn aside: hence the column passed through the country with no attempt at pacification.

FEBRUARY 18: A proclamation was issued by Firoz Shah at Bareilly: ...... *'Oh Hindoostanee Brethren! thus put on your guard against their subversive determinations, leave them to their folly, and all uniting break their head. When the army mutinied to preserve their faith, and in various places sent the kaffirs to hell, then the Padres and wise men amongst them, alarmed at the mutiny, the anarchy, and slaughter of the Europeans, concocted the following scheme, observing that if, on obtaining the supreme power, attention had been paid to the laws and rules then established, this would never have happened:- 1st. The families of Indian Chiefs and Kings were preserved, this should not have been: they ought now, all that remain, to be enticed on board the ship, under pretence of their being conveyed to England, and drowned. 2nd. 'All religious books, whether Hindoo or Mussalman ought to be collected by fraud or force and burned. 3rd Not a biswa of land ought to be left in the possession of any native. 4th 'The native officers ought to be bribed and intimidated into intermarriage with Europeans, that they may in a short time become the same as they. 5th. 'Natives ought not to be trained* *as Artillerists. 6th. 'All natives ought to he disarmed. 7th'No servant ought to be engaged until he has eaten and drunk with Europeans. 8th. 'Mosques and temples ought not to be allowed to be founded. 9th. Mahommedan and Hindoo worships ought to be proscribed. 10th. To adjudicate by Bible Law. 11th 'Marriage ought not to be celebrated according to Hindoo and Mahommedan ritual. This is to be special care of the Padres. 12th. To abolish Hindoo and Mussalman doctors. 13ln. 'Not to allow Hindoo or Mussalman doctors to educate disciples without the permission of the Padres. 14th. 'None but Doctors ought to be permitted to assist at the confinement of Hindoo and Mussalman women. 'These rules have not been adhered to: the worthless natives of Hindoostan have been treated with care and tenderness and the end of it has been that these very natives have got up the rebellion. If great attention is paid to the above principles for the future, and if all misconduct among the Hindoostanees is punished, then the English rule will remain established for thousands of years.....Before the commencement of these calamities of the English I went on a pilgrimage to Mecca....On my return I travelled from Bombay to Gwalior and made all chiefs and armies promise to exterminate the Nazarenes...from that time ... through the aid of God... 130,000 men, old and new soldiers. have been induced to swear to join me, and I will soon, collecting all these, purify the land from these Nazarenes.....the reason for the delay there has been in burying the English is that the commands of God have been disregarded in as much as the soldiers have wickedly put women and children to death, and have. without the orders of their leaders, given themselves up to loot in such a way that they generally convert victory into defeat and the common people have been much oppressed. Mien you have rectified these faults, you will succeed as I have promised you....My advice is this, abandon every other work: give your life to your beloved, or death will take it: decide which of these alternatives is preferable' Lithographed at Bareilly and issued by order of the Nawab of Kather.* For complete text *see* FSUP Voll p 459.

FEBRUARY 19: General Franks with 5,000 troops (including 2000 Nepalese) had been appointed to the command of the troops in the Azimgarh and Jaunpur districts, and given the job of defending Benares and the line of communication up country from thence; he now marched north from Allahabad and defeated Banda Hossein at Chundah, at 8am, and his leader, the Nazim Mehndi Hossein at Hamirpur in the evening.

FEBRUARY 20: Nana Sahib was reported to be at Birra and to be moving about on the frontier between Oude and Bareilly; other reports had him at Shahjehanpore *en route* to Bareilly city; there was even a report that he had crossed into Bundelkhand. to the south of Oude with a large force: British intelligence as to his movements was poor, and one conclusion is that few Indians were willing to betray him.

Palmerston Ministry resigned.

FEBRUARY 21: In London the Derby ministry was formed, with Ellenborough at the India Board.

Outram repulsed 20,000 rebels at the Alambagh. This, the fifth attack, was on the front of the position and on both faces, but before it came Outram had, providentially for him, been reinforced by additional troops, especially cavalry of which he had been deficient, and while containing the frontal attack, mainly by artillery fire, he launched his cavalry on the two flank attacks, who were thus assailed from their own flanks, and they suffered very severely.

Franks occupied the strong fort of Budhayan.

FEBRUARY 23: Franks defeated the rebels led by Mirza Gaffar Beg at the battle of Sultanpur. The rebel army, which consisted mainly of the troops of the Nazim Mehndi Hossein was scattered and left twenty guns on the Yield of battle.

Brigadier Hope Grant took Meeanganj from the Oude rebels.

FEBRUARY 25: Nana Sahib was today reported to be at Kalpi.

FEBRUARY 26: Whitlock relieved Damoh. but his actions were still ineffective: as his column passed, the rebels cleared off to the flanks but closed in again behind. A noted rebel. Kishor Singh. at Hindona near Damoh. was allowed to continue his depredations unmolested.

The Gurkhas of Jang Bahadur captured the fort of Mohbarakpur in Oude.

FEBRUARY 27: Rose, having received the supplies for which he was waiting, advanced northwards from Saugur and reached Ranipur: here he decided that the next place for his attack would be the Pass of Madanpur.

FEBRUARY 28: Campbell crossed the Ganges into Oude to head the British army again, and to launch the assault upon Lucknow.

MARCH 1: The Rani of Jhansi had not as yet had any encounters with British forces, but she had to repel the troops of neighbouring states, notably Orchha, which had attempted to conquer Jhansi, professing that they were agents of the British but in fact furthering their rajas' ancient claims to Jhansi territory. For months she had the worst of the encounters, indeed Jhansi city was besieged for six weeks, but today the Tehri[Orchha] troops were beaten in battle by the Rani of Jhansi's forces. See FSUP.

The raja of Charkhari in Bundelkhand was one of the few remaining loyal to the British in that province, and was consequently targeted by the rebels who today captured and sacked the town of Charkari. Significantly the rebels were led by Tatya Tope, the Nana Sahib's general. See Tapti Roy, *Sepoy Mutiny and the Uprising of 1857 in Bundelkhand,* Calcutta, 1991.

MARCH 2: The possession of arms by the local people in Northern India varied considerably from place to place. In Oude [Awadh] and Rohilkhand it was common-place for men to possess lethal weapons, although most of these would be the highly inaccurate and primitive matchlocks. As an example, today the populace of Saharunpur was disarmed by the British and 5,000 weapons were collected.

Campbell advanced to the Alambagh with the clear intention of conquering Lucknow.

MARCH 3: Canning's Proclamation to the people of Oude was prepared for issue in this month when it was assumed the city of Lucknow would have fallen to the British; it caused considerable controversy both in India (where the Chief Commissioner of Oude. Sir James Outram, feared it would harden resistance and delay pacification), and in England (where it led to the resignation of Lord Ellenborough the President of the Board of Control, a personal and political opponent of Canning). The disagreement centred round Canning's desire to punish those hereditary propritors of land, the *Taluqdars,* the majority of whom had joined the rebel cause: his opponents believed that to threaten confiscation of their land would be to delay indefinitely the pacification of the province. The full text of Canning's proclamation will be found in FSUP Vol II p 328, and in numerous other source books, but it is summarised as: *'Lucknow has been re-taken by the British army, and none can withstand the latter's*

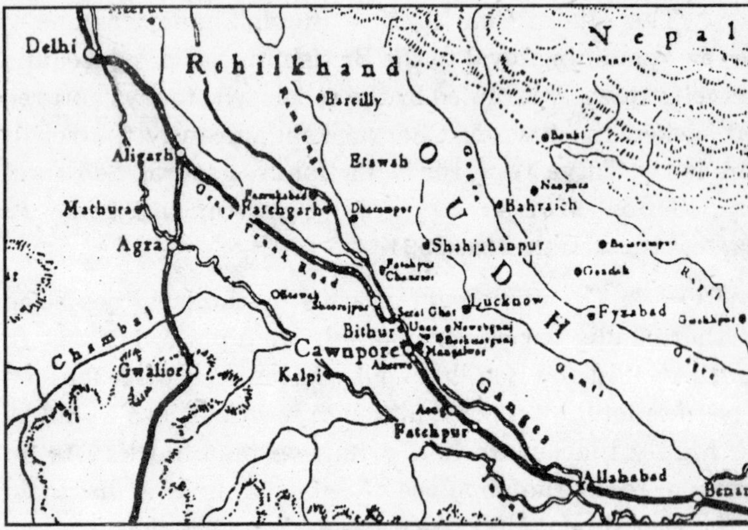

Oude and Rohilkhand

power; those who have fought against the government have committed a great crime and will be punished: the first care will be to reward those who have helped the British (eg Digbyjai Sing, Raja of Bulrampur, and Rao Hurdeo Buksh of Kathiari etc): others will be rewarded as their merits are revealed: for the rest the proprietary right in the soil is confiscated to the British government which would dispose of it as it saw fit: if taluqdars came forward now and helped the British then their lives and honour would be safe provided their hands were not stained with English blood 'murderously shed): they may even aspire to a restitution of their lands: all who had protected English lives should be specially entitled to consideration and leniency. It is on the latter grounds that Raja Man Singh profited although he had been a leading rebel.

On this day also the Raja of Banpur occupied the Narat Pass against Rose who attacked the Raja of Shahgarh holding the Madanpur Pass and drove them both out.

MARCH 5: The Raja of Rooroo in the Etawa District now in British hands was discovered in 'treasonable correspondence and committed suicide by poisoning himself: the *tehsildar* who had betrayed him to the British was threatened with death by the raja's relatives and supporters.

In the Gorakhpur District matters reached a significant crisis. The rebels were gathering in overwhelming numbers preparatory to crossing the Gogra river near Tandah: one estimate of their numbers put them at 15,000 of whom 4000 were regular sepoys including the 1st 53rd and 56th BNI from Cawnpore; they were led by Hurkishen a nephew of Kunwar Singh.

At a battle near Amorha Colonel Rowcroft with a greatly inferior force, repulsed 12000 rebels and killed nine hundred and took seven guns. Although Mohomed Hussun and the Gonda Raja made strenuous attempts to recruit more troops and re-group, the arrival of fugitives from Lucknow disheartened the rebels, and gave corresponding encouragement to those who had hesitated before joining the British side.

The Gurkha army of Jung Bahadur was marching steadily towards Lucknow to assist Campbell, and today was in action at the Kandoo Nuddee against the rebels led by Mehndi Hussein; although the latter was defeated he continued to harass the baggage and supply train of the Gurkhas.

MARCH 6: Mehndi Hussein attacked and plundered a British convoy which was travelling virtually without escort through Oude.

MARCH 9: The court trying Bahadur Shah Zafar in the Red Fort at Delhi found him guilty, as a 'false traitor and a rebel to the British government, and as an accessory to the massacre of Europeans at Delhi. He was sentenced to be transported beyond the seas as a felon 'where he will be entirely isolated from all other Mohammedans": Tungoo, 300 miles inland from Rangoon in Burma was selected.

Bahadur Shah,
King of Delhi

MARCH 10: By now Rose had completely defeated the Raja Shahgarh, and had annexed his territory, and the whole country between Sagar and Jhansi to the east of the river Betwa was now in British hands.

It was not until this date that the British were able to assemble a sufficient force in Rajputana to deals with the Kotah rebels: Major General H.G. Roberts from the Bombay Army was placed in command of what came to be called the Rajputana Field Force.

Raja Man Singh who had appeared to support both sides in turn today came into the British camp and tendered his submission. He was then told to return to his home and to report to the British at Lucknow within ten days.

MARCH 11: Jung Bahadur and his Gurkhas joined Campbell outside Lucknow.

In the Agra District the rebels still-virtually ruled much of the countryside, particularly to the south, and to the west of the Jumna in Scindia's territory where the maharaja though anxious to support the British was unable to do so. Brigadier Showers made a number of forays from Agra and today defeated a body of rebels at Bah.

MARCH 14: In one of the most decisive events of the struggle

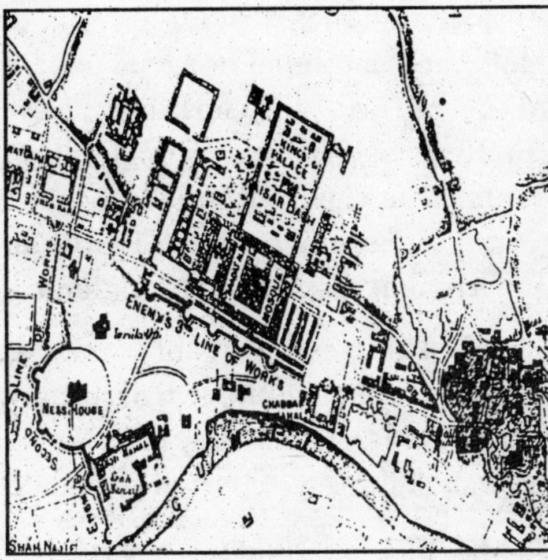

Lucknow, March 1858

Lucknow was today stormed by the British army under Campbell. Very heavy fighting took place, over the next seven days, but the rebels under the Begum Hazrat Mahal and the Maulvi of Fyzabad were eventually driven out. to the north, first to the area of the Musa Bagh and then scattering throughout northern Oude [Awadh]. Considerable criticism was levelled at Campbell for allowing the rebels to escape in such large numbers, as he had the ability and force in terms of cavalry and horse artillery to have pursued the rebel infantry. Lucknow may have fallen to the British but Oude [Awadh] was by no means conquered, and a fierce struggle was to continue for many months There are many accounts of the battles both in Lucknow and Oude the most succinct perhaps is in R. Montgomery Martin. *Indian Empire.* Vol II.

An example of the confused state of the countryside in the Doab comes from the Narrative of Events for Cawnpore at this time: today 2000 rebels from Hamirpur were reported as having crossed the Jumna: wherever they went they were either supported by the local population or took by force what they needed.

MARCH 16: Only with difficulty had Sir John Lawrence been prevented from ceding Peshawar to the Amir of

Afghanistan in return for his alliance: in fact the Amir, Dost Mohamed had remained true to his treaty promises and had needed no bribe to keep him so. Nevertheless the position on the Khyber Pass was critical still for the British had many enemies on the frontier. Today saw the return of the Guide Corps to Peshawar, from Delhi, and the reinforcement of government authority throughout the northern Punjab.

The movements of Nana Sahib during the past few months were never known accurately to the British, and it is clear he was protected by popular sentiment. Today however he was definitely reported to be at Shahjahanpur.

MARCH 17: Brigadier Stuart took the fort and town of Chanderi by storm, after a ten-day siege, and then marched to join Rose who was heading north towards Jhansi. and was encamped on the left bank of the Betwa river.

Kunwar Singh had. since the third battle of Cawnpore. been working his way back eastwards towards his ancestral home in Bihar: he displayed considerable strategic and tactical ability as a general and seeing the British pre-occupation with affairs in Lucknow and northern Oude he determined to make a strike for Azimgarh and possibly thence attack Allahabad or Benares. Today he joined up with a large number of rebels in eastern Oude at Atraulia, twenty-five miles from Azimgarh. This district had only a small British force to guard it, under the command of Colonel Milman.

MARCH 18: The Nawabs of Farruckabad and Banda Raja Tej Singh of Mainpuri Khan Bahadur Khan of Bareilly and Walidad Khan were specifically excluded from the benefit (free pardon etc) of a Proclamation offering 1 lakh rupees reward to any rebel betraying Nana Sahib. No one ever did betray him despite the enormous sum (=£10,000 at that time) offered.

MARCH 19: Rose reached Chachanpur fourteen miles from Jhansi.

MARCH 20: Showers made another foray from Agra and surprised a body of rebels at Kachru capturing the ring-leaders. But as British troops passed through an area the rebels closed in again behind.

MARCH 21: Rose with army and siege train arrived before Jhansi.

Lucknow was finally conquered by the British.

Kunwar Singh's advance guard was defeated by Milman who then halted to breakfast, near Atraulia and was suddenly attacked by Kunwar Singh's main body who advanced in good order and drove Milman back first into his camp at Koelsa and then in full retreat to Azimgarh, where the British built an entrenchment.

MARCH 22: Millman after being repulsed at Atraulia was besieged in Azimgarh by Kunwar Singh: a few British reinforcements joined Milman in his entrenchment and the command passed to Colonel Dames.

In Rajputana Roberts with a large force including a siege train arrived before Kotah. and encamped on the left bank of the Chambal.

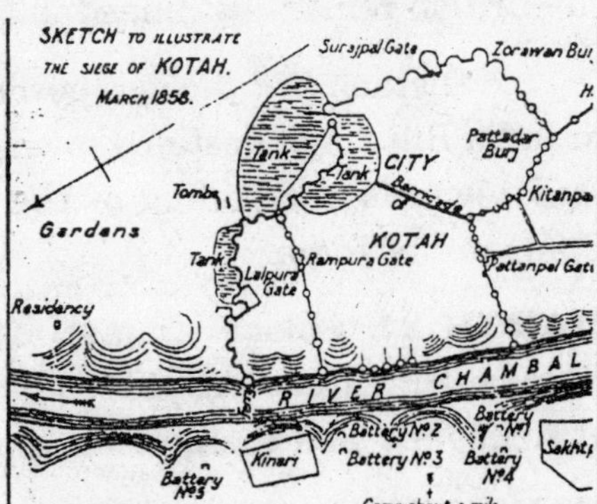

MARCH 23: The investment of Jhansi began. It was a formidable task: the fort had extensive and elaborate outworks: guns placed on the high towers commanded the surrounding country.

The fort stood on an elevated rock and was built of excellent and massive masonry, difficult to breach for it was sixteen to twenty feet in thickness. The fortress was surrounded by the city of Jhansi on all sides except the west and part of the south face. The city itself was about $4^1/_2$ miles in circumference and was surrounded by a fortified and massive wall, from 6 to 8 feet thick and up to 30 feet in height, with numerous flanking bastions.

MARCH 24: There was an explosion in Khan Bahadur Khan's gunpowder factory at Bareilly: nothing is known as to its cause, but many casualties resulted; sabotage was unlikely.

Nana Sahib arrived at Bareilly and was received by the rebels there with due ceremony but little warmth.

MARCH 25: In Chota Nagpur, Captain Moncrieff at the head of a wing of the 5th Madras NI routed a body of Kols at Chuckerderpore. but the rebellion in this district (which was of a most complicated nature) smouldered on for another year. The best explanation will be found in Gautam Bhadra's article Chotanagpur in 1857 in the *Companion,* p 83.

MARCH 26: Kunwar Singh occupied the city of Azimgarh, the British remaining pinned in their entrenchment.

Disraeli and the new government in London brought in India Bill 2. not destined to pass into law but one further step towards the ending of the power of the East India Company in India.

MARCH 27: Colonel Dames attempted a sortie against Kunwar Singh but was driven back into the entrenchment at Azimgarh and thereafter remained on the defensive.

MARCH 29: The British 'Army of Oude' was divided into

separate columns, each with a specific task and delegated area to pacify in the former Kingdom of Oude [Awadh] and with the eventual object of combining to move into Rohilkhand against Khan Bahadur Khan at Bareilly.

MARCH 30: Kotah was captured by the Rajputana Field Force under Roberts, after a considerable artillery bombardment of that section of the town occupied by the Kotah Contingent. The latter were either killed (400) or driven away and dispersed, and henceforth Rajputana remained quiet. This is one of the few occasions when a British commander had numerical superiority when dealing with the rebels.

MARCH 31: Kunwar Singh further strengthened his position in and around Azimgarh. His forces continued to grow as refugees from the rebel forces leaving Lucknow swelled his numbers.

9

April - December 1858

APRIL 1: Rose defeated Tatya Tope in the Battle of Betwa River. Sometimes inaccurately referred to as the Battle of Jhansi this was one of the most decisive engagements of the entire struggle. Sir Hugh Rose at the head of the Central India Force was besieging the city and fort of Jhansi in which the Rani was putting up a spirited defence. She had sent messengers to Tatya Tope and the Rao Sahib to come to her aid, and she had reason to know that efforts were being made for her relief. A force called the 'Army of the Peishwa estimated at 20,000 men and twenty guns crossed the river Betwa on 31 March 1858, and took up a position in rear of the British camp and lit an immense bonfire, as a signal to Jhansi of their arrival. This was welcomed by salutes from a1l the batteries of the fort and city, and shouts of joy from the defenders. Unfortunately for them, their joy was premature. Rose decided to plit his force, and while maintaining the siege, to invite a general action, despite his numerical weakness.

With silence and regularity he drew up his force, after dark, across the road from the Betwa. That night the two armies slept on their arms, opposite each other and not very far apart.. Today, before daybreak, Tatya Tope advanced to the attack, but was defeated, pursued for nine miles, and driven, on across the Betwa with the loss of 1500 men, eighteen guns, and large quantities of stores and ammunition. This destroyed the last hopes of the Rani, who fled from the fort of Jhansi with some of the garrison, altough some remained to defend unto death the city and foil. There are numerous accounts of this battle, in Chas. Ball and FSUP etc and in most of the 'heavyweight' versions of the mutiny/rebellion. In particular *see The Revolt in Central India,* Simla, 1908 p 110 *et seq., and* Thomas Lowe, *Central India during the Rebellion of 1857-58,* London, 1860. Tatya Tope, on the scaffold, claimed he would have won this battle if his men had obeyed him.

APRIL 2: Colonel Lord Mark Kerr on his way up country with a motley collection of reinforcements and small detachments was ordered by Canning to digress and move to the aid of the British holed up in the Azimgarh entrenchment.

Death of Capt Sir William Peel R.N. the commander of the Naval Brigade at Kanpur: although he had been wounded it was not this that killed him but small-pox.

APRIL 3: Jhansi city was captured by Rose by assault and sacked. By all accounts the population was treated with some brutality by the British troops, remembering the massacre of British civilians at the beginning of the Mutiny: up to 5,000 rebels of the garrison were said to have been killed, although Rose claimed that no Indian women or children were harmed by his men. The Rani escaped, with her three-year old ward and a few hundred of her personal troops, by jumping on horseback down the steep slope on the south side of the fort.

APRIL 5: Jhansi Fort was taken by the British: many of its defenders fought to the death. The Rani with her stepson reached Kunch.

APRIL 6: Lord Mark Kerr at the head of 300 British troops, fought a strangely unreal action against the forces, estimated at 4,000 men of Kunwar Singh eight miles from Azimgarh. He defeated the greatly augmented Danapur Brigade and marched into Azimgarh. Kunwar Singh was still in a strong position but his plan to attack the British in Benares and cut them off from the NW Provinces had tobe abandoned.

In the Doab, Brigadier Seaton defeated the Mainpuri raja at Kankur, twenty-two miles from Fatehgarh, and the rebels virtually abandoned all hope of holding this area.

APRIL 7: In London the East India Company continued to protest against both India Bills.

APRIL 11: The Sagar Field Division under General Whitlock had made very slow progress since leaving Damoh in February. Today he fought an action against some 2.000 rebels at Jhigan and destroyed the fort and village after driving the garrison away. He then marched to Mahoba and turned towards Banda where the Nawab Ali Bahadur, was preparing to meet the column in open battle.

General Lugard had been sent from Lucknow. on 29 March, also to try to relieve Azimgarh. and today defeated a rebel force of about 3,000 of whom 1000 were trained sepoys, at the village of Tigra not far from Jaunpur.

APRIL 12: The House of Commons in London determined to proceed by Resolutions on the India Bill, and to dismiss the complaints of the East India Company.

APRIL 15: General Walpole had been despatched from Lucknow on 7 April with orders to advance up the left bank of the Ganges and so penetrate into Rohilkhand. Today he reached Royah (Rhodamow) fifty miles north of Lucknow a fort occupied by Nirpat Singh and some 300 rebels. Walpole sent his force gainst the strongest face of the fort, and they were beaten off with over one hundred killed, including the very popular Highland Colonel, Adrian Hope.

Lugard now moved in on Azimgarh occupied by Kunwar Singh and some 15,000 rebels, but was held up by determined resistance on the river Tons. Kunwar Singh had divided his forces, he greater part, including the Danapur Brigade, heading for the Ganges with the intention of crossing into Bihar and his home territory. Lugard eventually occupied Azimgarh but had not defeated the rebels. Kunwar Singh was pursued by Brigadier Douglas

APR1L 16: Kunwar Singh readied Naghai not far from Azimgarh and occupied a strong position.

APRIL 17: Douglas attacked Kunwar Singh at Naghai but did not defeat him; he continued his retreat towards the Ganges, and breached Mannahar in the Ghazipur district. Rao Sahib issued a proclamation to the chiefs of Bundelkhand: in particular he called for the chief of Charkari, who. despite considerable loss had sided with the British.*'To be considered as an Englishman and sent to Hell'*.

Kunwar Singh was attacked by Brigadier Douglas at Muneer Khas[Mannahar] and this time his force fled in disorder; breaking into a number of different columns, by prior arrangement, they headed for Sheopur Ghat on the Ganges.

Rowcroft defeated the rebels at Amorah. Jones defeated the Rohilkhand rebels at Nagul.

In a skirmish at Kabrai, twenty-four miles west of Banda. Whitlock's fforce came under heavy fire and was temporarily checked: the rebels withdrew to Banda and claimed to the Nawab that the British had no stomach for a fight and were few in number.

APRIL 18: The Nawab took up a strong position at Goora Mughali about eight miles west of Banda, with a force of approximately 9,000 well-armed men including some former sepoys. At this, the Battle of Banda, Whitlock successfully defeated the Nawab and his allies. His force of 2.000 included 400 of the Raja of Charkari's men.

Campbell resumed operations from Cawnpore.

Douglas having defeated Kunwar Singh at Azmatgarh and at Muneer Khas [Mannahar] continued the pursuit but was confused by the local people who supported the rebels and gave the British false information.

APRIL 19: Lord Ellenborough's 'Secret Dispatch was written. He was President of the India Board, and he wrote to Canning a strong condemnation of the Oude Proclamation which had in effect confiscated all the estates of Oude with the exception of seven or eight small chiefs land. The matter however became a party political one and Ellenborough resigned his office. There is an excellent explanation of the affair in Martin Vol II pp 482-83.

Whitlock took the town of Banda and found there immense quantities of valuable property. It is said that the Nawab had passed through the town weeping bitterly; he and the remainder of his forces marched to Kalpi and joined the rebels there under the Rao Sahib and the Rani of Jhansi; Sir Hugh Rose was advancing on that stronghold.

APRIL 21: Kunwar Singh reached Sheopur Ghat and there crossed the Ganges by boats previously collected, although he had spread the rumour that he would cross, by elephants, at another place. Douglas arrived at the river bank in time only to sink the last of the boats; what was not known until afterwards was that Kunwar Singh was wounded in one of the boats, by artillery fire, and actually cut off his own shattered arm. Once in Bihar he found his brother Amar with several thousand armed villagers and made his way to his old home in the Jagdishpur jungles.

Brigadier General Jones, commanding a small column operating from Roorkee, crossed the Ganges at Hardwar unopposed, and defeated a very large body of Rohilkhand rebels, estimated at 12,000 with fifteen guns, at Nagina. The victory was decisive and Jones was able to re-occupy Bijnor without opposition and then push on towards Moradabad.

APRIL 22: Firoz Shah reached Moradabad and demanded money, supplies etc from the citizens, but they, aware of the approach of British forces, refused. Walpole defeated a large body of rebels at Sirsa on the right bank of the Ramgunga, not far from Aliganj: this time he was more careful in the use of his infantry, but still failed to follow up the rebels as they fled in disorder.

APRIL 23: Kunwar Singh defeated Captain Le Grand and a body of the 35th Regiment at Jagdishpur. inflicting many casualties' and pursuing the British back to Arrah. Lieutenant Richard Parsons was a survivor of this particularly badly organised British expedition against Jagdishpur in Bihar, he wrote frankly and honestly of this British defeat at the hands of the (dying) Kunwar Singh. See R. Parsons, A Story of Jugdespore, London. 1904.

APRIL 24: The forces of the Nawab of Rampur were helping to drive out Firoz Shah from Moradabad to which he had secretly returned.

APRIL 25: Jones encamped a few miles from Moradabad.

Campbell reached Fatehgarh.

APRIL 26: Under Jones's orders Brigadier Coke entered

Moradabad and encountered little resistance: during house-to-house searches twenty-one rebel ringleaders were take prisoner. but Firoz Shah escaped.

Kunwar Singh died of his wounds at Jagdishpur.

Jung Bahadur left Gorakhpur for Butwal, en route for Nepal.

APRIL 27: Campbell entered Rohilkhand, and joined Walpole to the north of Fatehgarh. the combined force then marching towards Shahjehanpur.

APRIL 28: The Rao Sahib with a large army encamped at Jalalpur to oppose Whitlock.

The Gurkha army reached Faizabad and Ayodhya.

APRIL 30: Campbell entered Shahjehanpur.

General Penny's column was ambushed and he was killed at Kakrauli.Disraeli brought in the 'Resolutions' in the House of Commons.

MAY 2: Rose was marching upon Kunch and Kalpi but today sent a party under Major Gall to take the town and fort of Lohari. The sepoys of the fort's garrison were all from the 12th BNI which had mutinied at Jhansi: they died, to a man in a gallant defence of the fort: not one man got away.

Moradabad district was made over to the Nawab of Rampore to garrison and administer.

MAY 3: As Campbell had moved north against Bareilly the Maulvi Ahmadullah Shah, ie the Fyzabad Maulvi with a large force came from Mohamdi to Shahjehanpur where Colonel Hale held the gaol until 11 May against 8 000 rebels.

Lugard crossed the Ganges in pursuit of the late Kunwar Singh's forces.

MAY 5: Campbell defeated the rebels in the Battle of Bareilly including the famous charge of the Ghazis of whom 133 were bayonetted: Bareilly was taken but the rebel leaders and the great mass of their trained soldiers escaped to the north-east to Pilibhit.

MAY 6: Jones's column marching from Moradabad also approached Bareilly and today joined Campbell.

MAY 7: A Corps of Bengal European Cavalry was determined on.

In the Battle of Kunch, Rose defeated Tatya Tope, but the latter's men especially the infantry, fought with great courage and discipline. The 52nd BNI which covered the rebel retreat as skirmishers was almost entirely destroyed. Five hundred of the rebels were killed, to eight on the British side, but the latter suffered greatly from the effects of the sun: forty-five men succumbed to sunstroke. It was reported that there was great dissension among the rebels, and that Tatya Tope was accused by them of running away. Months' later on the scaffold he claimed he was never more than number four in the rebel hierarchy.

MAY 9: Lugard defeated a party at Jagdishpur. but by no means cleared the area of rebels who were supported by the local population.

Rose marched in pursuit of Tatya Tope and Rani of Jhansi.

MAY 10: Lugard occupied Jagdishpur.

Today was the anniversary of the outbreak of the Mutiny, and although Delhi. Lucknow, Cawnpore. Jhansi and Bareilly had all been retaken by the British the rebellion was still far from over. In Central India in Oude [Awadh] in Rohilkhand and in rural Bihar the rebels were still active and determined to continue the struggle and many others watched and waited to see which side would win before committing themselves irrevocably.

MAY 11: Amar Singh the brother of Kunwar Singh was defeated by Brigadier Corfield near Piru in Bihar but managed to escape.

In the inconclusive Battle of Shahjehanpur, Jones relieved Hall but was then himself placed on the defensive by the forces of the Maulvi. The latter was constantly reinforced, by the Begum of Oude and Firoz Shah and some of the followers Nana Sahib Lord Stanley was appointed to the Board of Control for India in place of Ellenborough.

MAY 12: Lugard defeated Amar Singh near Jagdishpur. Again, this was far from decisive. Brigadier General Hope Grant to whom the campaign in Oude had been virtually delegated fought an indecisive battle with Beni Madho and 16,000 Oude rebels at Sirsi: although the rebels retired they were not pursued.

MAY 13: The rebels continued to menace the British position camp at Jagdishpur.

MAY 14-21: Great debates took place in Parliament on Canning's Proclamation and Ellenborough's Dispatch. The split came on party lines and Canning found himself considerably strengthend because the party that supported him was now the government.

MAY 15: Rebel leaders including Nana Sahib. Khan Bahadur Khan and Maulvi Ahmadullah Shah, the Begum of Oude and Firoz Shah were all in the vicinity of Shahjehanpur and today they attacked Jones there in great force, but were unable to dislodge the British.

Rose was involved in a fierce conflict with the forces

of Tatya Tope and his allies near Kalpi; sun-stroke, the great heat and a shortage of water increased his difficulties, but it is quite clear also that the local population were entirely on Nana Sahib's side in the struggle; Rose reported 'the inhabitants of the valley of the Jumna were the most disaffected my force had yet met with. One result was that he was unable to find reliable spies or to communicate with other British forces. Added to this there was a big problem, in the heat, with ammunition for the Enfield rifles which became almost useless. At sunset the rebels withdrew into Kalpi and the entrenchments they had built there.

MAY 17: Jung Bahadur returned to Nepal; his army had started with 2,000 carts loaded with loot, but much was stolen from the Gurkhas on their way home.

Rose's force had to deal with determined mass attacks by the rebels outside Kalpi.

MAY 18: Campbell, marching down from Bareilly, repulsed the rebels at Shahjehanpur, and effected a junction with Jones and Hale but was unable to defeat the enemy as he was considerably out-numbered in cavalry.

MAY 21: Light summer clothing was ordered for the British troops. Until now they had marched and fought, no matter what the temperature, in the heavy woollen uniforms they had brought from Europe.

MAY 22: For the British Kalpi was of great significance. Junction had been made here between the men of the Bombay army commanded by Rose, and men of the Bengal army commanded by Colonel Maxwell (on the left bank of the Jumna). Failure now would have led to a revival of the struggle throughout India, and '*lit the torch of rebellion in the Deccan and Southern Marathas, full of ill-disposed Arabs and Rohillas and partizans of Nana Sahib*. The Battle of Kalpi took place today: the rebels came out in great numbers and attacked with courage but were beaten by superior generalship. The best acount of this battle in Revolt in Central India 1857-59. Simla 1908 Produced by the Intelligence Branch Army HQ India.

Coke Joined Campbell from Pilibhit.

MAY 23: Rose occupied Kalpi town and fortress which were found deserted. The Rao Sahib, Tatya Tope, Rani of Jhansi and Nawab of Banda and large numbers of the rebels all moved out of the town on the Jalaun road. The value of the stores found in the arsenal at Kalpi was estimated at 3 Lakh of rupees. An attempt to rally some of the retreating sepoys and to cut the British off from Jhansi was made by Barjur Singh in his stronghold at Bilayan on the Jhansi road.

MAY 24: There was a further outbreak of incendiarism at

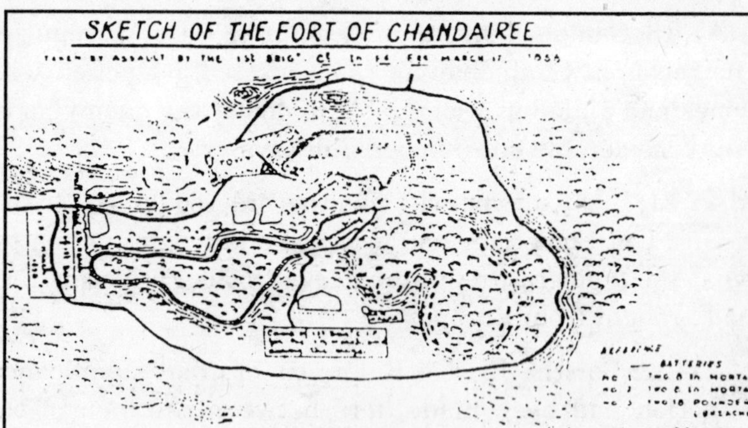

Allahabad showing quite clearly that the rebellion there was fact from ended.

Campbell'followed up the Maulvi who have retired from Shahjehanpur and captured the fort at Mohamadpur.

While Campbell could claim he had cleared Bareilly and much of Rohilkhan his victory was only partial where British troops withdrew the rebels moved in behind, and none of the major bodies of rebel troops had been destroyed or dispersed.

Nizam Ali Khan, in former times the *kotwal* of Shahjehanpur, and now a leading rebel in Rohilkhand, was reported to be in the Shahi *pargana.* He was attacked at Kuthura but escaped with his small force of infantry and cavalry intact.

May 25: Hamirpur was occupied by the British; more and more territory that had been in rebel hands for twelve months or so was coming back into government control.

May 26: The railway from Allahabad to Fatehpur was completed, but Raniganj to Allahabad was still to be built.

May 27: Chanderi and its fort in Bundelkhand were evacuated by the rebels, and it seemed that Kalpi was the last battle in this land and that the rebels would soon be dispered for ever, but in fact news was about to break that had as much impact as the first outbreak over a year before. Acting on a daring plan that has been ascribed to the Rani of Jhansi, the rebel leaders in this part of India decided to move upon Gwalior where the massive fortress and equally firm support of much of the local people would guarantee success. So confident had the British been that the campaign was over that Sir Hugh Rose had issued his valedictory general order to the troops and prepared to depart for Bombay and then to England. He had perforce to cancel these arrangements at short notice.

It is often misleadingly tsserted that there was no mutiny or rebellion except in Northern India but today Mr Manson, a political agent, was murdered by the Raja of Nargund between Kolapur and Belgaum in Southern

Maratha country. An excellent account of the affair, together with a statement of the true nature of the rebellion in this part of India is to be found in Sir George le Grand Jacob. *Western India before and during the Mutinies*, London, 1871.

MAY 28: Dara Shikoh and Haji Shikoh. princes of the Delhi Royal family were arrested at Hasanpur in the Moradabad district.

Campbell returned to Fatehgarh, and in a General order thanked his army for past services, from which it may be inferred that he too thought, prematurely, that the rebellion was coming to an end.

MAY 30: The rebel leaders, Rao Sahib, Tatya Tope, the Rani Jhansi and the Nawab of Banda arrived at Gwalior, with considerable forces, including many of the former Gwalior Contingent. Reports were that they had 7,000 trained infantry, 4,000 /airy and twelve guns: they entered Morar just to the east of Gwalior and occupied the old cantonment area.

MAY 31: At daybreak Maharaja Scindia marched out with 8,000 men and eight guns and took up a position two miles east Morar and awaited the rebel attack. When the attack came, the whole of Scindia's army, with the exception of his bodyguard, went over to the rebels, and Scindia himself fled to Dholpur and then to Agra with a few faithful retainers.

JUNE 1: The rebels captured Gwalior. The area of the city own as Lashkar where Scindia's palace was and Gwalior fort were also occupied. Dramatically the rebels who had fled from Kalpi in a disorderly state were now set up with great wealth an artillry park of some sixty guns, a fine arsenal filled with warlike stores and with Scindia's army as their allies. The British realised that they had it all to do over again. Moreover the matter appeared urgent as the rains would be due shortly, and troop movements, particularly of large guns, would be most difficult. If Tatya or the Rao Sahib were able to head south through Sciendia's territory into Maratha country the whole of western India might have joined the rebellion. The Hyderabad Contingent which had performed so well for government was actually on its home to the Deccan when the message came to return to the rural India Field Force.

Whitlock today marched to Kirwi and the two Raos deserted by their armies, surrendered.

JUNE 3: There was an engagement at Rath between the Chankari Raja and the rebel leader. Martand Rao Tatya. and the latter was killed.

The Raja of Nargund was captured and his town and fort destroyed.

JUNE 4: Lugard again defeated a party of rebels in the Jagdishpur jungles. In Gwalior the Nana was proclaimed Peishwa and the Rao Sahib his deputy, and Tatya Tope the Diwan: much feasting and rejoicing took place, but were to prove premature.

JUNE 6: Kirwi was captured by Whitlock and immense treasure and jewels (later to be distributed as prize money to the British troops) and forty-two guns were taken. News came from Etawa that one Ganga Singh had been appointed Nazim for the Gwalior area.

JUNE 7: Lord Stanley resumed the India debates in the House of Commons.

JUNE 9: There was still considerable small scale rebel activity wherever British columns were not physically present; in Gorakhpur District in particular certain rebel leaders had considerable success. One. Mahomed Hussain was today defeated at Amorah but retreated with his army intact.

Captain Moncrizeff with Madras troops defeated rebels at Chuckerderpur in Chota Nagpur, but it was not until the end of the year that order was finally restored to this area.

JUNE 11: Tej Singh, Raja of Mainpuri surrendered on guarantee of his life.

The Raja of Nargund was tried and executed at Belgaum: his wife and mother had drowned themselves in despair at the disgrace.

JUNE 12: In the final decisive battle in Oude[Awadh] Hope Grant defeated 16,000 rebels at Nawabganj, on the road between Faizabad and Lucknow. Grant had been reinforced by the Raja of Kapurthala, Ranbir Singh with a thousand Sikhs. The rebels in this area of Oude were commanded by Beni Madho but he was not present at this battle. The zamindari men in the rebel army fought with great courage and determination to conquer or die but once again they were not well led. The battle lasted three hours, and the rebels lost six guns and six hundred dead, while the British losses amounted to sixty-seven in dead and wounded, beside thirty-three who died of sun-stroke, and two hundred and fifty in hospital from the same cause. The rebels had been flocking to Nawabganj from all sides to join the formidable numbers already there, but the crushing defeat had very important results upon rebel morale.

Amar Singh returned to Buxar on the Ganges where he had considerable local support. Khan Bahadur Khan, still active in the north of Rohilkhand was reported as having attacked Shahjehanpur: he had with him 5,000 cavalry, six hundred infantry and eighteen light guns.

JUNE 15: Maulvi Ahmadullah Shah attacked Pawayan. near Mahomdi and in a fight with its raja Jagannath Singh, he was killedi. His head was then struck off and sent in to the magistrate at Shahjehanpur and the reward of 50,000 rupees claimed.

JUNE 16: Rose arrived from Kalpi more quickly than the rebels had anticipated and their preparations were incomplete. In the Battle of Morar, therefore Rose was able to defeat the combined forces of the Kalpi rebels and the Gwalior army, and to drive them back into Gwalior much disheartened by their defeat. Many of Scindia's troops now deserted and rejoined the maharaja who was making his way south again from Dholpur.

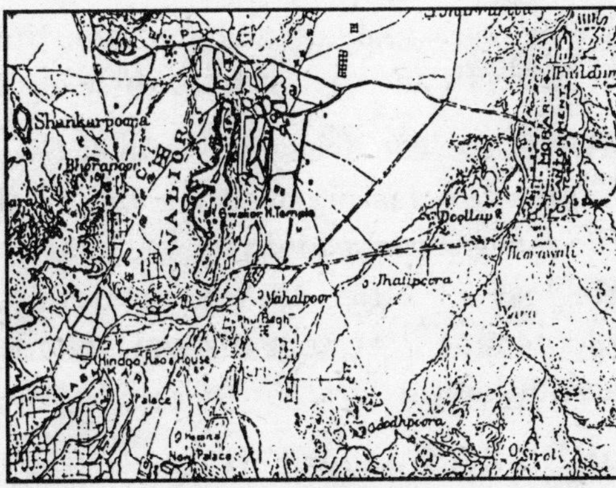

JUNE 17: The Battle of Kotah-ki-Serui some five miles from Gwalior was a small affair but highly significant for it was here that the Rani of Jhansi dressed as a cavalry soldier, was killed by a British Hussar (who had no idea what he had done).

The British were by now paying particular attention to the detection and punishment of those they considered guilty, particularly of the murder of Europeans. Former officials of government who had become rebels were also pursued relentlessly; as an example Mahbub Khan qualified on both counts: he was a former *tehsildar* of Aligarh and he was convicted of having murdered the judge. Tucker, in

Fatehpur: he was today hanged at Aligarh.

Lord Stanley brought in India Bill No 3 to Parliament.

Canning who can have had no idea that Ellenborough had already resigned, sent a reasoned reply to the latter's Dispatch.

JUNE 18: Mahomed Hussain with an army estimated at 4,000 men was again defeated, this tune by Colonel Rowcroft at Harriah and driven from the Gorakhpur district

JUNE 19: The decisive Battle of Gwalior took place today: in an action lasting over five and a half hours Rose defeated the rebels marched into the Lashkar and re-occupied the city. He lost 21 killed and 44 wounded, including his ADC Lieutenant Rose (not his son) who was killed in the final assault on the fort.

JUNE 20: Gwalior Fort was captured by Rose: despite its great strength, no real attempt was made to hold it by the rebels who now retreated to the westward via the Residency. General Napier at Morar was ordered to pursue the rebels, and he marched twenty-five miles that same day to Samaoli where they learned that the rebel force numbered 12,000 men with 22 guns and that it was commanded by Tatya Tope. Maharaja Scindia returned to Gwalior under escort of British troops and was reinstated.

JUNE 21: At the Battle of Jaora-Alipur. some thirty-two miles west of Gwalior Napier with a numerically far inferior force, completely routed the rebel army, captured all their guns and scattered them in every direction. This dispersal brought Sir Hugh Rose's regular campaign to an end. although the long pursuit of Tatya Tope was to occupy another ten months.

JUNE 23: The East India Company's objections to Bill No 3

were published but by now it was clear to all that the Company is fighting a losing battle.

JUNE 24: The India Bill was read a second time in the Commons.

JUNE 29: Rose handed over his command to Napier, and left for Poona via Mhow.

JUNE 30: The 30th and 31st Bombay N.I. were formed to contain faithful men from the mutinous 21st and 27th. This again makes it clear that the mutiny existed outside the Bengal army. Similarly faithful men from the 3rd 36th and 61st Bengal N.I. were formed into a new regiment in the Punjab. The authorities were assuming, prematurely, that the rebellion was coming to an end every where.

JULY: The Mutiny and the rebellion in general were by no means over, although this month saw little in the way of grand campaigns. Tatya Tope presented the greatest threat to the British: he carried neither tents nor provisions and when unencumbered by guns could move far more quickly than his pursuers: the sympathy of the people was with him and he got both information and supplies without difficulty. Active rebel bands around Jagdishpur are frequently mentioned in official reports. Numerous *talukhdars* of Oude were still engaged in active hostilities with the British directly, and more particularly, in punishing those who had shown friendship for the British. The Begum of Oude also still held a large body of insurgents under her command. All attempts to arrest Nana Sahib had failed. In other-words the process of pacification was not far advanced. It is highly significant that by this time the number of mutinied sepoys still engaged in active hostilities had dwindled dramatically, from death or desertion or rejection by potential patrons: perhaps 100,000 had mutinied, but no more than 15,000 were still in arms.

Truly the Mutiny now had the appearance more of a civil Rebellion, and lends credence to the idea of a Freedom Struggle.

JULY 2: General Roberts with the Rajputana Field Force reached Jaipur, for which city Tatya Tope was reported to be heading. At this time Tatya was still accompanied by the Rao Sahib and the Nawab of Banda: these three now turned southwards towards Tonk.

JULY 5: The Banpur Raja surrendered to the British, but was temporarily allowed to return to the Chanderi district where he continued to intrigue.

JULY 8: Tonk saw another success on the part of the rebels the Nawab shut himself up in the fortress and left a part of his forces outside with four guns to oppose Tatya Tope, but they welcomed the rebels and today gave them their guns.

The India Bill passed all stages in the House of Commons.

JULY 9: Tatya Tope plundered Tonk; Firoz Shah was reported to be with him. Soon afterwards Colonel Holmes with a Light Field Force drove them out of the city, but inflicted no damage or casualties upon them.

JULY 10: The Shargarh raja surrendered.

Amar Singh re-occupied Jagdishpur and the entire district was kept in disturbance by small parties of rebels, although they operated mostly south of the Ganges and west of the Son. Today they reached Rampur.

JULY 11: In the Etawa and Mainpuri districts there was still considerable small scale rebel activity: Ramnagar was temporarily occupied by these rebels, being driven out by local levies raised and officered by the British

JULY 14-21: Brigadier Berkeley, operating from Allahabad captured and destroyed a number of small forts in Oude[Awadh], and made contact with Hope Grant operating from Lucknow. Southern Oude was thus brought under firm government control for the first time.

JULY 17: In a typical affair at this juncture Rattray operating from Jagdishpur captured some rebel chiefs, including Sangram Singh at Dehri yet almost immediately Jagdishpur was re-occupied by Amar Singh.

JULY 21: Hope Grant set out from Lucknow to confront rebels: his specific task was to relieve Raja Man Singh who was besieged in his fort at Shahganj by up to 20,000 rebels all anxious to punish him for going over to the British.

JULY 23: Roberts left Tonk in pursuit of Tatya Tope; it was to be a prolonged and frustrating task for the British.

Where British power was restored retribution followed and many who had been active on the rebel side were apprehended and hanged eg today the kotwal of Aligarh. Hussun Khan Mewatti, was hanged, also the former *tehsildar,* Mahbub Khan. Mutiny within the armed forces still occurred: today Kishan Singh, a naik of the Aligarh Levy was hanged, for attempting to tamper with sundry troopers of Captain Murray's Jat Horse and to persuade them to join in refusing the messing system and to eat bread backed except by themselves'.

JULY 25: Two rebels. Barjur Singh and Daulat Singh reinforced by Deshpat of Jaitpur from the Hamirpur district, were active and unopposed at this time in the Kunch, Jhansi and Jalaun stricts: they had local support and in the absence of a British column they held power.

JULY 26: Pawayan and Shahjehanpur were reported as seriously threatened by Oude rebels.

JULY 27: The rebel force besieging Shahganj broke up on the news of the approach of Hope Grant.

JULY 28: Hope Grant relieved Raja Man Singh at Shahganj.

JULY 29: Hope Grant entered Faizabad and drove out the rebel.

Still active in Oude against the British were the begum Beni Madho, Babu Rambaksh, Behinath Singh, Chandabaksh, Gholab Singh, Nirput Singh the Shahzada Firoz Shah, Bhopal Singh and between them they had around seventy thousand armed men and fifty guns.

JULY 30: Cavanagh defeated a body of rebels in Muhiabad.

JULY 31: The India Bill passed the House of Lords: it had a stormy passage because complicated by the contest concerning Canning and Ellenborough which had eventually divided Parliament on party lines, ie Whigs and Tories. Canning's reply to Ellenborough was not known in England until October and his defence of his Oude Proclamation became academic as it was never issued in its original form, but there seems little doubt that its tenor influenced many of the *talukdars* to fight on against the British.

There was an outbreak of prisoners at the gaol Mymensing in Eastern Bengal: six hundred escaped of whom half were afterwards killed or recaptured: it was never established as to whether these men had any connections with the mutiny/rebellion.

AUGUST 1: The Bundela rebels, many of them led by Vlansaram a follower of the late Rani of Jhansi seized Jaloun; after a couple of days they abandoned it on hearing of the approach of a column from Jhansi, led by Colonel Macduff. At the same time Kunch was attacked by Barjur Singh.

AUGUST 2: By Act 21 and 22 Victoria c. 106 all the East India Company's territories became vested in Her Majesty, and all its powers were to be exercised in her name. To take effect on 1 November 1858.

AUGUST 3: Man Singh, the Raja of Narwar (who claimed that his quarrel was with Scindia not the British, and who should not be confused with Man Singh of Shahganj in Oude) captured Paori, a town and fort twenty miles north of Sipri he had a force of 4,000 men of whom 700 were sepoys.

The Banpur Raja and the Shargarh raja were sent under escort into Gwalior.

AUGUST 7: The Court of Directors elected seven members for the new Council of India.

AUGUST 8: Roberts caught up with and defeated Tatya Tope at Sanganir on the Nasirabad - Neemuch road. Tatya and his 'great force' then retreated into Udaipur territory.

AUGUST 11: Colonel Parke headed a column from Neemuch to halt Tatya Tope.

AUGUST 12: Tatya Tope was checked at the Marwar frontier by the Erinpura force.

AUGUST 13: Horsford was despatched by Hope Grant to retake Sultanpur from the Oude rebels, but found it strongly held by some 14,000 men with fifteen guns and awaited reinforcements.

Brigadier Carpenter from the Sagar Field Division defeated a party of 2,000 rebels near Kirwi.

AUGUST 14: After marching seventy miles in three days Roberts again defeated Tatya Tope at Kattara an action ajso referred to as the Battle of Banas River. The rebels lost about a thousand men many from the Kotah Contingent and the

5th B. Irregular Cavalry, and were scattered, only to reform later at a distance.

AUGUST 20: Tatya Tope crossed the Chambal to Jalta Pattan where the Rana was loyal to the British, but his troops sided with the rebels. Tatya took possession of some thirty small guns and ammunition, and received an unwilling contribution of fifteen lakhs of rupees from the Rana; he then headed for Rajgarh intending to reach Indore and rouse Holkar's troops.

AUGUST 23: Napier drove Man Singh out of Paori.

AUGUST 25-29: Hope Grant who had come to the relief of Horsford was engaged in fighting with the Oude rebels outside Sultanpur. The city was finally abandoned by the rebels after an inconclusive action: they retired to Amethi, a fort twenty-five miles away, the residence of Lal Madho Singh a devoted follower of the Begum, and then to Mozaffarnagar. Heavy rains then put an end to operations for six weeks.

AUGUST 27: Carpenter came up again with the rebels at the Panghati Pass and again dispersed them: they numbered some 7,000 men of whom 500 were mutineers.

AUGUST 29: A 'Brahmin plot' was discovered at Gwalior: some troops of the 25th Bombay NI disclosed it to the adjutant. Enquiries led to the belief that the Nana Sahib was intriguing here through his emissaries.

AUGUST 31 : The disarmed 62nd and 69th BNI mutinied at Multan in the Punjab, it seems they thought the plan to disband and despatch them to their homes piecemeal covered an intention to kill them: they seized clubs and other weapons and beat five Sikh guards to death: the reaction was a furious massacre by the 11th Punjabis in particular and up to 1.300 "mutineers" were summarily killed.

Man Singh encamped at Sirsi north of Guna, with a considerable force of trained sepoys.

SEPTEMBER 1: Captain Ashburner marched against Barjur Singh, Jowahir Singh, Debi Singh and three thousand rebel followers and defeated them near Mahoni on the river Pahuj and depersed the survivors.

This was the last day of the governing power of the Honourable East India Company.

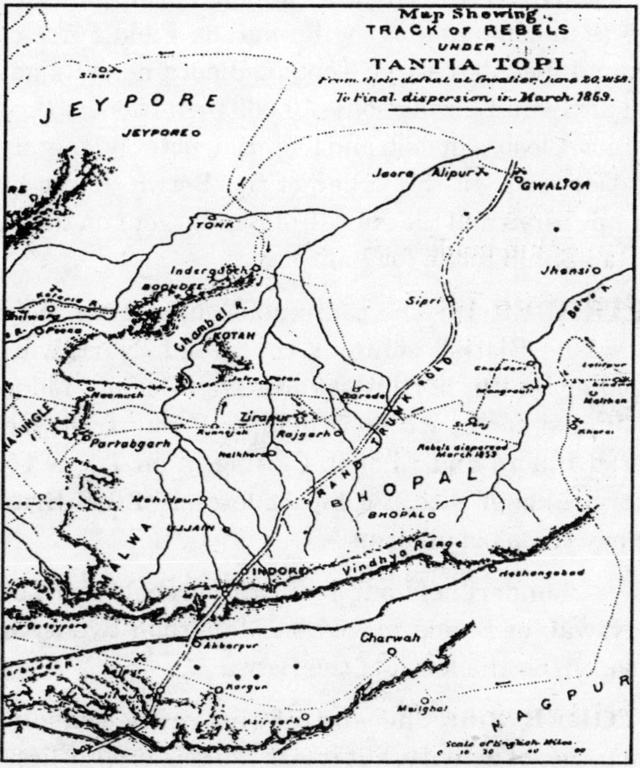

SEPTEMBER 2: The few survivors of the Multan mutineer regiments now fled.

The new Council of India commenced its sittings.

SEPTEMBER 5: Napier defeated Man Sing at the Battle of Bijapur near Guna. The rebels who came mainly from the remains of the Gwalior Contingent and from the 40th, 50th and 52nd BNI were heavily defeated, losing at least 450 men and were now dispersed.

SEPTEMBER 7: Four conspirators in the 'Brahmin Plot' at Gwalior were blown from guns, and the Nana Sahib's perwunnah seized.

SEPTEMBER 15: General Michael who had succeeded Roberts in command of the Rajputana Field Force came up with and defeated Tatya Tope at Biaora near Rajgarh. The rebel army numbering some 10,000 men was dispersed with considerable loss in men and material, notably 27 guns. Tatya fled eastwards to the valley of the Betwa where his force split up: Tatya and the Nawab of Banda went on to Chanderi; the Rao Sahib made for Lalitpur.

SEPTEMBER 16: The continuous chase after Tatya Tope by various British columns continued. Northwards was Brigadier Smith, northeastwards was Colonel Liddell with the Jhansi force, while Brigadier Parke from Neemuch covered Indore and Bhopal. Closing in on Tatya Tope was General Michel with a compact force of 1,000 British and Bombay troops of all arms.

Chanderi held out against the rebels and Tatya and the Nawab of Banda moved on Mangraoli twenty miles to the south, on the left k of the Betwa.

OCTOBER 3-8: The end of the rainy season saw a resumption of activity, but it was the rebels who first moved in Oude [Awadh]. Captain Dawson was besieged by the Oude rebels, led by Harichand with 6,000 men and eight guns at Sandila.

OCTOBER 5: Brigadier Eveleigh defeated a body of rebels

at Mianganj, between Lucknow and Cawnpore, taking two guns: it is significant that this area, constantly patrolled by British troops yet managed to resist strongly.

OCTOBER 8: Pawayan was attacked by a large rebel force no doubt inspired by the killing of the Maulvi there, but they had to retire. The Raja of Pawayan now had little option but to actively support the British.

Brigadiers Barker and Dawson, breaking out from Sandila defeated the rebels at Pannu but only after a very severe action in which British casualties were eighty-two killed and wounded.

OCTOBER 19: Tatya Tope was defeated by Michel at Sindwah. but these actions were inconclusive since the rebels were able to slip away and reform, by arrangement, elsewhere. It was this type of activity that gained Tatya Tope his reputation as a guerilla fighter.

OCTOBER 25: Again Tatya Tope was defeated' at Malthone but was neither captured nor was his army dispersed.

OCTOBER 29: Beni Madhoo was defeated at Poorwa.

OCTOBER 30: Mehndi Hussein, the leading Oude rebel was defeated at Sufderganj but still refused to surrender.

OCTOBER 31: Tatya Tope, with the main body of his army. passed through Rajgarh and crossed the Narbada forty miles above Hoshangabad and headed for Nagpur but was turned side by the Nagpur Force, and he went westwards, hoping to move to the south through the wild country of the Melghat Forest but his way was barred by the Berar Field Force of the Hyderabad Contingent, and he turned northwestwards into Holkar's territory, making for Baroda. Had he not been thus diverted the rebellion might have developed very differently.

NOVEMBER 1: Queen Victoria's Proclamation to the Princes Chiefs, and People of India was read in the principal cities of India. It was to be of great significance not only in the story of the mutiny but also in subsequent Indian history:- *'Victoria by the Grace of God of the United kingdom of Great Britain and Ireland, and of the Colonies and Dependencies thereof in Europe, Asia, Africa, America and Australasia, Queen. Defender of the Faith. Whereas, for divers eighty reasons we have resolved, by and with the advice and consent of the Lords Spiritual and Temporal, and Commons in Parliament assembled, to take upon ourselves the government of the territories in India, heretofore adminstered in trust for us by the Honourable East India Company: Now, therefore, we do by these presents notify and declare that, by the advice and consent aforesaid, we have taken upon ourselves the said government; and we hereby call upon all our subjects within the said terrotories to be faithful and to bear true allegiance to us, our heirs and successors, and to submit themselves to the authority of those whom we may hereafter from time to time see fit to appoint to adminster the government of our said territories, in our name and on our behalf.... We hereby announce to the native Princes of India that all treaties and engagements mode with the by or under the authority of the Honourable East India Company are by us accepted, and will be scrupulously maintained... We desire no extension of our present territorial possessions.... We shall respect the rights, dignity and honour of native Princes as our own: and we desire that they, as well as our own subjects, should enjoy that prosperity and that social advancement which can only be secured by internal peace and good government. We hold ourselves bound to the natives of our Indian territories by the same obligations of duty which bind us to all our other subjects: and those obligations, by the blessing of Almighty God, we shall faithfully and conscientiously fulfil. Firmly relying ourselves on the truth* *of Christianity and acknowledging with gratitude the solace of religion, we disclaim alike the right and the desire to impose our convictions on any of our subjects. We declare it to be our Royal will and pleasure that none be in anywise favoured, none molested or disquieted, by reason of their religious faith or observances, but that all shall alike enjoy the equal and impartial protection of the law: and we do strictly charge and enjoin all those who may be in authority under us that they abstain from all interference with the religious belief or worship of any of our subjects, on pain of our highest displeasure. And it is our further will that, so far as may be, our subjects of whatever race or creed, be freely and impartially admitted to offices in our service, the duties of which they may be qualified, by their education, ability, and integrity, duly to discharge. We know and respect the feelings of attachment with which the natives of India regard the lands inherited by them from their ancestors, and we desire to protect them in all rights connected therewith subject to the equitable demands of the State and we will that, generally, in framing and administering the law, due regard be paid to the ancient rights, usages, and customs of India. We deeply lament the evils and misery which have been brought upon India by the acts of ambitious men, who have deceived their countrymen by false reports, and led them into open rebellion. Our power has been shewn by the suppression of that rebellion in the field: we desire to shew our mercy by pardoning the offences of those who have been thus misled, but who desire to return to the path of duty. Already in one province, with a view to stop the further effusion of blood, and to hasten the pacification of our Indian dominions, our Viceroy and Governor General has held out the expectation of pardon, on certain terms, to the great majority of those who in the late unhappy disturbances have been guilty of offences against our government and has declared the punishment which will be inflicted on those whose crimes place them beyond the reach of forgiveness. We approve and confirm the said act of our Viceroy and Governor General, and do further announce and proclaim as follows:-our elemency will be extended to all offenders, save and except those who have been or shall be convicted of having taken part in the murder of British subjects. With regard to such, the demands of justice forbid exercise of mercy. To those who have willingly given asylum murderers, knowing them to be such, or who may have acted as leaders or instigators in revolt, their lives alone can be guaranteed: but in appointing the penalty due to such persons, full consideration will be given to the circumstances under which they have been induced to throw off their allegiance: and indulgence will be shown to those whose crimes may appear to have originated in a too credulous acceptance of the false reports circulated by designing men. To all others in arms against the government, we hereby promise unconditional pardon, amnesty, and oblivion of all offences against ourselves, our crown and dignity, on their return to their homes and peaceful pursuits. It is our royal pleasure that those terms of grace and amnesty should be extended to all those who comply with their conditions before the first day of January next. When by the blessing of Providence, internal tranquillity shall be restored, it is our earnest desire to stimulate the peaceful industry of India, to promote works of public utility and improvement, and to adminster its government for the benefit of all our subjects resident therein. In their prosperity will be our strength in their contentment our security, and in their gratitude our best reward. And may the God of all power grant unto us and to those in authority under us strength to carry out these our wishes for the good of our people.'*

NOVEMBER 3: Men of the 32nd BNI formed part of the garrision of 4,000 in the Fort at Rampur Russia, held by Ram Ghulam Singh for the Oude rebels: today the stronghold was stormed by Brigadier Weatherall and twenty three guns captured. By all accounts Weatherall was very lucky, chancing by accident upon the only spot where the ramparts had not been completed.

NOVEMBER 8: The Raja of Amethi, Lal Madho Singh submitted and yielded his fortress without a fight to the combined forces of Campbell (now Lord Clyde) and Hope Grant. This submission had a profound effect upon the attitude of other *taluqdars* in Oude.

NOVEMBER 12: At the significant action at Shankerpur Rana Beni Madho was forced to yield his fort and was driven northwards, with an estimated army of fifteen thousand men and reported as joining forces with Bala Rao. Beni Madho was offered favourable terms for surrender by Clyde but proudly refused, saying he would always remain loyal to his King. Few of the *taluqdars* showed the same spirit now and Oude was being rapidly pacified by the British columns under Clyde, Grant, Eveleigh, Gordon, Carmichael and Horsford.

NOVEMBER 19: Tatya Tope arrived at Kargaon in Nimar where a detachment of Holkar's troops joined him.

NOVEMBER 24: Amar Singh and the Bihar rebels had retreated to the Palamau district, but were today caught by Brigadier Douglas and completely defeated at Salia Dahar in the Kaimur hills: all their arms and ammunition were captured and many killed.

NOVEMBER 25: The Raja of Gonda was defeated by Hope Grant, and Gonda occupied.

DECEMBER 4: Bahadur Shah Zafar ex-King of Delhi, with his Queen, Zinat Mahal, his young son Jamma Bakht and his half-brother Shah Abbas (a mere child), with some women of the *zenana* embarked in HM steamship Megera. The destination of the captives (Rangoon) was kept secret until after their departure.

DECEMBER 5: Nana Sahib was reported as crossing the

Ganges between Fatehgarh and Kanpur, but these reports were most unreliable.

DECEMBER 6: Firoz Shah and Walidad Khan were reported at Aroul. Firoz Shah had clearly made up his mind that Rohilkhand and Oude were lost to the British and that his best plan was to head south and west and try to join Tatya Tope. This at an a amazing speed, he now attempted.

DECEMBER 17: Firoz Shah had a brief encounter with a British force under Napier, at a place called Ranod near Chanderi.

DECEMBER 23: Bala Rao was driven by Grant from Tulsipur and retreated with six thousand men and fifteen guns towards Nepal.

DECEMBER 29: In an engagement at Partabgarh Tatya Tope defeated the small force of Major Rocke and succeeded in getting his baggage and his force through the pass the British were guarding, and marched towards Mandsaur. Thence he marched very rapidly - far out pacing any pursuers-to Zirapur a hundred miles south east of Neemuch, thus returning to the country almost directly South of Gwalior.

DECEMBER 29: There was an engagement at Zirapur, and Tatya Tope and the Rao Sahib were again defeated. The rebels now marched for Indragarh being joined for a short time by Man Singh, who then for reasons unknown, left them on reaching the banks of the Chambel. The pursuit of Tatya Tope continued, but he, fighting in the old Maratha way and never committing himself to one great battle, continued to avoid capture. He could march at twice the pace of any British pursuer.

DECEMBER 31: The Bihar rebels were reported as finally dispred and the area completely back under British control.

10

January 1859 - December 1877

JANUARY 2: Mohamed Hassan Khan, the Nazim or Chuckledar of Gorakhpur who had played a highly ambivalent role in the rebellion, was reported to be at Tulsipur, and to be in combination with Bala Rao. Mohamed Hassan had be friended Colonel Lennox and his family on the latter's escape from Faizabad in December 1857 but had then been one of the Begum's most active supporters.

JANUARY 4: Grant moved against the remaining forces of Bala Rao and took all their guns and drove them over the Nepal Border. He then reported that he considered the mutiny finally extinguished in Oude. an opinion with which Clyde who had just driven the Begum and the Nana Sahib also into Nepal, concurred. Grant was left in military charge with orders to keep the frontier with Nepal strictly closed.

JANUARY 7: The rebellion in Oude [AWadh] was officially declared to be at an end, but Grant's troops remained actively engaged.

JANUARY 9: Prince Firoz Shah who had cut his way across Oude and the Ganges joined Tatya Tope at Indragarh with his bodyguard and the 12th Irregulars.

JANUARY 16: Tatya Tope was usually well informed of British troop movements, but this morning was surprised in the town of Dewassa while holding a council of war with the Rao Sahib and Firoz Shah; Brigadier Showers killed three hundred of the rebels but the remainder fled, into Marwar territory.

JANUARY 21: Colonel Holmes with a force from Nasirabad caught up with Tatya Tope at Sikar and completely defeated him: the rebels abandoned horses, camels, arms and fled, six hundred of them surrendering later to the Raja of Bikaner. This defeat began the break-up of Tatya's army: Firoz Shah and the 12th Irregulars rode off. Tatya himself now parted from Rao Sahib with whom he was on bad terms, and almost alone, went off to join Raja Man Singh of Narwar.

JANUARY 29: Tafuzzul Husam Khan, the Nawab of Farrukhabad arrived at Fatehgarh under arrest. At his subsequent trial he was defended by English barristers but found guilty and sentenced to death; the sentence was then commuted to banishment, to Mecca.

FEBRUARY 10: The Rao Sahib, still with 3-4.000 men was caught at Kushani, eighty miles east of Jodhpur. by Brigadier Honner and defeated, losing about two hundred killed: he now fled southwards and then turned to the north-east. But his followers were now weary of being hunted, and many deserted and made their way to their homes: two hundred, mainly Muslims from Cawnpore and Bareilly gave themselves up to the British.

MARCH 9: Major Meade acting under the orders of Brigadier General Napier, met one Naraiyan Singh. an old friend of

Raja Man Singh of Narwar and discussed with him the possibility of persuading the latter to surrender. Man Smgh's quarrel was not with the British but with his feudal lord, Scindia of Gwalior, who had unjustly deprived him of some territory. A message was sent to Man Singh.

MARCH 25: Raja Man Singh's womenfolk, seventy in all, surrendered to Major Meade clearly in anti-cipation of the raja's own surrender.

MARCH 28: Nana Sahib and the Begum of Oude were reported to be at Butwal.

APRIL 2: Man Singh entered the British camp at Mahudra and surrendered to Major Meade on condition that his life and liberty be spared. Meade now attempted to persuade the raja to perform some signal service for the British that should earn him total restitution of his lands and dignity. This took, surprisingly, the offer by Man Singh to capture his own uncle. Ajit Singh for the British!' This plan failed and Ajit Singh escaped.

APRIL 7: Although Tatya Tope knew Man Singh had surrendered he still trusted him completely and actually consulted him as to what his next move should be. Man Singh betrayed him and led a party of Bombay sepoys sent by Meade to arrest Tatya Tope in the Paron jungles.

Khan Bahadur Khan, the Begum of Oude. Nana Sahib and the young prince Birjis Qadr were reported as being in the fort of Niacote in Nepal. They had with them no more than 500 men at most. Bala Rao still had about 2,000 fighting men and was still paying them. The sepoys knew about the amnesty extending to them but were distrustful and reluctant to submit.

APRIL 8: Tatya Tope, betrayed and captured, was taken

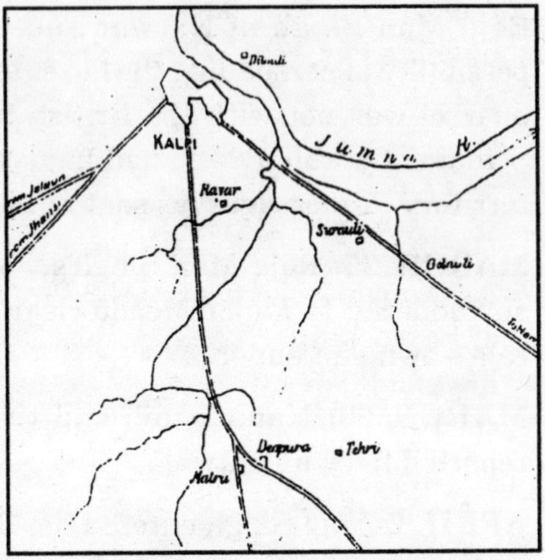

Country around Kalpi

into Meade's camp, and immediately marched off to Sipri where he was put on trial. The charge was a grossly unfair one ie '*having been in rebellion against the British Government.*' His defence was simple and straightforward: that he had only obeyed the law-ful orders of his master the Nana up to the fall of Kalpi and thereafter of Rao Sahib; he rightly claimed that he was in no way a British subject. But he was sentenced to be hanged.

APRIL 18: Tatya Tope was hanged at Sipri. He had successfully eluded the British pursuers for more than nine months and demonstrated his ability as a guerilla leader: it is estimated he had covered in that period a distance of three thousand miles. With his death and the surrender of Man Singh of Narwar an entire change came upon the revolt. In effect the people of central India surrendered with Man Singh.

APRIL 20: Nana Sahib sent an *Ishtiharnama* a formal letter addressed to Queen Victoria, to Major Richardson the nearest British officer. He declared his innocence of murder or massacre and wondered why he had not been pardoned as others had; he also declared his intention to fight to the death.

A petition to the English from Bala Rao was also

received, asking for favourable terms for surrender and blaming everything upon his brother Nana Sahib.

APRIL 30: To both Nana Sahib and to Bala Rao replies were sent with copies of the Queen's Proclamation explaining the terms on which surrender could be arranged. Unfortunately Richardson mentioned as examples or inducements the cases of the Nawab of Banda and the Nawab of Farruckabad both of whom had eventually been granted life and liberty. Had the Nana or Bala Rao now surrendered the British might have been highly embarrassed: they would not have wished to spare either man, yet their representative had clearly hinted at the possibility But neither man took the bait.

MAY-JUNE: Under the arrangements made for the transfer of power from the Company to the Crown, all European troops of the HEIC were transferred to the Queen's service. No one anticipated they would object, but they did. violently, and a state of mutiny resulted. Their major objection was that no form of signing-on bounty was on offer. Ironically this 'White Mutiny', as it came to be called, also began in Meerut. Although certain individual mutineers were punished the mutiny was successful and government had to repatriate and discharge a large number of the Company's European soldiers, with whom Clyde, though he disapproved of their methods, had much sympathy.

JULY 8: Although events showed it to be somewhat premature a 'State of Peace" was officially declared throughout India.

JULY 31: There was still some rebel activity in Central India reported, notably under Barjur Singh but his gang were now behaving more like dacoits than rebels: they raided villages and carried off the principal inhabitants for ransom.

AUGUST 2: 500 rebels under Firoz Shah entered the Bala Behat jungles, having passed through the Sagar district. It was reported that the local people received him well and made supplies freely available. He was defeated in an action with some Madras troops at Putrai and the band dispersed.

SEPTEMBER 24: In a letter written on 8 October, 1859. Lieutenant Colonel Ramsay, the Resident of Nepal, wrote to Beadon that he had received a report from the Nana's camp in the Deokur Valley that the Nana had died on 24 September, according to the females of his family, '*now residing at Tara Gurrhee*. *But ...clear authentication of Nana's death will be very desirable, as the Nana is a Brahmin and is reputed to be very wealthy, and, in the present temper and spirit of the local authorities in the teraie, it is not at all unlikely that they may be conniving at his escape into the mountains. The 'Englishman' reported that Nana Sahib died on 24 September of fever at a place called Tara Ghurrie near to Dhang and Deokhur. He had suffered previously from repealed attacks and at one time was so ill that his attendants believed him to be dead, and the usual gifts were distributed amongst the Brahmins: he however recovered partially and did not die till 24 September. His dead body is said to have been seen by creditable witnesses, and to have been burnt in their presence with the usual Hindoo rites.'*

DECEMBER : Amar Singh. the brother of Kunwar Singh, was captured in the *Terai* by Jung Bahadur's troops and handed over to the British.

DECEMBER 9: The capture in Nepal of Khan Bahadur Khan of Bareilly by Jung Bahadur was reported.

DECEMBER 17: Khan Bahadur Khan and Mammu Khan, (the minister and paramour of the Begum of Oude), were lodged in Lucknow Gaol.

DECEMBER 31: At the end of the year there was still rebel

Neill contrasting avenger

activity in the Jhansi Division, and evidence that some of the smaller native states (and some officials of larger states such as Gwalior) were still giving assistance to the rebel bands. Jhansi itself was occupied in April, 1958. Jalaun in May Hamirpur in June and the Chanderi district in November, but even after these dates considerable portions of the districts were at times in the hands of the rebels. The best known rebel leaders were Dowlat Singh. Barjur Singh. Rao Humeer Singh, Debi Singh and Desh Pat a Rajput of the family of Chatarpur and with considerable local influence and support. Desh Pat was still in rebellion in 1860.

Havelock, British supreme hero

FEBRUARY 5: 1860: Amar Singh died in Gorakhpur hospital gaol of natural causes while awaiting trial.

MARCH 24: Khan Bahadur Khan of Bareilly was hanged on the spot where he had raised the flag of revolt.

MAY 3: Jwala Prasad was hanged the Satichaura Ghat, in Cawnpore. Firoz Shah was reported to be in Kandahar.

1861: Firoz Shah was reported at Bokhara.

1862: Firoz Shah was reported in Teheran.

APRIL 9: The Rao Sahib nephew of Dondhu Pant, the Nana Sahib, had avoided capture until this year when he was arrested in the hills to the north of the Punjab, and was sent to Kanpur; there he was tried and found guilty of having been concerned in the murder of Europeans, and was hanged on 20 August 1862 at the Satichaura Ghat (aka the Massacre Ghat). Documentation on his capture and trial, and *a rare photograph* are contained in the papers of James William Macnabb which are preserved in the Oriental and India Office Collections of the British Library.

AUGUST 20: The Rao Sahib was tried and hanged.

1863 APRIL 4: The Calcutta Times reported the names of the Lucknow Begum and her son Birjis Kudr as having been expunged from the list of proscribed outlaws. Nonetheless she refused to return to India and died in Nepal, although her son eventually came back to Lucknow.

1867 FEBRUARY 23: *'Mr J Burton,' a police assistant in Lucknow, had shown considerable detective ability - has hunted up his father's murderer: also some of those who killed our officers at Chitramow, and some other Mutineers who were 'wanted'. Major Burton, that young man's father, was political Agent at Kotah in Rajpootanah and was killed by the rebels at Awah while gallantly defending himself and his famity.* General Charles Hervey, *Some Records of Crime*, London, 1892,

This story is typical: the British retained long memories for the events of the rebellion, and. despite proclamations and amnesties for many of the lesser rebel participants, continued to hunt down individuals for many years. It was also believed by many that the Nana Sahib had not died of fever in the Terai, and for thirty years after 1857 reports were coming in of sightings and arrests.

1877 DECEMBER 17: Firoz Shah was reported as having

died at Mecca. His widow was awarded a miserly Rs 5 p.m. 'pension' by the British, but this was later increased to Rs 100 subsistence allowance. At long last the Mutiny/Rebellion could be said to have finally ended at least in a military sense. The Sepoy had a Grievance but no Cause, but the struggle which had begun in 1857 as a Milary mutiny now became the inspiration for a nationalist drive for independence which gathered pace and conviction as the century wore on. The British had unwittingly united the peoples India in a manner that had never existed before in historical times. This unity trans-cended ancient state boundaries, rivalries, language barriers and religious divides until, at the moment of the winning of independence in 1947 old hatreds and suspicions were revived by the imminent departure of the common enemy the sub-continent was split into three.

11

Causes of the Mutiny

What caused the Mutiny?

Even before the last embers of the mutiny had been trampled out, the question which had from the first puzzled every man, from the Governor-General in Council to the subaltern in his modest bungalow, the question as to the original cause of the mutiny became the burning question of the day. It was a question which required a complete and accurate reply, because prompt reorganisation was necessary, and to carry out a complete scheme of re-organisation a knowledge of the circumstances which had caused the collapse of the system to be reorganised was indispensable.

Opinion of Sir John Lawrence

The opinion of no man was looked forward to with so much eagerness, so much anxiety, and,I may add, with so much curiosity, as the opinion of the great Indian official whose daring and unselfish policy had made possible the storming of Delhi. It was very natural that this should be so. Few men had more thoroughly piered to the core the national character, and few men possessed a more complete power of metal analysis. People, for the most part, did not stop to remember that, with all his gifts, Sir John Lawrence had ever been the partisan of a school–a school opposed to the tenure of land by great families; that he had favoured Lord Dalhousie's policy of annexation; and that, althogh he was thoroughly acquinted with the feelings of the agricultural class, he contemned those of the large proprietors, and that he knew little of the Sipahis. Further-more, and especially, that he possessed no personal knowledge of Oudh and of its people.

Greased Cartridges

It will readily be believed, then, that when the opinion of Sir John Lawrence was published it gave satisfaction only to the heedless many, none at all to the thinking few.

After an exhaustive argument, Sir John Lawrence arrived at the conlusion that the mutiny was due to the greased cartridges, and to the greased cartridges only. The public applauded a result so beautiful in its simplicity so easy of comprehension. It chimed so entirely with the ideas of men who never take the trouble to think for themselves, that by the masses, which are mainly composed of such men, it was promptly and thankfully accepted. With them it remains still the un-answerable reason for the mutiny of the Indian army. They did not stop to consider that to declare that the greased cartridges caused the mutiny was in all respects similar to the declaration of a man who, if asked what causes a gun to discharge, sould reply—the powder. True it is that the powder, when exploided, forces out the bullet: but who ignites the powder? That the greased cartridges were the lever used in many instances to excite the Sipahis is incontestable; they were explosive subdtances. But, though explosive, they had been perfectly harmless had the minds of the Sipahis not been perpared to act upon them in the same manner that the percussion-cap acts upon gunpowder.

The chapatis

It should never be forgotten that the greased cartridges were not the only instrument employed to create discontent in 1856-7. Before a greased cartridge had been issued the chapatis had been circulated by thousands in many rural districts. The chapati was, it is true, a weapon far less perfect than the greesed cartridge. It was, nevertheless, sufficiently adapted to the comprehensions of the class to whom it was addressed–the class given to agriculture. To minds, simple, impressionable, suspicious, prompt to receive ideas, the chapati acted as a warning of an impending calamity. A Hindu can conceive nothing more dreadful than a violation of his caste and his religion. The conculusion was a foregone one. The receipt of the chapatis foreshadowed a great attempt to be made to upset the national religion.

Though we might even grant, then, for the sake of argument, that the greased cartridges were not in themselves harmless, yet the chapatis certainly were so. But it was these harmeless chapatis which stirred up the rural populations, especially those in Oudh and in Bundelkhand, to participate in the rebellion. What becomes, then, of Sir John Lawrences's conclusion? It simply vanishes. The greased cartridges became dangerous only when used by other as a means to an end. Before the plans of leaders of the revolt were ripe the cartridge and the chapatis were nothing more than gunpowder strored in a magazine. When the opportune moment arrived, when the minds of the Sipahis and the agricultural classes had been instructed to receive any ideas, however absurd, then the cartridges and the chapatis were rammed into them, and were exploded.

But what was it that made the minds of the Sipahis, what was it that made the minds of the agricultral classes prone to conceive suspicions alike regarding the greased cartridges and the chapatis? The answere to these two questions will bring us to the real cause of the mutiny. Sir John Lawrence's conclusions were not pushed to their legitimate issue. He named only one of the means. I must go back to the cause.

Native opinion as to the cause of the mutiny

Before I express my own opinions on the matter I think it only proper that I should state the views of some thoughtful and well-educated natives, with whom I have had the opportunity of discussing the subject. I may premise that it is not an easy matter to obtain the real opinions of native gentlemen on matters regarding which they know, not only that those opinions would be distasteful to the listener, but that his ignorance of aught but the superficial life of a native of position, his absolute want of knowledge regarding the religious obligations which affect every thought of his life, act as a bar to comprehension. There are few Englishmen, for instance, even amongst those who have served long in India and who have obtained credit there for understanding the native character, who will not be amazed at the revelation regarding the origin of the mutiny, or rather of the causes which led up to it, which I am about to place on record as the real opinion of thoughtful and educated natives of India. That it is their real opinion I, who enjoyed special opportunities of conversing with them without restraint, and who possessed their confidence as far as an Englishman can possess it, know most certainly. And, what is more, there are living men, Englishmen, whose opportunities have been even greater, and who have communicated to me impressions absolutely confirming my views on the subject. From one of these gentlemen, a perfect linguist, and whose opportunities have been unrivalled, I have received the follwing reply to my query as to the cause to which the educated Hindus with whom he was in the habit of associating attributed the mutiny.

"In the opinion of the educated natives of India," was his answer, "the gross wrongs inflicted on Nana Sahib; the injustice done to Kunwar Singh; the injuries inflicted on the Rani of Jhansi; the seizure of the kingdom of Oudh; the fraudulent embezzlement perpetrated with regard to the Rao of Kirwi, and the scores of lesser wrongs done in reckless insolence to the landowners under the administration of the north-west provinces. Were Indians ever to write their account of the causes of the mutiny, it would astonish many in this country."

These views may be disputed. Indeed, I am confident that not one ex-Indian offical among a hundred will read them with aught but a contemptuous smile. It requires that a man shall have lived with the educated natives as intimate friends associate together in Europe that he should be able to understand it. There is too little of such intercourse in India. In fact, it is only those officers who have enjoyed the opportunity of a long residence at a native court to whom the chance of such intercourse is available.

Bad faith, and the attempt to force western ideas on an eastern people

In the first edition of this volume I expressed as my own an opinion in entire conformity with the general views I have just quoted as the views of the natives of India as to the origin of the great outbreak. I wrote-and I may say that time, and a subsequent visit to India, have confirmed my view- "The real cause of the mutiniy may be expressed in a condensed form in two words-bad faith. It was bad faith to our Sipahis which made their minds prone to suspicion; it was our policy of annexation, of refusing to Hindu chiefs the permission to adopt, with them, a necessary religious rite; of suddenly bringing a whole people under the operation of complex rules to which they were unaccustomed, as in Oudh, in the Sagar and Narbada territory and in Bundelkhand, and our branches of customs more sacred to the natives than laws, which roused the large landowners and the rural population against the British rule." This was my opinion then, and it is, if possible, more strongly my opinion now. I shall proceed to support it by examples.

The bad faith towards the Sipahis goes back so far as the period immediately succeeding the first Afghan war. In that war the Sipahis had behaved splendidly; they had fought well, they had suffered privations without a murmur, they had borne with cheerfulness absence from their country and their families, in a cause which was only theirs because it was the cause of their foreign masters. I recollect well meeting in 1844 at Allahabad a political officer whose conduct during his mission at Herat can never be mentioned without admiration-the late D' Arcy Todd. Speaking to me of the difficulties of his position at Herat; D' Arcy Todd stated that but for the zeal, the energy, and the fidelity of the few Sipahis who were with him he could not have stayed at Herat; he added, "When properly treated the Bengal Sipahi will go anywhere and do anything." Well, these men returned from Afghanistan. Immediately afterwards we annexed Sindh. The Bengal Sipahis were sent to garrison a country then notoriosly unhealthy. How were they treated? The timehonoured rule which provided that they should receive a fixed extra food allowance on proceeding to certain localities was rescinded, in one instance after the men had reached one of the indicated localities, in another instance when the regiment was in full march to it. Is it to be wondered at that the men grumbled and then actually refused to march? They committed no violence. They simply said, "You are guilty of bad faith; we contracted to enter your service and to perform all the duties entrusted to us on certain conditions, of which the payment to us of food allowance under certain circumstances was one. We have fulfilled our share of the contract, and now you refuse to fulfil your share. We decline to work until you fulfil it." In equity the Sipahis were right; but the Government, instead of soothing them, acted in a high-handed manner, disbanded one regiment and severely punished the men of another.

Bad effect produced on the Indian Army

The conduct produced a very bad effect throughout the Indian army. It was felt in every regiment that the word of the Government could no longer be depended upon. Nevertheless, no open indignation was manifested. The Satlaj campaign ensued, and again the Sipahis fought well. The annexation of the Panjab followed. Then succeeded a long period of quiescence a period during which seeds, sown some time before, took root, sprang up, and blossomed into regulations fraught with danger to the discipline of the Indian army.

The native of India serve a master well once he has shown himself capable of wielding authority. But should that authority slacken, or wrose still, should they find out that the Government they serve has placed at their disposal the means not only of shaking but even of upsetting it, then the nominal master wielding it ceases to be their real master; the substance of his power vanishes; the shadow only remains. The occurrences in the Indian army during the several years immediately preceding 1857 completely illustrate this assertion.

In former days, in the time of Lake, in the time of

Hastings, and even later, the commanding officer of a native regiment was supreme in all matters of discipline. Responsible immediately to his divisional commander, he could promote, he could reduce, he could punish. But, as time passed on, men were appointed to the general staff of the Indian army whose visions became clouded and whose brains became turned by the air of the new regions to which they had been transferred. Forgetting their own regimental experience, not caring to know that the routine system which suits a British regiment formed of men taught to obey the law, no matter by whom administered, is not applicable to a regiment composed of Asiatics bred to obey the man in whose hands they see authority centred and him only, these men began, step by step, to introduce the British system into the native army.

It would take too long to tell how gradually the real power of the commanding officer was underminded; how the Sipahi was, by degrees, taught to look upon him, not as a superior who must be obeyed, but as a very fallible mortal, peculiarly liable to err, and against whose lightest exercise of authority he had the right to appeal to the one central power, the Commander-in-Chief. Suffice it to say that this process of sapping the power of the commanding officer was carried to so great an extent that immediately prior to the mutiny the Sipahis had lost all respect for the authority he only nominally wielded. Nor had the Sipahi imbibed for the Commander-in-Chief the feeling which he had ceased to entertain towards his commanding officer. To him the Commander-in-Chief was but a name; he was a lay figure living in the clounds of the Himalayas, rerely, often never, seen, but whose interposition enabled him to defy his own colonel and to set discipline at nought! The extent to which this interposition was exercised before the mutiny was dangerous in the extreme. It succeeded before 1857 in weakening the influence of all the regimental officers, and in undermining the discipline of the army.

Progress of demoralisation between 1843 and 1852

I have said that the refusal of the Government of India in 1843 to act up to their contract with regard to the Sipahis sent to occupy Sindh had been felt throughout the Indian army. Immediately subsequent to that event, the process of undermining the powers of commanding officers had made swift progress. When, then, in 1852, the Government most unadvisedly again attempted another breach of contract, the Sipahis, demoralised by the process I have alluded to, were even more inclined to resent it.

The breach of contract referred to occurred in this manner. With the exception of six or seven regiments the Sipahis of the Bengal army were enlisted for service in India only; they were never to be required to cross the sea. But with the view of supplying the necessities of the state in Arakan and the Tenasserim provinces, Six or seven regiments had been specially raised for general service, and these regiments were invariably despatched thither by sea whenever their services were there required. Lord Dalhousie, however, who had ridden roughshod over so many native customs, considered that he might set aside this one also. Accordingly, when, during the Burmese war, he wanted to send an additional regiment to Burmah, instead of despatching a general service regiment or of inviting a regiment to volunteer, he ordered a regiment stationed at Barrackpur to proceed when, during the Burmese war, he wanted to send an additional regiment to Burmah, instead of despatching a general service regiment or of inviting af regiment to volunteer, he ordered a regiment stationed at Barrackpur to proceed thither.

The men of the regiment refused to go. "You ask us,"

they said, "to embark upon a service for which we have not enlisted, and which many of us regard as imperilling our caste. We will not do it." Lord Dalhousie was forced to submit. He was very angry, but there was no help for it.

But the result on the minds of the Sipahis was most disastrous. For the first time in the history of India the orders of the Governor - General had been successfully resisted. It was little to the purpose to argue that the Governor - General had exceeded his powers: the blow to the discipline of the native army was not the less deadly.

Annexation of Oudh

The minds of the Sipahis were under the influence of this blow, and by the insane action of the head-quarter staff they were becoming more and more released from the bands of displine towards their own officers, when the annexation of Oudh took place. How this affected them I shall as briefly as possible.

A very large proportion of the army of the Bengal Presidency, and a smaller proportion of the army of the Bombay Presidency, were recruited from the kingdom of Oudh. It is scarcely too much to affirm that there was not a single agricultural family in that country which was not represented by at least one of its members in the Indian army. Service in that army, in fact, offered no incosiderable advantages to the subjects of the king of Oudh. It made them clients, and favoured clients, of the paramount power. Every Sipahi was, so to speak, represented at the court of Lakhnao by the British Resident. His commanding officer was authorised to frank any petititon he might present addressed to the Resident, and the fact that the Resident had received such petition ensured substantial justice to the claims of the petitioner at the hands of the court of Lakhnao. Every one familiar with the workings of a native court will at once recognise the value at which service in the Indian army was rated by the natives of Oudh. By accepting such service they obtained an all-powerful advocate to plead their cause whenever thier property might be threatened, or their civil rights endangered.

The Nawabs and kings of Oudh had from the time of Warren Hastings shown a loyalty to the British Government not to be surpassed. During the Afghan disasters, the Gwalior campaign, the battles on the Satlaj and in the Panjab, Oudh had been the milch-cow of the paramount power. She had lent that power money, she had given her best sons as soldiers, she had done all that she could do to maintain unimpaired the relations between the prince independent only in his own country and the paramount overlord.

"But," exclaimed the advocates for annexation, "she has misgoverned." Misgovernment is a relative term. There can be no question but that in the English sense of the term there had been no good government in Oudh. But a kind of administrative system had, nevertheless, prevailed which induced the Sipahis, after the term of their service under the British flag had expired, to settle in their native country. More than that, after the native of Oudh had one year's exeprience of British government as administerd by Mr. Coverley Jackson and Mr. Martin Gubbins, they, one and all, evinced a strong preference for the native government which had been superseded.

It is necessary to take all these circumstances into consideration when one analyses the effect which the annexation of Oudh produced upon the Sipahis of the Bengal army. In my belief that annexation gave them the greatest shock they had felt since the occurrences, already adverted to, of 1843-4. It was the last and the most fatal blow to their belief in British honesty. That belief had been greatly shaken by the proceedings of Lord Dalhousie with respect to Karauli, the dominions of the Bhonsla, and Jhansi. The annexation of Oudh pressed them still more closely. It made them ready to become the tools of any adventurer.

It was not only that they beheld in that annexation a lowering of their own position as men represented at their sovereign's court by a British Resident, though that was a blow under which the Indian army yet reels, for it accounts for the difficulty of procuring recruits, which subsequently embarrassed the Government. They beheld in that act, and in the manner in which it was carried out, a deliberate infringement of promises they had ever looked upon as sacred - a repayment for the good services of nearly a century, such as even the most abandoned amongst their own princes would have hesitated to enforce.

There are not statements made at rendom. I was myself an eye-witness to the effect produced upon the Sipahis by the order to annex Oudh. It devolved upon me, as Commissariat Officer of the Kanpur division, to supply carriage and provisions for the force which, under Outram, crossed the Gangs into Oudh at the end of 1855. Over my house and office, which were in the same compound, was a Sipahi guard - a hawaldar's party. Contrary to custom and to departmental instructions, no written orders were given to me for the requisitons. The expedition was to be a secret, I was told, and I must obey verbal orders. But, in spite of this mystery, the destination of the force became known before it set out to every Sipahi in the cantonment - to every native in the town. The effect was alarming. The natives had no doubt whatever as to the real meaning of the demonstration. For the first time in the memory of man an English regiment was about to march on Lacknow, and an English regiment would march on Lakhnao with but one object. The agitation of the Sipahis of my guard was most marked. It was with the greastest difficulty that I was able to control them. Had they had any warning of the intended movement they would, I am confident, have broken out then and there. The subordinates of the Commissariat Department, themselves greatly moved, assured me that a similar feeling was manifesting itself in every regiment in the place. I made no secert of these manifestations. I reported them in the proper quarter. I communicated them even to one of the officials, a man of remarkable gifts, who had accepted a high post in Oudh, but my warnings found no more credence that did the warnings of Cassandra. They were remembered afterwards.

The annexation of Oudh, keeping in view the way in which it was carried out, was in very deed, the act which broke the trust of the Sipahis in their English masters. The perpetration of that deed prepared their minds to receive and to believe any matter, however absurd in itself, which might betoken English perfidy. How their minds were played upon I shall show presently. Meanwhile, it is necessary that I should indicate how it was that the landowners and agricultural classes of India become impressed with the "bad faith" of their rulers.

Princes, Chiefs, and Landowners of India lost faith in the British

The internal annexation policy inaugurted by Lord Dalhousie was, in many instances, based upon his refusal to recognise a right which the Hindus hold as an essential part of their religion- the right to adopt an heir on the failure of children lawfully begotten. In the early part of this volume I have spoken of the disaffection, the terror, the hatred of the English which this policy produced in the southern Maratha country. Carrying out this principle, Lord Dalhousie had annexed the territory of the Bhonslas; he had annexed the states of Jhansi, he had endeavoured to annex the state of Karauli, and had only been prevented by the interference of the Home Government on a threatend motion in the House of Commons. Still he continued to hold the principle in terrrorem over the heads of the princes and chiefs of India, and the fact that the policy of "grab all" was the policy, the paramount power, and might, on the occurrence of dath without natural hreirs, be applied to any coveted territory, produced, it is not too much to say, "a terror" in the minds of the Hindu princes throughout India,

But in another and a far more guiltless manner the Government had sown the seeds of hatred in the minds of the representatives of great families whose ancestors they had deprived of their dominions. Two instances of the action of this policy will occur at once to the reader - Nana Sahib and the Rao of Kirwi. Nana Sahib was indubitably the lawful representative, according to Hindu law, of the last of the Peshwas. When, in June, 1818, Baji Rao surrendered to Sir John Malcolm, the Court of Directors considered that an annuity of eighty thousand pounds was more than an adequate compensation for the loss of an empire. Baji Rao lived in the enjoyment of this pension nearly thirty-five years. When he died, in January 1853, Lord Dalhousie refused either to recognise his adopted son or to continue the pension.

According to European ideas this ruling was perfectly just. It strictly carried out the agreement as understood by Sir John Malcolm in 1818. But neither Baji Rao nor his retainers had so understood it. Such a settlement would have been so repugnant to the ideas and customs of the races of Hindustan, that they could not be expected to understand it. As the son of Baji Rao would have succeeded that prince as Peshwa had he remained Peshwa, so would he succeed naturally to all rights for which Baji Rao had exchanged the dignity of Peshwa. With them it was a point of honour to recognise in the son, whether begotten or adopted, the successor to the titles and estates of his father. Whether the English recognised him or not, Nana Sahib was still Peshwa in the eyes of every true Maratha. The refusal to recognise him and the stoppage of the pension forced the heir of the Peshwa to conspire. It can easily be conceived how readily such a man, occupying a fortified palace close to the Oudh frontier, would hail and encourage the discondered it, could not fail to produce.

The story of the Rao of Kirwi, whilst reflecting still more disadvantageously on the conduct of the British Government, is similar in character and in application.

We see, then, how many of the princes and the chiefs of India in possession, and all the chiefs not in possession, were predisposed to view with at least indifference any troubles which might assail their British over-lord. Incidents like that of the Rajah of Dilheri, of Kunwar Singh of Jugdispur, driven into revolt by the action of a revenue system which he did not understand, came at uncertain intervals to add to the general mistrust. Such incidents affected alike chieftain and retainer, noble and peasant, for, in almost every part of the country, the retainers considered their interests as bound up with those of the former.

Western Principle pushed to its logical extreme allienates an Eastern Race

It was when the minds of all were thus distrustful that the annexation of Oudh - of Oudh which had ever been faithful, always true and loyal-came to startle them still more. It is just within the bounds of possibilty that, if the system introduced by the English into Oudh had been administrated in a conciliatory manner, the result might have been similar to that which was produced in a few years in the central provinces. But the Englishmen to whom the administration of the new-annexed province was intrusted were men with fixed ideas, which they rode to death; the slaves of a system which had sown disaffection all over the North-Western provinces and in Bundelkhand, and which they carried out without regard to the feelings and previous habits of those with whose lands and property they were dealing. In less than twelve months the result was disaffection and dismay; the new settlement made every man in Oudh an enemy to British rule.

With Oudh thus disaffected, the chiefs and the territorial interest doubting and trembling, with the Sipahis alienated and mistrustful, there needed but one other element to produce insurrection. The country, the army, the newly-annexed province were alike ready for the machinations of conspirators.

Authors of the Mutiny

The conspirators, too, were ready. Who all those conspirators were may never certainly be known. Most of them died and made no sign. It is, however, a fact be-beyond question that the Maulavi of Faizabad- the man who was killed at Powain - was one of them. I have already given a sketch of the previous career of this remarkable man. I have shown how, after the annexation of Oudh, he travelled over the north-western provinces on a mission which was a mystery to the Europeans, how he was suspected even then of conspiring. Abundant proofs were subsequently obtained that a conspiracy had been formed by some influential people in Oudh in the interval between the annexation and the outbreak of the mutiny. Of this conspiracy the Maulavi was undoubtedly a leader. It had its ramifications all over India - certainly at Agra, where the Maulwavi stayed some time - and almost certainly at Delhi, at Mirath, at Patna, and at Calcutta where the ex-King of Oudh and a large following were residing.

For some time there was one thing wanting to the conspirators - the means, the instrument - with which to kindle to action the great body of their countrymen. Especially were they at a loss how to devise a scheme by which the minds of the Sipahis serving throughout the Bengal Presidency should ne simultaneously affected. They were in this perplexity when they heard of the new cartridge - a cartridge smeared with animal fat and which they were told was to be bitten.

It was easy for them to make this discovery. Their spies were everywhere. The cartridge were openly manufactured at Damdamah. Eagerly looking out for a novelty to be introduced from Europe into the native army, they were the most likely men of all to detect the instrument they required in the greased cartridge. They had no sooner found it than they realised that it corresponded exactly to their hopes. It was the weapon they wanted. Instantly the chapatis were distributed by thousands to the rural population, whilst means were employed to disseminate in every military station in Bengal suspicion regarding the cartridge.

To tell a body of Hindus, already suspicious of their foreign master, that they would be required to bite a cartridge smeared with the fat of their sacred animal, and to tell Muhammadans that they would be required to bite a cartridge smeared with the fat of an animal whose flesh was forbidden to them, was tantamount to tell them that their foreign master intended to make them break with their religion. Certainly that result was produced. When the new cartridges were issued, suspicion and calumny had done their work. The Sipahis even believed that cartridges made of paper had been feloniously tampered with; and, when they were issued to them, they broke into revolt.

In this lesser sense, then, and in this only, did the

cartridges produce the mutiny. They were the instruments used by conspirators; and those conspirators were succussful in their use of the instruments only because, in the manner I have endeavoured to point out, the minds of the Sipahis and of certain sections of the population had been prepared to believe every act testifying to bad faith on the part of their foreign masters.

I have said that the mistrust of the British faith had, towards the year 1857, become as great in the minds of the princes and chiefs and landowners of India as in the minds of the Sipahis. There were, however, a few exceptions and, when the country rose, those exceptions saved us. I will briefly refer to the most prominent amongst them.

Provinces which rose against us

In four great provinces of our empire - in Oudh, in Rohilkhand, in Bundelkhand, and in the Sagar and Narbada territory - the great bulk of the people rose against British rule. In western Bihar, using that geographical expression as inclusive of the districts subordinate to the Commissioner of Patna; in many districts of the Allahabad division, of the Agra division, and in many parts of the Mirath division, the risings of the people and the Sipahis were almost simultaneous in point of time. Had the revolt been universal, had the chiefs, the people, and the Sipahis risen at one and the same moment, India could not have been held. Fortunately for British interests, the great prince who occupied the most central position in India, and whose action, had he risen, would have been felt to the extermities of western India, was throughout the crisis, loyal to his suzerain. Throughout the period between the 12th of May and the 1st of September, 1857, Sindhia held the fate of India in his hands.

I have described very beriefly how it was that, in an

unexampled crisis in the fortunes of the people with whom his ancestors had contended for empire, Sindhia did remain loyal. I have shown that the loyalty did not proceed from affection towards the English. His minister and confidant, Dinkar Rao, had no love for our nation. Sindhia's people were, almost to a man, against us. Yet Dinkar Rao used all his great influence in favour of a loyal policy, and his representations, backed by the solid arguments of the able representative of the Bristish power at the court of Sindhia, Major Charters Macpherson, prevailed over national sentiment, the solicitations of other courtiers, and the boisterous demonstrations of the people. The importance of the result of English interests cannot be over-estimated. Sindhia's loyalty alone made possible Havelock's march on, and the retention of Kanpur. It acted at the same time on the rebels like a wedge which pierces the centre of an army, dividing the wings, and preventing concentrated action. Nor, when, after the back of the rebellion had been broken, Sindhia's army revolted against himself, was the effect much lessened. Sindhia's great influence was still used for the English.

In considering Sindhia's loyalty in connnection with the risings of others - of all, or almost all, the rajahs and talukadars, of Oudh, of the cheifs in Bundelkhand, in the Sagar and Narbada territory, in the Southern Maratha country, and in western Bihar - it is impossible to shut our eyes to the fact that there had been a marked difference in the behaviour of the British Government towards Sindhia on the one side, and towards the rajahs and landowners of the countries mentioned on the other. Under circumstances of a peculiarly tempting character, Lord Ellenborough had behaved with the greatest generosity and forbearance towards Sindhia in 1844. The Government had kept faith with him ever since. The reader of this volume will see that towards the rajahs and landowners of the other provinces mentioned the British Government had shown neither generosity nor forbearance. In some instances they had not even kept faith. It is scarcely necessary to point the moral.

It is, indeed, a very remarkable fact, and one which the rulers of India at the present moment would do well to bear in mind, that in the several provices and districts traversed by our troops in 1857-8-9, the behaviour of the people corresponded to the character of our rule. Thus, in the central provinces, to which the regulation system had never penetrated, the people were loyal and contented, and refused all aid to Tantia Topi. In the Sagar and Narbada territories, in Oudh and in the districts bordering on that province, in the Agra division - in all of which the Bristish hand had been heavy, and the British acts opposed to the national sentiment - the people showed a spirit of opposition, a resolution to fight to the last, and in many cases a detestation of their masters, such as no one would before have credited. Cases similar to that of the Rajah of Dilheri, referred to in the earlier part of this volume, had sown far and wide the seed of disaffection and revolt.

Mutiny the result of a rude attempt

If these facts are, as I believe them to be, correct, we have not to go far to seek the conclusion. The mutiny of the army and the insurrection in the provinces I have named were the nutural consequences of an attempt to govern a great Eastern empire according to purely Western ideas.

The civilisation, over-refined though it might be, of thousands of years was ridiculed by the rougher race which scorning sentiment, regarded utilitarianism as its foundation - stone. The governing members of that race failed to recognise the great truth upon which their forefathers had built their

Indian empire, that the Western race can gain the confidence of the Eastern only when it scrupulously respects the long-cherished customs of the latter, and impresses upon it the conviction that its word is better than its bond. This is just the conviction which, during thirty years immediately actecedent to 1856, the majority of the Hindus and Muhammadans of India had been gradually losing, and which in 1857 they had lost.

If Lord Canning had any idea in the early part of 1857 that the isolated out breaks which then disturbed the general serenity were part of an organised plot, he would, I believe, have at once taken measures to meet the diffculty. Not that at any time in 1857, he could have prevented a mutiny, but he could easily have made better arrangements to meet one. I am far, however from imputing any blame to lord Canning in this respect. He had but recently arrived in India. His predecessor, when making over to him charge of the empire, had exspressed his conviction that never had the country been in so satisfactory a condition. All the time ground was undermined, the train was being laid, the miners were at work. But how was lord Canning to know this? He inherited Lord Dalhousie's councillors. They were as satisfied, and as ignorant of the real state of the country, as was Lord Dalhousie. Lord Dalhousie had quitted India in a blaze of glory; and the new Governor-General, unsed to the currents of Indian thought, could for some months only steer the vessel by the advice of the officers who had helped to bring to Lord Dalhousie a renown far-reaching and seemingly well deserved.

Lord Canning

But, in fact, upon no men did the news of the mutiny descend with so starteling a suprise as upon the concillors of Lord Canning. They could not comprehend it. Weeks and weeks elapsed before they could bring themselves to believe that it was anything more than a fortuitous explosion at various points, each having no concert and no connection with the other. The Home Secretary's assurances that the apprehensions expressed regarding its nature were "a passing and groundless panic," that "there is every hope that in a few days tranquillity will be restored throughout the presidency," testify to the ideas that filled the minds of these men. The admission at least is due to them that they were honest - they believed what they said. But those saying betrayed a complete ignorance, of the country and of the situation. This ignorance this blindness to the fact that it was more even than a mutiny of the Bengal army, and not merely a series of isolated revolts, with which they had to cope, was illustrated in a thousand ways, but in none more strongly than in the refusal to disarm regiments which were known to be mutinous. The consequences of this refusal were most serious. In the case of the regiments at Danapur, the reader will have seen that it brought revolt into western Bihar, added enormously to the dangers of Havelock and even imperilled Calcutta.

How great Lord Canning really was, how small were his councillors, was shown when, having completely shaken off their influence, he stood alone and unshakled at Allahabad in the early part of 1858. A different man was he then from the Lord Canning of April and May 1857. His nature then displayed its real nobility. His grasp of affairs, at Calcutta apparently so small, excited at Allahabad the admiration of all who came in contact with him. He showed a turner insight into the military position than the Commander-in-Cheif himself. It was entirely owing to Lord Canning's insistance that campaign in Rohilkhand followed close upon the capture of Lakhnao. Sir Colin Campbell would have postponed it. But Lord Canning was too convinced of the danger of allowing a province to continue to flaunt rebellion, unchecked, in the face of the Government, to permit the delay. He insisted with all the determination of a man whose resolution, based on the logic of facts, was not to be shaken. It was Lord Canning at Allahabad who sent Lord Mark Kerr to Azamgarh; who gave his fullest support to Sir Hugh Rose, and to the generals engaged against Tantia Topi; and if, in one respect, to which I have adverted, his judgment was faulty, his companion in error was the Commander-in-Chief, and the error was solitary one.

Nor is lesser praise due to him for the measures inaugurated at Allahabad to heal the wounds caused – he must then have seen — in a great measure by the mistakes of his predecessor. His Oudh proclamation, despite of the apparently harsh terms which it promulgated, was intended as a message of mercy, and, in its application, was a massage of mercy. It gave every landowner in Oudh a title better, safer, more valid, than the title he had lost. It insured mercy to all except to those who by their crimes had forfeited all right to it. Interpreted, as Lord Canning meant it to be interpreted, by one of the ablest administrators in India it became the charter upon which the position now occupaied by the people of Oudh has been built up and secured.

Never was the real greatness of Lord Canning's character more completely displayed than when the galling strictures of Lord Ellenborough's despatch were published to the world. At the moment the insult, the breach of etiquette, were lost sight of in the fear lest the condemnation of his policy proceeding from so high a quarter should afford encouragement to the rebels or weaken the attachment of native tributaries. As soon as he ascertained that the despatch had not produced that result he was calm. He could not help seeing that it was designedly impetinent, that it was intended to provoke him to resign. Conscious of the rectitude of his motives and of the soundness of his views, he laughed at the pettiness of the display. In his calm and statesman-like answer he sought neighter revenge nor triumph. But both soon came to him. The news the Lord Ellenborough had been hoisted with his own petard, the receipt of Lord Derby's almost imploring letter not to resign, followed the insulting missive with a rapidity almost startling

Towards the men who served under him, Lord Canning displayed generosity, kindness, and forbearance. He knew that in many departments he had been badly served, yet he would rather bear the burden himself than dismiss the incapable minister. But so low did he rate the abilities of men about him, that when he had resolved to appoint Mr. Edmonstone, till then his Foreign Secretary, to be Lieutenant-Governor of the North - West Provinces, he cast his eyes far from the men surrounding him to select a successor to that official. He had actully resolved to offer the post to Herbert Edwardes when the publication by that officer of a letter, violently polemical, caused him to reconsider his resolve. For the moment he was cast back upon the clique about him, but finally he made an admirable choice in Colonel Durand.

Judging Lord Canning's conduct after his arrival at Allahabad, it is difficult to find a fault in it. He was then the lofty-minded English gentleman, the trained and skilful statesman. Every day made it more clear that the mistakes of the Calcutta period, mistakes which have been fully recorded in these volumes were due to the inexperience of generous nature guided by men whom he had been told to look upon as masters of the situations, but who were in fact hopelessly ignorant and incaplable. That Lord Canning came to know this himself was evidenced by the generosity he displayed, after the munity had been quelled, the those who had ventured to express very boldly their disagreement with his policy of 1857.

Lord Elphinstone

But, if Lord Canning was to be admired from the time of his arrival at Allahabad, Lord Elphinstone deserves the fullest meed of praise that can be accorded to him from the very first. Lord Elephinstone possessed this advantage over Lord Canning – his previous experience in India had given him a thorough knowledge of the country and the people. When the mutiny broke out at Mirath he saw it as it really was; he saw that it was no isolated outbreak, no local discontent, but part and parcel of an organised rebellion which had its main roots, intleed, in the North West Provinces, but the dovelopment of which especially in the direction of Bombay, was certain, unless it could be promptly stopped. The Bombay Presidency, in fact, with an army partly recruted from Oudh, and composed mainly of conglomeration of Maratha states, was in a peculiar degree susceptible. Lord Elphinstone understood the situation at once. He dealt with it in a manner possible only to a statesman of high and lofty courage, of clear intellect, and of far-seeing views. The idea of waiting for the mutiny within his own borders, if, indeed, it ever occured to him, came only to be promptly rejected. To mass the greatest number of men on the decisive point of the scene of action – that Napoleonic motto became at once his guiding principle. For that purpose he denuded his own Presidency, highly sensitive as it was, of European troops, and despatched them, as fast as he could force them to move, to the threatened points outside of it. He, too, like Lord Canning, had colleagues in his government, but here again his previous experience saved him from the mistakes which marred Lord Canning's administration during the first seven months of the mutiny. Knowing his counsellors thoroughly, he listened to them with courtesy—but he acted on his own convictions. To the men who were the instruments of his policy he gave the most complete and generous confidence. How large was his trust when he once gave it Mr. Frere in Sindh, Mr. Forjett is a living evidence. Mr. Seton-Karr and afterwards Colonel Le G. Jacob in the southern Maratha country, Mr. John Rose in Satarah, and Colonel Malcolm, are instance of a similar import. When, in spite of all his measures to keep the mutiny from Bombay by a policy of offensive defence, the poison crept in and infected the regiments of the regular army in the southern Maratha country, how vigorous, how decided is his policy! We see here none of the hesitation, of the half-heartedness, the halting between two extremes, which enabled the mutinous regiments of Danapur to disturb all the plans of the Governments and to imperil the safety of the empire. Promptly, without an hour's delay, Lord Elphinstone sent for the fittest man at his disposal and told him to go to Kolhapur and at all costs quell the mutiny. Le Grand Jacob went and disarmed the rebellious. How Lord Elephinstone was occasionally thwarted by the man not immediately under his orders has been shown in the case of Woodburn. But his firmness was proof even against opposition of this description, and, after some vexatious delay, he carried out his policy.

Only those who have enjoyed the privilege of reading his voluminous correspondence during 1857-58 can form an idea of the remarkable perspicity which characterised Lord Elphinstones's views on every point connected with the stirring events of those years. The strong and the weak points of a case, the true policy to be pursued, the proper time for putting it in action, when to withhold the blow, when to strike, the reasons for withholding or for striking, are laid down in clear and vigorous language in his letters. Reading them after the events, it seems marvellous how a man standing alone should have judged so clearly, so truly. Many of the military movements which tended to the pacification of the country had their first inspiration from Lord Elphinstone, and the smallest of the tardy tributes that can be paid him is this—that no man in India contributed so much as he contributed to check the mutiny at its outset; no man contributed more to dominate it after it had risen to greatest height.

In the glory of the victory, amid the bestowal of well merited rewards for military services, the great deserts of Lord Elphinstone received but small notice from the public. But it is a remarkable fact that after the death of Sir Henry Lawrence he was nominated by three successive Secretaries of State—by Mr. Vernon Smith, by Lord Ellenborough, and by Lord Stanley — to be sucessor to Lord Canning in the event of a vacancy occurring in the office of Governor-General. It now becomes the duty of the historian to place him on the lofty pedestal to which his great service and his pure and noble character entitle him.

The southern Presidency was never invaded by the mutioous spirit. But not the less is a large share of credit due to its governer, Lord Harris. The responsibility which weighed upon this nobleman was very great indeed. The immunity of Madras depended upon the loyalty of the Nizam, and, at the outset, the Nizam had much to apprehend from his own people. It was in the height of the crisis that Lord Harris denuded his own Presidency to send troops to Hydrabad and it cannot be doubted but that their opportune arrival tended greatly to the pacification of the Nizam's dominions. The formation of the Kamthi column, of whitlock's force, of the brigade which fought under Carthew at Kanpur, the despatch to Bengal of the regiments which kept open the grand trunk road in western Bihar and which afterwards co-operated against Kunwar Singh, of the troops who rendered good service in Chutia Nagpur, testify to the energy, the foresight, the devotion of the Governor of Madras. He used all the resources of his Presidency to crush outside the rebellion which never penetrated within his own borders.

Deserts of Englishmen in the crisis of 1857-8-9

Of other actors in the rise, progress, and suppression of the rebellion I have written in the body of this history, not always, perhaps, in as full detail as their splendid services demanded, but, I would fain hope, in full proportion to the scope and requirements of the work instrusted to me. It may be that some incidents have escaped me. I shall regret it much should such prove to be so, for my chief anxiety has been to render full justice to every man. This at least, I may say, that however ineffectively the History of the suppressions of the Indian Mutiny may have been told, the character of our countrymen must be seen to emerge from the terrible ordeal of 1857-58 in a form that would gratify the most exacting people. We are, fortunately, as a nation, accustomed to success in the field, but on no occasion in our history has the nerve and fibre of our troops, the fortitude and manliness of our countrymen of all ranks, been more conspicuous—often in the face of death itself, and under circumstances which would have seemed to justify despair. But with life they never dispaired. They endured all that had to be endured, with a patience and cheerfulness never to be surpassed, and sought victory when it was possible with a determination before which the strongest opposition had to yield. And in all this they were sustained and animated by our country women, who, in positions and under trials to which few gently - nurtured women have been subjected, showed all the noblest and most lovable aspects of woman's character.

The History of the Indian Mutiny is, in fact, a record of the display of all the qualities for which Englishmen have been famous of the qualities which have enabled the inhabitants of a small island in the Atlantic to accumulate the noblest and largest empire in the world, and which, so long as they remain unimpaired in their descendants, will enable them still to maintain it.

12

Varieties of Rebellion

Most of the writers represented in this volume would have claimed to have examined their sources objectively and then, without bias in their selection of facts, to have stated their interpretation of these facts warranted. All of them, therefore, could be said to have presented a summary of the evidence. Yet it is obvious that many of the writers sought to make a case, even though they were doubtlessly persuaded of the genuineness of their argument. There are, however, a number of writers who have made a particular effort to examine the conflicting theories and to sum up existing knowledge. Four such accounts are given in this section. The first is by Haraprasad Chattopadhyaya, Professor of History of Asutosh College, Calcutta University. The selection given here is from two different works. In the first part he examines one of the most lively facets of the controversy about the nature of the war: the role of Hindus and Muslims as religious communities. In the second part he argues that no consistent pattern or unity emerges, but that rather one sees a variety of rebellions.

(I)

The socio-religious policy of the Government of India during the year preceding the Mutiny and the introduction of greased cartridges towards the close of 1856 reacted adversely on both the Hindus and Muslims of the country. When, through the initiative of the sepoys, the Mutiny broke out in 1857, both the Hindus and Muslims joined it in protest against the attitude of Government towards their religious feelings and social prejudices. It is not, however, a fact that all the Hindus and Muslims of the country rose in revolt. As the Mutiny progressed, Government found its supporters among both the communities of the Indian society. Sometimes in the course of the Mutiny they renewed their old feuds and fell foul of each other. But such Hindu-Muslim feuds were sporadic and were confined to certain districts of the then North-western provinces only, Those Hindus and Muslims, who arrayed themselves against Government stood, on the whole, united in common opposition to Government during the Mutiny.

The Mutiny thrived on the disaffection of both the Hindus and Muslims. Both of them had grievances against the British Government before the outbreak of 1857. So far as the Muslims were concerned, they could not forget that not long ago the political destiny of India was in their hands. They still sighed for their lost Empire and longed for its restoration on the ruins of the British power in India. The Muslims of those areas, where Muslim fanaticism ran high, swelled the ranks of the mutineers with political motives. Consequently they came into hostility with the British Government so much so that they had to suffer much at the hands of the British Government for some years after the sky of India was cleared of the cloud of the Mutiny. In fact, the failure of the revolt was much more disastrous to the Muslims than to the Hindus. The spread of higher education through the medium of English, though much appreciated by the Hindus, did not find favour with the Muslims who had pre-judices against learning English. The "mollas" used to forbid it on religious grounds. Status in society then depended much on the knowledge of English. But the aversion of the Muslims to it closed to them every avenue of prosperity in public life and arrested the growth of the Muslim middle-class in the pre-Mutiny days. The eagerness of the Hindus for imbibing western culture, on the other hand, raised their social prestige and decidedly gave them a primacy over the followers of Islam in India. Most of the appointments in the executive and judicial departments of Government were then meant not for the Muslims but for the Hindus, as the latter adapted themselves to the western culture, and the former were loud and strident in their opposition to it. Though the Muslims were thus themselves responsible for being debarred from Government service and for having to face a grave economic hardship consequently, still they entertained ill feeling against Government for their hard economic lot and low status before the Mutiny. The annexation of Oudh in 1856 also wounded their feelings and left them meditating a revenge on the British Government on the eve of the Mutiny....

In spite of the grievances of the Muslims of India against the British Government the Mutiny did not find favour with the entire Muslim community. Muslims from several parts of the country were reported to have openly sympathised with Government during the Mutiny. The Muhammadans of Calcutta reposed their entire faith in the policy of the British Government and pledged themselves to support Government during the crisis of 1857-59. On May 27, 1857, the members of the Muhammadan Association of Calcutta held a special meeting...and passed resolutions, expressing their loyalty to Government and promising their entire aid and support to the suppression of the Mutiny. Some of the resolutions, which were passed by them, are cited below :

> The meeting having heard of the havoc and devastation, lately committed in some towns of the North-western provinces, and of the sacrifice of life and property, caused by the disaffection and Mutiny of a small portion of the native' soldiery of the British Government, do hereby express their sincere regret and heartfelt sorrow at these lamen-table and dissastrous proceedings.
>
> The Committee learn...that the cause of the present Mutiny may be traced to an unfounded report, maliciously spread by ill-disposed men, of a contemplated interference on the part of the Government with the religious rites, ceremonies and persuasions of the natives of this country...

In Southern Bibar the Muhammadans were reputed to be the foremost in acts of devotion to Government. The attitude of the Nizam of Hyderabad towards Government was friendly. While the so-called Bengal Army was carrying fire and sword from one, station to another, Hyderabad was in a ferment. Still Hyderabad remained immune from mutinous outbreaks, thanks mainly to the endeavours of the faithful Nizam, Afzul-oo-Dowlah and of his faithful minister, Salar Jung. Wherever in Hyderabad disturbances were apprehended, the Nizam and his minister took prompt action to nip them in the bud. Both of them received thanks from Government in recognition of the services, rendered by them during the disturbances of 1857-58. If the Nizam turned against Government, Southern India would have been in a blaze of insurrection, Again, when the regiments at Chittagong and Dacca mutinied, the Muhammadans of Eastern Bengal treated the mutinous sepoys with much hostility and hunted them out with much pluck.

Surely then, the entire Muhammadan civil population did not rise in revolt in 1857. The Mutiny, in other words, did not thrive on the support of the entire Muslim civil community.

Though a fanatic section of the Muslims of Delhi joined the mutineers, the majority of the Muslim population of the district appeared to have kept aloof from the Mutiny. During the siege of Delhi in May, 1857, the mutineers wanted to have King Bahadur Shah II as their leader. But the titular Padshah was then too old to assume the leadership of the mutineers. The court, that was formed at Delhi under the presidentship of Lieutenant Colonel M. Dawes for the trial of Bahadur Shah, found him guilty not only of open sympathy with the mutineers but also of fomenting sedition by assuming active leadership of the mutineers. But the statement made by the King in the Court in self-defence indicates that he was a prisoner in the hands of the mutineers and that he had no genuine sympathy with them. If he supplied his leadership to the mutineers, he did it most reluctantly.

So, then, the Mutiny should not be ascribed solely to the disaffection of the Muslim community. The entire Muhammadan civil population did not rebel, though many from the Muslim civil society joined the movement; the Muslim mutinous sepoys were numerically inferior to non-Muslim mutinous sepoys; and the Mutiny did not start in the Muslim-dominated areas of the country, as the foregoing paragraphs would show. In the circumstances the Mutiny should not be treated as an exclusively Muhammadan rising on an all-India basis. The Muslim character of the revolt was prominent only in certain parts of the country. In some districts of the North-western provinces, for instance, the Mutiny assumed a Muslim colour. In such districts the hostility of the Muslims towards Government during the Mutiny was quite conspicuous. In Patna also the Muslims stood opposed to Government....

The reaction of the Mutiny on the Hindus may now be studied here. The Hindus also, like the Muslims, had grievances, many and varied, against the Government. The attempt at westernising the Indian society caused much irritation and discontent among the caste-conscious Hindus of the country. The Brahmins and other upper class Hindus stood seething with thousand and one complaints against the governmental encroachment on their sacred domains of caste and prejudices. The spread of English education, systematic policy of Christianising the native population, legal protection, afforded to widows and converts produced a serious Brahmanic reaction in the country. Government was alleged to have violated the sanctity of caste by bringing the highest and the-lewcst castes together in schools, in the ranks of the Army and in the railways carriages. The sati system was abolished and withji was abolished a source of income of the priestly class. The remarriage of widows was encouraged; the use of common utensils in goals was insisted on. All such steps proved revolting to the caste-ridden and superstitious Hindu population of the country.

The British Government was looked upon by the Brahmins as a menace to Hinduism, as they believed in the current prophecies that Brahmanism would be abolished and that a new doctrine namely Christianity would come to prevail. Such prophecies about the end of Brahmanical religion excited among the Hindus the apprehension of a mighty change in religious systems. Among the Brahmins of the pre-Mutiny period there was superstitious belief that in the existing "kali yuga" all distinctions of caste would be obliterated, and that all men should be of one faith, forsaking the idolatry and worshipping one Supreme Being. Such a superstitious belief caste a gloom on the Hindu society and caused much uneasiness in it. When, however, the Mutiny broke out, it did not find favour with the entire Hindu community. The Hindu inhabitants of the Bhowanipur area in Calcutta remained loyal of Government. On May 23, 1857 a meeting was held by them at the premises of Guru Charan De of the Chakraberia locality of Bhowanipur to consider the best means of maintaining peace in the Bhowanipur area. A committee was formed...and the following propositions were carried out:

> The Committee being apprehensive of the most deplorable state of things, created by the disaffected sepoys in some parts of the country consider it as a duty of every loyal subject of Her Majesty's empire to be true to her Government.
>
> As false apprehensions and unfounded tales regarding the exaggerated affairs of Mutiny have prevailed in and about the town through the maliciously disposed persons, the committee feels it as a necessity to remove them from the minds of peaceful subjects.
>
> The committee after mature deliberation comes to the conclusion that some of the members,...will by every means in their power impress upon the minds of the timid and

> credulous people the idea of the mightiness of the power of the British Government to repel the aggressions of any foreign enemy, however powerful and indomitable, or to put down any internal disturbance of order.
>
> The committee determine that these noble feelings of loyalty and attachment to the beneficial British rule that had actuated them to meet (here) be most respectfully communicated to the Governor-General in Council.

The inhabitants of the town and district of Barasat in Bengal submitted to the Governor-General in Council an address, in which they recorded their high appreciation of the tolerant attitude of Government towards the people of the country of India, and conveyed their assurance that they would be unsparing in their efforts to maintain order and discipline amongst themselves during the Mutiny....

The entire Hindu community thus refrained from rising in arms in 1857. There is, however, no gainsaying the fact that a large portion of the Hindu society then stood in opposition to Government. The Mutiny, in fact, fattened on the hostility of both the Hindus and Muslims of the country. Though both of them participated in the Mutiny, it was neither the fruit of the conspiracy of the Hindus only nor the result of the hostility of the Muslims exclusively. The Mutiny was a joint movement of both the Hindus and Muslims of the country.

II

The nature of the Sepoy Mutiny may now be briefly reviewed thus: In the North-Western provinces,

Bundelkhand, Saugor and Narbada had a popular basis. In the rest of the country including the South, the Punjab, Rajputana, Sind, Hyderabad, Bengal, East Bihar, Orissa and Assam, though there were risings of the native soldiery here and there, the civil population remained, on they whole, quiet and peaceful. The Mutiny, in other words, was not a popular movement on an all-India basis. It was popular only region-wise, that is, on a zonal basis. In the regions or zones which witnessed popular risings, the civil population rose in arms? against Government not, however, with the political motive of liberating India from the British yoke. In fact, the Mutiny was not a rising of the people for achieving their political freedom. Neither the revolted sepoys nor the rebels from the civil society had the common and positive ideal of realising their political self determination. The motives with which they were actuated to rise in revolt during the Mutiny were selfish in nature. The Hindus joined the Mutiny in protest against the interference by the Government with their caste and religion. The Muslims also raised the cry of religion being in danger. The dispossessed Muslim ruling class at the same time sought to avail itself of the opportunity to reestablish Muslim sovereignty in India. The dispossessed zamindars and talukdars joined the Mutiny to reverse the agrarian decisions of the civil courts and to recover their lands from the auction-purchasers. The villagers, city-rabble and run-away convicts and even many of the sepoys hailed the Mutiny as the most suitable opportunity to plunder treasuries, burn Government buildings and destroy state-records. The sepoys rose in arms to preserve the sanctity of their ancestral caste and religion which were in the danger of being defiled by the introduction of the Enfield life equipped with greased cartridges. Beyond the above-mentioned motives the participants in the Mutiny had no such common political, aim in view as India's emancipation from British authority.

There were leaders, it is true, at the head of the rebels in different Mutiny stricken parts of the country but the leaders themselves could not work in harmony with one another in the course of the Mutiny. Neither could they set up an organisation like the Indian National Congress of the later days. An Administrative Court was, of course, set up in Delhi after its capture by the rebels. But this Court was not formed on an all-India basis. Its sessions were held in the Red Fort, Like the members of the Frankfurt Parliament, the members of the Administrative Court had no practical political training and could not, therefore, evolve any policy or programme from the point of view of practical statesmanship. The Court had no achievement to its credit.

Again, the leaders had their activities, if not exclusively, at least largely, confined to their respective areas with the result that the movement failed to have an all-India basis. Kumar Singh, Lakshmi Bai, the Nana Saheb, Maulavi Ahmad Shah and Tantia Tope who are generally honoured as the foremost among the leaders of the Mutiny could not enlist the co-operation of other local leaders like Khan Bahadur Khan, Muhammad Khan and Maulavi Liaqat Ali to work towards a common end. Such leaders as Khan Bahadur Khan, Muhammad Khan and Maulavi Liaqat Ali often sank into local factions and in some cases pursued anti-Hindu policies, which spelled disaster for the course of the Mutiny. Khan Bahadur Khan, the ruined Nawab of Rohilkhand, entered into a rivalry with another such Nawab of Rohilkhand, Mobarik Shah, both of whom hoped to obtain supremacy on the expulsion of the British....Such a leadership could not command the confidence of the nation at large. Maulavi Liaqat Ali ended his leadership merely by proclaiming himself Governor of Allahabad. Evidently such local leaders were mostly self-centred and only thought of their own immediate gains. They identified themselves with their regional or local interests. They were not inspired by pan-Indianism. Even Rani Lakshmi Bai, Kumar Singh and the Nana Saheb rose in arms out of local and personal grievances against Government.

It is idle, indeed, to plead that the Mutiny was a freedom movement. It may be argued that since the dispossessed Muslim ruling class sought to avail itself of the Sepoy Revolt to overthrow the British Empire in India and to restore in its place the former Mughal Empire with Bahadur Shah at its head, the Revolt should merit to rank as a War of Independence. The argument might have, carried sense, if, in the first place, Bahadur Shah had really been in sympathy with the rebels and could be looked upon by all the communities of the country as their rightful representative, and secondly, if the Muslim Government could be treated as the Government of the entire Indian people. But the above assumptions have little to support them. Bahadur Shah had not evinced any genuine sympathy for the rebels. He was never sincerely interested in the cause of the rebels. He played a double game in the course of the Mutiny. Again, to the Muslims, Bahadur Shah, who had kinship with the Great Mughals, might have appeared as the representative of the entire country, but in the eyes of the Hindus and Sikhs he was a leader of the Muslim community only. Both the Hindus and the Sikhs were opposed to the revival of the Muslim Empire in India. It will, therefore, be anything but just the maintain that the attempt of the dispossessed Muslim ruling class to restore the Mughal Empire during the Mutiny lends it the character of a war of Independence.

There is yet another aspect of the Indian Mutiny. Behind the outbreak of the Mutiny in different regions of India the same set of causes had not been equally prominent everywhere. In some regions, the Mutiny broke out for the predominance of certain, factors, while in others, it broke out because of the preponderance of other factors. In other words, regional factors predominated over any general or any single common factor in bringing about the Mutiny of 1857. In the North-Western provinces, for instance, the predominant causes of the Mutiny were the resumption of rent-free tenures, auction-sale of estates as a penalty for default under the newly introduced land-revenue system, the play of passions and prejudices of the native people and their apprehension regarding the loss of caste and religion. Again, the fact that North-Western provinces were an important centre of recruitment of the sepoys of the mutinous Bengal Army supplied another predominant cause of the Mutiny in that region. One or other of these predominant causes played its role effectively in hastening the outbreak of the Mutiny in one district or another, in one group of districts or, another group in the North-Western provinces. In such districts as Meerut, Allahabad and others, the play of passions and prejudices of the native people and their apprehension regarding the loss of caste and religion mainly caused the Mutiny. In the Revolt in such districts as Budaun, Saharanpur, and Muzaffarnagar, the resentment for the land-revenue policy of Government found a prominent expression. In Moradabad, Bareilly, Budaun, Bijnor and Shahjahanpur, the hostility of the Muslim community towards Government was conspicuous during the Mutiny. In Delhi also a fanatic section of the Muslims stood aggressive during the Mutiny. In the Saugor and Narbada territories, the apprehension regarding the loss of caste and religion and the application of the Thomasonian principles to the land-revenue settlement were the predominant causes of the Mutiny. In Jhansi, the fact of annexation and the alarm, produced by the rumour that Government was seeking to invade the sacred domains of the native caste and religion, made the civil and military classes rebellious. The Rani was also ultimately forced by circumstances to throw herself into the thick of the struggle with Government to fight out her own cause. After a display of unique heroism she embraced death on the battle-field. Again, the revolt in Oudh was due to such principal causes as its annexation by Lord Dalhousie, introduction of a revenue-system, which abolished the rank of talukdars, and the disbandment of the native Army of the deposed Nuvvab. Again, Oudh was the nursery of the Bengal Army. The revolt of the Bengal Army naturally also paved the way for the outbreak of revolt in Oudh...

To conclude, the Sepoy Mutiny, as the foregoing analysis shows, did not find favour with the entire civil population of the country. The entire native Army had not revolted and the majority of the landed and territorial aristocrats of the country were then favourably disposed towards the British Government. The so-called leaders of the Mutiny could set up no such central organisation with a clear-cut, commonly accepted and positive political programme as the Indian National Congress of the later days. How can, then, the Sepoy Mutiny be treated as a national or freedom movement. It was, no doubt, a popular movement on a regional basis. But a popular movement is not necessarily a national or freedom movement. People of a country may support a movement on grounds other than political. Such a movement *sans* political basis is not national, though it is popular in character, A freedom movement has a positive political ideal to attain, the ideal of building up a free and sovereign state. The movement of 1857 had no such political ideal before it. The leaders of a freedom movement instill into the minds of the people they lead decisive political doctrines, equip them with phrases, formulas and augments and give their mind a revolutionary tone and cast. They destroy the prevailing regime but have at the same time a constructive programme to follow after the independence is achieved. They establish a centralised state to which common allegiance of the people is demanded, provide them with an organisation of revolutionary activities. The leaders also seek to arouse the people to their national consciousness, to the sense of their ethnological, flinguistic and cultural unity in the course of the freedom movement. The leaders of the Sepoy Mutiny had no such political part to play, no such political missions to fulfil. There was then no Jefferson or Mazzini to inspire the Indian people with the ideal of fighting for freeing their country from the British control, to stamp them with oneness of political feeling and to make them conscious of their unity in the midst of diversity. They could establish no such central organisation as could claim common allegiance of the people of the country. Their motives, above all were selfish and their interests, local. The people also were actuated, in their opposition to the established authorities, by their selfish and particular motives. The Sepoy Mutiny thus lacks the characteristics of a freedom movement. The end of the Mutiny did not see India freed from the British yoke. Rather it saw the completion of the work initiated by the battles of Plassey and Buxur.

Dr. Harprasad Chattopadhyaya

13

A Military Revolt

In contrast to those observers who, like Alexander Duff, saw the uprisings in the summer of 1857 as evidence of a great conspiracy, or like Disraeli, saw it as an expression of alarm occasioned among the people by unnecessary reform, there were many who insisted that it was fundamentally an army mutiny. Among those who held this view, few had better sources of information than Sir John Lawrence (1811-1879). He had been appointed assistant-magistrate of Delhi in 1830, then, after holding various other important posts, had become one of three members of the Board that administered the Panjab after its conquest from the Sikhs. In 1857 he was Chief Commissioner and was largely responsible for the consideration and planning that led to the recapture of Delhi. After a few years in England he returned to India as Governor-General (1863-69).

Lawrence was convinced that the real explanation of the war was the inefficiency and lack of discipline in the

Bengal Army, and that this could be traced to a considerable degree to the system used for recruiting officers. He also advocated having a larger number of British troops than had been the case before 1857. Reliance on Indian troops for the maintenance of British control was, he believed, a dangerous practice likely to lead to further outbreaks. He expanded on these ideas, while he was actively engaged in the fighting, in a series of letters to Sir Charles Trevelyan, a former member of the Company's Civil Service.

Dec. 16, 1857

My Dear Trevelyan, Many thanks for your letter of October 20 and kind congratulations. We have just been passing through a frightful ordeal. It is by God's mercy alone that an English person is alive on this side of India. I recognised your old signature (in The "Times") at once. I don't think I saw all your letters, but I did see most of them, and liked all I saw, though I do not think that Delhi would answer for our metropolis, in consequence of its insalubrity. I am glad you do not advocate its destruction. It is a position of great importance, and should be held by us.... We have been almost as much to blame for what has occurred as have the people.

I have as yet neither seen nor heard anything to make me believe that any conspiracy existed beyond the army; and even in it, one can scarcely say there was a conspiracy. The cartridge question was to my mind, indubitably, the immediate cause of the revolt. But the army had for a long time been in an unsatisfactory state, It had long seen and felt its power. We had gone on, year by year, adding to its numbers; without adding to our European force. Our contingents, which, under better arrangements, might, like the Punjab troops, have acted as a counterpoise, were really a part of the army. All the men were "Poorbeas" i.e. from

Eastern India. The Bengal army was one great brotherhood, in which all the members felt and acted in union.

Our treasuries, arsenals, forts were all garrisoned by them. As one letter I intercepted said, it was a *saf imydan* (a clear level) from Delhi to Calcutta, and as a Hindustani observed to a Sikh friend of mine, the proportion of European soldiers to Hindustanis was about equal to the salt a man consumed in his Chupatti. The Mohammedans took advantage of the revolt to convert it into a religious and political affair. The missionaries and indeed religion, really speaking, had nothing to do with the mutter. It was an all affair of caste, of personal impurity. Both Hindu and Mohammedan believed that we meant by a bit of legerdemain to make them all Christians. Religion, as you know, with them, consists in matters of ceremony. Provided missionaries talked to them without acrimony, I believe they would never have objected to their talking for ever on religion. This, however, only applies to the body of the people, including the soldiers. Of course there are many fanatics. A sense of power, then, defective discipline, and want of sufficient employment ruined the Bengal army. Reform was impracticable, for the officers would not admit that any was necessary, and nobody not in the army was supposed to know anything about it.

I think that we have now weathered the storm, The worst seems over. But great and radical changes are necessary, and who is to effect them? Wt need a man at the head of affairs of great heart and head, and of vast experience. Nothing short of this will do what is necessary. Condign punishment should of course be meted out to all murderers and the leaders of mutiny. But I see every danger of justice degenerating into revenge of a savage character. Already we hear of strange deeds being perpetrated by private individuals at Delhi and elsewhere. Already it looks too like a general war of white man against black. There is little fear that offenders will escape the just penalty of their crimes; there is much that many innocent people will suffer. It was a great misfortune that troops, even in small numbers, were not sent out overland. Thousands of natives who in the first instance kept aloof, fell off, thinking that our hour was come. They would have sided with us if they had seen a chance; but with the general defection around, and no aid within hail, it was not surprising if they were carried away also.

We should have a European army of at least double its former strength in India, carefully kept up to the maximum strength. The native army should be no greater than is absolutely necessary. It should be officered by men carefully selected and removable simply because they were not successful in the discharge of their duties. The Mutiny Act, as regards native soldiers, should be abolished— at any rate, made to accord with common sense. No man should escape punishment for technical reasons. The officers should be selected in England by competition, as is done with civilians. They should join European corps and learn their duty and habits of discipline, and selections should be made from this body for native corps. Officers so selected should receive extra pay, and so have a strong inducement to exert themselves and give satisfaction. The cry for numbers of officers for native corps is merely a cry for rapid promotion.... The police should be reorganised and divided into two bodies—organised police on military principles for guards of gaols, treasuries and the like, and detective police for other duties. The latter will not be benefited by drill. This does not give discipline and moral training, which is what is wanted. Select such men carefully, pay them properly, look after them thoroughly, reward and punish promptly, and you will have good police. So far from being surprised at their faults, I only wonder, they did so much as they did. The Sepoys in the army would never have done one-forth of their work,

April 23, 1858

My dear Trevelyan, The mail is about to go out, and I have little time to answer your letter of March 11. However, I have often thought over many of the points discussed in your memorandum, and will give you my opinion to the best of my ability.

I am a strong advocate for extending the competition system throughout all branches of the army. I am sure it will work well. As yet, time has not allowed for a fair trial in our Civil Service, but the specimens which it has furnished to the Punjab have been favourable....I think, with Dr. Vaughan, that it is a mistake to think that a clever boy, who has obtained high proficiency at school, cannot be an adept at manly exercises. I think also that mere bookworms are not likely to be candidates for the English services. The circumstance that a boy is willing to come forward and compete for an appointment where the standard is high, is indicative of a certain amount of "grit" in his composition. Moreover, admitting that a few bookworms do find their way into the service, there are parts which will suit them and in which they may do good service. Such men are in every respect superior as public officers to a regular dunce—a thorough hard bargain...

Nothing can be more important than to secure for the army a body of really able officers, of men who have received a good education, and, from boyhood, have been accustomed to use their intellects. With an army so officered it would be impossible for any government to appoint incapable commanders. Public opinion would not permit such abuses. As it is now, mediocrity is the rule of the day; capacity the exception. Public sympathy, even in the army, is in favour of a chief of inferior talents. It is considered cruel to pass him over. Nothing short of a calamity will ensure a proper selection. The zeal, energy, ability, and real experience which prevent misfortune, are seldom to be found in high quarters....

I have always considered that the maximum age for civilians might be reduced with advantage. We want well-educated gentlemen rather than first-rate scholars. Men who come to India at a comparatively mature age, such as clergymen and lawyers, seldom like the country and are apt not to sympathise, as they should do, with the natives....

Sir John Lawrence

14

A Social Revolution

A Modern Marxist interpretation of the war as a social revolution expressive of class antagonism is given in the following selection by P.C. Joshi, who was Secretary of the Communist Party of India from 1937 to 1945. Noting as did many students of the period, the apparently important role of religion, Joshi argues that the people were forced to use religious terminology since they were familiar with no other idiom. Like many other modern Indian writers, Joshi regards the war as the source spring of our national movement, the moment in History when the Indian people in a great upsurge of nationalist sentiment "laid the foundation for the world-wide democratic solidarity....."

The British, under the East India Company's rule, disrupted the whole economic order of India, they turned the traditional land system topsy turvy, they smashed the trades and manufactures of the land and disrupted the relationship between these two sectors of economy, systematically drained the wealth of our country to their own, and destroyed the very springs of production of our economy. Every class of Indian society suffered at this new spoliators hands. The landlords were dispossessed and the peasants rendered paupers, the merchant bourgeoisie of India liquidated as an independent class and the artisans and craftsmen deprived of their productive professions. Such unprecedented destruction of a whole economic order and of every class within it could not but produce a great social upheaval and that was the national uprising of 1857. The all-destructive British policy produced a broad popular rebellion against its rule.

Within Indian society, however, those productive forces and classes had not yet grown (in fact early British policy had itself destroyed their first off-shoots) that could lead this revolution to victory. The revolt of 1857 as also its failure were both historical inevitabilities. But it also was a historical necessity, for after it followed those modern developments (which we will later analyse), from which emerged the modern national liberation movement of the Indian people and those new social forces which led it to victory.

The religious factor played a big part in the revolt of 1857. The British statesmen and chroniclers exaggerated and deliberately misinterpreted the role played by this factor to prove their thesis that the 1857 uprising was reactionary, revivalist and directed against the progressive reforms that they were introducing in Indian society. The early generation of English-educated Indian intellectuals swallowed this imperialist thesis uncritically because they themselves had suffered under the old reactionary religious influences. A true historical outlook demands that we do not forget the historical stage which Indian society had reached on the eve of 1857, the ideological values which would be normal to this society and the ideological forms in which the Indian people could formulate their aspirations.

Indian feudal society in the middle of the 19th century was rapidly disintegrating and alien conquerors were seeking to exploit our weaknesses to their own advantage. They were conducting a furious well planned, economic, political and ideological offensive against our country. The biggest problem facing all classes of the Indian people was to save India for the Indians and defend it from the Firinghis' all-sided onslaughts. In the then historical context, traditional religious-cultural concepts could not but be a very important constituent of the Indian ideological struggle against the foreigner's rule. From his own study of history and people's age-old struggles to remake their destiny, Marx had come to the conclusion:

> Men make their own history, but they do not make it just as they please; they do not make it under circumstances chosen by themselves, given and transmitted from the past. The tradition of all the dead generations weighs like a nightmare on the brain of the living. And just when they seem engaged in revolutionising themselves and things, in creating something that has never yet existed, precisely in such periods of revolutionary crisis they anxiously conjure up the spirits of the past to their service and borrow from them names, battle cries and costumes in order to present the new scene of world history in the time honoured disguise and this borrowed language.

It is not at all true that the British rulers were responsible for the major reforms then introduced, for example, the abolition of sati widow remarriage, etc. For purely political propaganda purposes, the British chroniclers subsequently made this claim. The truth is that the initiative, the popular compaign, etc. for these long-needed reforms came from the Indian reformers themselves.

By the beginning of the 19th century, British rulers had become so arrogant and power-drunk that in administrative methods they wilfully ignored and trampled under foot Indian customs and the mass of Indians concluded that all this was designed with a view to gradually convert them to Christianity. For example, common messing was introduced in jails. Much more serious was the Act 21 of 1850 which enabled converts to inherit their ancestral property. The reaction produced by this Act and how it made easier the task of converting Indians to Christianity is described by Sir Syed Ahmad Khan in the following words :

> The Legislative Council is not free from the charge of having meddled with religious matters. Act 21 of 1850 was without doubt prejudicial to the professors of other creeds. This Act was thought to have been passed with the view of cozening men into Christianity. The Hindu faith, as is known, allows no converts. To the Hindus, therefore, this Act brought no benefit. If a man again becomes a convert to Islam, he is forbidden by the laws of his own religion, from inheriting property left to him by men of another creed. No Mohammudan convert, therefore, could profit by this Act. To such men, however, as became Christians it offered great advantages. Hence this Act was said not only to interfere with people's religion but to hold out strong inducement to conversion.

This interference with traditional forms also invaded the sepoy army. They were banned from using their caste marks, compelled to "cross the seas," go abroad to fight Britain's wars, and most serious of all was the introduction of the greased cartridges. The British commanders and statesmen indignantly denied that any fat or lard objectionable to the Hindus and Muslims had been used. It was subsequently proved that they told a deliberate lie. . . .

The suspicion that the British government was out to Christianise the Indian people was widespread. Let us quote a contemporary Muslim divine's statement. "They left no stone unturned and tried their utmost to bring to an end, the various religions (excepting Christianity) by inventing devices...They established schools in towns and cities in order to teach books of their language and faith to the children and illiterate adults. They wiped out of existence the centres of knowledge and learning and *madrasahs* and institutions which have been established in earlier days."

The suspicions of the Indians were thoroughly justified, The Chairman of the Directors of the East India Company, Mr. Mangles said in the House of Commons in 1857 ;

> Providence has entrusted the extensive empire of Hindustan to England, in order that the banner of Christ should wave triumphant from one end of India to the other. Everyone must exert all his strength that there may be no dilatoriness on any account in continuing in the country the grand work of making India Christian.

The missionary propaganda was not only violently aggressive and widespread but also supported by the government agency. Syed Ahmad Khan states: "In some districts, the missionaries were actually attended by policemen from the station. And then the missionaries did not confine themselves to explain the doctrines of their own books. In violent and unmeasured language, they attacked the followers and the holy places of other creeds; annoying and insulting beyond expression the feelings of those who listen to them. In this way, too, the seeds of discontent were sown deep in the hearts of the people."...

The introduction of English education was also not motivated, by the pure desire to introduce European science and enlightenment into India but by its very protagonists themselves, directly related to the aim of converting the newly-educated Indians. For example, Macaulay wrote in a letter to his mother on October 12, 1836: "It is my firm belief that if our plan of education is followed up, there would not be a single idolator in Bengal thirty years hence!"...

It is abundantly clear, therefore, that the British rulers purely for their imperialist motives were out for some decades preceding 1857 to culturally denationalise India by the method of mass conversion to Christianity. This was seen as a menacing danger by the mass of Indians, irrespective of their viewpoint whether it was Sir Syed Ahmad Khan or Bahadur Shah, whether it was the enlightened Bengali intellectual in Calcutta or the Nana Saheb at Bithoor, by the mass of sepoys both Hindu and Muslim. Thus when the religious factor played a big role as it did in the struggle of 1857, it was as a part of the national factor. The mass of Indians took up arms to defend their own religions and they were fighting not only in defence of their religion but to defend their way of life and their nationhood. Of course, there were several reactionary features within Indian society but then the only healthy way to change them was through the struggle of the Indian people themselves.

This is not all. Our rebel ancestors used religion to advance the revolutionary struggle. They did not let religion stupefy them....

During the siege of Delhi, British agents repeatedly tried to transform the joint Hindu-Muslim struggle into a fratricidal Hindu-Muslim civil war. Even as early as May 1857, British agents began inciting the Muslims against the Hindus in the name of *jihad* and the matter was brought before Bahadur Shah. "The king answered that such a *jihad* was quite impossible, and that such an idea an act of extreme folly, for the majority of the *Purbeah* soldiers were Hindus. Moreover, such an act could create internecine war, and the result would be deplorable. It was fitting that sympathy should exist among all classes.... A deputation of Hindu officers arrived to complain of the war against Hindus being preached. The king replied, The holy war is against the English; I have forbidden it against the Hindus.

Thus did our rebel ancestors use religion to organise and conduct a united revolutionary struggle against foreign domination. In the historic conditions of 1857, the ideological form of the struggle could not but assume religious forms. To expect anything else would be unrealistic and unscientific.

P.C.Joshi

Bibliography

Anderson (Capt. R.P.): A Personal Journal of the Seige of Lucknow (1858).

Ball (Charles): The History of the Indian Mutiny (1859).

Bartrum (K.M.): A Widow's Reminiscences of the Seige of Lucknow (1858).

Bonham (Col. John): Oude in 1857

Bourchier (Col. G.): Eight Month' Campaign against the Bengal Sepoy Army (1858).

Cavenagh (O.): Reminiscences of an Indian Official (1884).

Chaudhur (S.B.): Civil Disturnances during the British Rule in India (1765-1857) (1955).

Chick (N. A.): The Annals of the Indian Rebellion (1860).

Cooper (F.): The Crisis in the Punjab (1858).

Cosens and Wallace: Fatehgarh and the Mutiny (1933).

Crawshay (G.): The Immediate Cause of the Indian Mutiny (London Effingham Wilson, Royal Exchange)

Dodd (G.): The History of the Indian Revolt (known as Chambers's History) (1859).

Edwards (W.): Facts and Reflections connected with Indian Rebellion (1859).

------- Personal Adventures during the Indian Rebellion (1858).

Forbes-Mitchell (W.): Reminiscences of the Great Mutiny (1893).

Forrest (G. W.): Selection from the Letters Despatches and other State Papers preserved in the Milltary Deptt. of the Government of India, 1857-58—(1893, 1902)

-------- History of the Indian Mutiny (1904)

Gough (General, Sir Hugh) Old Memories (1897)

Gubbins (M.): An Account of the Mutinies in Oudh (1859).

Gupta, Rajani Kanta: Sipahi Juddher Itihas (1886-1900).

Halls (J.J): Two Months in Arrah in 1857.

Hansard's: Parliamentary Debates (1857).

Hilton, Richard: The Indian Mutiny (1957).

Holloway (J.): Essays on the Indian Mutiny (1864)

Holmes (T. R.): A History of the Indian Mutiny (1913)

Hope Grant and Knollys (H.): Incidents in the Sepoy War (1857-58) (1873).

Hutchinson (Capt. G.): Narrative of the Mutinies in Oude (1859).

Inglis (Mrs.): The Siege of Lucknow (1892).

Innes (McLeod): Lucknow and Oude in the Mutiny (1896).

Jacob (Maj.Gen. Sir George Le Grand):The Causes of the Crisis of 1857-58.

Jones (Capt. Oliver J.): Recollections of a Winter Campaign in India (1859).

Joyce (Michael): Ordeal at Lucknow (1938).

Kaye (J.W.): A History of the Sepoy War in India(1880).

Keith Young (Col.): Delhi—1857 (1902).

Kincaid (C. A.): Lakshmi Bai, Rani of Jhansi.

Lang (John): Wanderings in India (1859).

Ludlow (J.M.): A Pamphlet on the War in Oudh.

Mackenzie (Col.A.R.D.): Mutiny Memoirs (1892).

Majendie (Lt. V.D.): Up among the Pandies (1859).

Majumdar (R. C.): The Sepoy Mutiny and the Revolt of 1857 (1957).

Malleson (G. B.): History of the Indian Mutiny 1857- 58 (1878, 1879,1888).

Mariam: A Story of the Indian Mutiny of 1857, reproduced by J.F. Fanthorne (1896).

Martin (R. M.): The Indian Empire (1858-61).

Maude and Sherer: Memories of the Mutiny (1894).

Medley (J. G.): A Year's Campaigning in India (1858).

Metcalfe (C. T.): Two Native Narratives of the Mutiny at Delhi (1898).

Montalembert: A Debate on India in the English Parliament (Published at the Office of the Continental Review, Bedford Street, Strand, London, 1858).

Mowbray Thomson: The Story of Cawnpore (1859).

Muir (Sir William): Records of the Intelligence Deptt. of the Government of the North - West Provinces of India during the Mutiny of 1857, ed. by William Coldstream (1902).

Nash (J. T.): Volunteering in India (1893).

Norton (J.B.): The Rebellion in India (1857).

Proceedings on the trial of Muhammad Bahadur Shah, titular king of Delhi, etc. Office of the Superintendent of Government Printing, India, Calcutta, 1895.

Raikes (C.): Notes on the Revolt in the North-West Provinces of India (1858).

Red Pamphlet: The Mutiny of the Bengal Army, by one who served under Sir Charles Napier (ascribed to Malleson) (1857).

Rees (L.E.R.): A Personal Narrative of the Siege of Lucknow (1858).

Robertson (H.D.): District Duties during the Revolt (1859).

Rotton (J.E.): The Chaplain's Narrative of the Siege of Delhi (1858).

Sen (S.N.): Eighteen Fifty-Seven (The Publications Division, Government of India, 1957).

Shepherd (W.J.): A Personal Narrative of the Outbreak and Massacre at Cawnpore (1879).

Sherring (Rev. M.A.): The Indian Church during the Great Rebellion (1859).

Sita Ram: From Sepoy to Subadar (Trans. by Norgate, 1911).

Showers (Lt.General, C.L.): A Missing Chapter of the India Mutiny (1888).

Syed Ahmed Khan: An Essay on the Causes of the Indian

Revolt. Trans, by Captain W.N. Less, Calcutta, 1870.

Sylvester (J.H.): Recollection of the Campaign in Malwa and Central India (1860).

Thackeray (Col. Sir Edward): Reminiscences of the Indian Mutiny (1916).

Thornhill (M.): The Personal Adventures and Experiences of a Magistrate during the Indian Mutiny (1884).

Townsend: The Annals of Indian Administration.

Urquhart (D.): The Rebellion in India (London, Paternoster Row).

Vincent (Benjamin): Haydn's Dictionary of Dates (22nd Edition, 1898).

Wilberforce (R. G.): An Unrecorded Chapter of the Indian Mutiny (1894).